NEW WORLD SYMPHONIES

New World Symphonies

HOW AMERICAN CULTURE
CHANGED EUROPEAN MUSIC

JACK SULLIVAN

Yale University Press   New Haven & London

Designed by James J. Johnson and set in
Electra types by Rainsford Type, Danbury,
Connecticut.

Printed in the United States of America.

The paper in this book meets the guidelines
for permanence and durability of the
Committee on Production Guidelines for
Book Longevity of the Council on Library
Resources.

*Library of Congress Cataloging-in-Publication
Data*

Sullivan, Jack, 1946–
New World symphonies : how American
culture changed European music / Jack
Sullivan.
p.   cm.
Includes bibliographical references and index.
ISBN 0–300–07231–7

1. Music—Europe—American influences. 2.
Music—United States—History and critiicism.
I. Title.
ML240.S89   1999   98–3641
780'.94—dc21

A catalogue record for this book is available
from the British Library.

10 9 8 7 6 5 4 3 2 1

For my sons, Geoffrey and David, two New Worlds

Contents

Acknowledgments

For the third time in a decade, I owe thanks to Jacques Barzun for his help in completing a book. His encouragement and seasoned insights into Poe, Varèse, French verse, and numerous other subjects have proved invaluable. I also wish to thank friends and colleagues who contributed leads and ideas, including Tom Barran, Michael Beckerman, Jack Belsom, Michael Blaine, Sedgewick Clark, Shirley Fleming, Thomas Gunn, Charles Hobson, Joseph Horowitz, Allen Hughes, Art Paxton, Helen Paxton, Seymour Solomon, and Alan D. Williams. Special thanks go to Charles Simmons and Gladys Topkis, who helped launch the book's publication. I am greatly touched by the generosity of Richard Lieberman, who has helped with the entire publishing process.

I am grateful to Rider University for a generous grant and to my colleagues there for their support and encouragement, especially Katherine Maynard, Deborah Rosenthal, Pearlie Peters, Carol Brown, Dominick Finello, and Phyllis Frakt. A special thanks goes to Jim Guimond, who critiqued the manuscript in its early stages and has continued to offer sound advice.

Portions of Chapter 3 originally appeared in *Lit: Literature Interpretation Theory* (5 [1994]: 83–93). I gratefully acknowledge their permission to reprint.

I am fortunate to have Harry Haskell for an editor at Yale University Press. Encouraging and astonishingly knowledgeable, he has given helpful suggestions about everything from overall conception to intricate details.

My main thanks go to my wife, Robin, a great editor and mom who read the manuscript and enabled this book to survive the joyous but anarchic din of two new babies.

Introduction

The youth of America is their oldest tradition.
—Oscar Wilde

Michael Wood once pointed out that it is possible to practice idolatry for a country other than one's own. Indeed, that is what other countries are for; it is why people travel—to celebrate freshness, otherness, foreignness, as ideal states of being.[1] Calling this need a "necessary exotic," the narrator of Julian Barnes's short story "Tunnel" goes so far as to say, "It is unhealthy to be idealistic about your own country, since the least clarity of vision quickly led to disenchantment. Other countries, therefore, existed to supply the idealism: they were a version of pastoral."[2]

Since the mid-nineteenth century, when an identifiably American literature and music began traveling across the Atlantic, when Berlioz heard Gottschalk and Dvořák read Longfellow, European composers have increasingly found this idealism in America, a new world where a lack of tradition and convention makes it possible to continually find a new version of pastoral. Because music itself is an ideal state, less representational than the other arts, this idea of America has been embodied in its purest form by composers. And it is pure idea. Although every country has a self-concept, it is usually backward-looking, based on history. Only in America, as the English expatriate Wood notes, is the self-perception "a picture of possibility. To be un-American is to be unfaithful to what the place might be."[3] This ideology of Americanness has little to do with reality; when Europeans take the latter into account, as Tocqueville did, their musings become decidedly more measured and melancholy. As C. Vann Woodward puts it, Europeans have always regarded America as a "metaphor adapted to their uses. . . . Any resemblance to geographic or social realities was purely coincidental."[4] Going a step further, Wood says that "America is no different from other countries except in its exaggerated notion of its own idea of difference—and that *makes* a difference."

It has certainly made a difference in music, where a New World tradition based on America's picture of possibility has been sounding out from both sides of the Atlantic since the mid-nineteenth century. The Polish composer Joanna Bruzdowicz, a late twentieth-century avatar of this tradition, called this fundamental sense of renewal *Spring in America*, the title of a 1994 chamber work she dedicated to the "United States of America and what I feel for this country." What she felt was adulation, made clear by a quotation from Sinclair Lewis she used in explaining her dedication of the piece: "Intellectually, I know that America is no better than any other country; emotionally, I know she is better than any other country."[5] With this chauvinistic gesture, one an American could never get away with, Bruzdowicz joined company with Frederick Delius, Samuel Coleridge-Taylor, Edgard Varèse, Kurt Weill, and numerous other America-worshipers from across the Atlantic. Her statement is a bit more blunt than those of her predecessors, but many voiced similar sentiments.

Like the Americana of many of its European antecedents, *Spring in America* is a vision of the New World from the vantage point of the Old, with swingy syncopations and open harmonies, plus a European sense of logic and structure. Whether it is really European music speaking "in jazz American," as Jack Kerouac put it, or American music speaking with a foreign accent is difficult to pinpoint, especially in a postmodern corporate world where culture is increasingly blurred and internationalized. To some extent that is the point of *Spring in America*: it is intended to break down nationalist distinctions and boundaries, to celebrate America and Europe simultaneously. This goal resembles that of Bruzdowicz's earlier piece in the tradition, the 1980 *Trio of Two Worlds*, "inspired by the friendship and musical heritage that unite the old continent of Europe and the Americas."[6] Even so, as Bruzdowicz's reference to Sinclair Lewis makes clear, this Old World artist regards the New World as the superior one, at least emotionally.

She is by no means alone. Conceived just over a hundred years after Dvořák's *New World* Symphony, this New World sonata is a 1990s sample of an American musical hegemony that has steadily solidified, even as Americans worried about being unduly influenced by Europe. In a peculiarly defensive key, American critics often downplay or fret about the New World elements in Dvořák, Weill, Milhaud, Hindemith, and other European composers, while hyping homegrown American music. They might as well relax; the influence came from America in the first place, demonstrating its potency rather than vulnerability. As David Drew pointed out at the Dvořák New World Centennial at Alice Tully Hall, American music seems to require a foreign accent to carry authority in American culture, but this is more projection than reality. As far as the actual composers are concerned, from Coleridge-Taylor to Bruzdowicz, it is America that carries the authority, occupying an importance in musical culture similar to what the Austro-German empire once enjoyed,

The anxiety about Americanness goes back to Emerson, who in "Self-Reliance" and "The American Scholar" deplored his compatriots' worship of the "courtly muses of Europe." Emerson called for an art that would be new and native, allowing Americans to "speak our own minds," and for a "philosophy of the street" that would cause Europe to imitate America for a change. In short, the American artist should be strong enough to make the world "come round to him."[7] Emerson could not have known that his fantasy of reverse imitation would be fulfilled in an unlikely place, music. Indeed, the early New World composer Louis Moreau Gottschalk would soon carry New Orleans music to the capitals of Europe. By the end of the nineteenth century, Dvořák and Delius would be singing of the prairies, rivers, and cotton fields, leaving the philosophy of the street to later émigrés such as Edgard Varèse and Kurt Weill. By the end of the twentieth century, even rock and roll, already dominating the European pop scene, had grown into art music such as the rock landscapes of Steve Martland and the Frank Zappa-esque collages of Klaus König.

With short histories and scant traditions, American idioms offer a seductive openness and malleability. The French composer Olivier Messiaen, an uncompromising elitist who deplored the influence of jazz on his compatriots, nonetheless understood the freedom conferred by America's lack of tradition. "With the exception of the American Indian," he said in 1986, "[Americans] have no past of their own; they've no reason to be troubled."[8] An exaggeration? Perhaps to an American, but it expresses the point of view of those for whom tradition is trouble. "History is a nightmare from which I am trying to awake," says James Joyce's Stephen Dedalus. Composers often experience a similar claustrophobia.

Inspired by everything from African-American hymns to the poetry of Walt Whitman, from the remoteness of the frontier to the brutal energy of the American city, these European composers forged a New World art characterized by bold intensity and experimentation, resulting in permanent changes in musical art. Seizing upon American stereotypes, they turned them to their own expressive purposes, eagerly exploiting Americanisms such as frankness, funkiness, innocence, wide open spaces, and a certain mindlessness—but always with an Old World sophistication that threw these clichés into a new, often startling context. Some, such as Debussy and Delius, went in the opposite direction, toward mystery and ambiguity. The darker, swampier aspects of American culture told a story about the New World that differed from what the clichés suggested, and these two were among the first to divine it.

These composers—herewith called New World Symphonists, after Dvořák's famous example--create a personal configuration of influences, often with a writer at the center, to construct their version of the American myth. Lukas Foss told me that when he came to New York at age fifteen, he fell under the sway of Aaron Copland, then Carl Sandburg. It was Sandburg who "took me by the hand and introduced me to America." The result of this tutelage was *The Prairie*, Foss's first masterpiece, written when he was nineteen, based on Sandburg's *Corn Huskers*. "Those were the days," said Foss: "America influenced everybody."[9]

The mythmaking frequently comes close to a religion, sometimes accompanied by a diatribe against the Old World, as illustrated by a fantasy obituary written by Percy Grainger, an émigré from a continent that is also a New World: "Grainger's religion—if any—is Walt Whitmanism, for since about 1897 . . . he has revered the personality and teachings of the great American seer much as Christians revere Christ or Buddhists revere Buddha. This predilection for an American Messiah in place of a European or Asiatic religion is typical of his Australian championship of the New World at the expense of the Old World, so strong in his teens and never since abandoned. Since his mid-teens he has always regarded the European continent as hopelessly sunk in conventionality, sham intellectuality, and parochialness."[10]

Aside from its characteristic Grainger tartness, this statement is not unusual for musical sojourners seeking a New World to liberate them from the conventionality and parochialism of the Old, although some express an equally powerful nostalgia for the Europe left behind. The writers they cite, often with the same messianic reverence, are varied and personal: for Dvořák, the inspiration was Longfellow; for Debussy and Ravel, Poe; for Delius, Parry, Vaughan Williams, Hindemith, and many others, Whitman; for Kurt Weill, Twain, Whitman, and a large cluster of contemporary writers. The configuration usually includes a favored idiom of American folk or popular music, often jazz or spirituals, and sometimes the work of vernacular composers such as Ives or Gershwin. It also includes a favorite landscape, the expected open space of the prairie or an exotic version of the American jungle such as the Everglades or the Amazon rain forests. Although the United States receives the most attention, South America is very much in play, in a merging of the Americas that began with Gottschalk and continued with Lambert, Milhaud, and Varèse. As the latter two demonstrate, the European version of pastoral can even be the funkiness and grandeur of the American city.

The British composer Michael Tippett is typical. Speaking of America as "my dream country," he writes that he is swept away by the "exhilaration of New York" and "deeply moved" by Gershwin's *Porgy and Bess*, a work "staking out its own territory, independent of the musical traditions of Europe."[11] Like his predecessors, he places a special value on a transcendence of Old World tradition. Tippett is also riveted by jazz and the blues, by Miles Davis and Bessie Smith. His literary list is a long one, from Hawthorne and Melville through Fitzgerald and Faulkner to John Updike and Gore Vidal, but it typically begins with Whitman, Tippett's first and most lasting entrée into the New World. As with many composers, this unwieldy grab bag of New World influences produced some of his most original and important music.

Most of the artists covered in this book had one or two pet American obsessions as well as a broad interest in the culture. Tremendously curious and highly cultivated, they were well read in American literature at a time when what is now canonical was still on the fringe. Debussy and Ravel, like their literary counterparts in France, regarded Poe with an awe bordering on reverence when Americans saw him as something of a crackpot; the many European Whitman-worshipers, especially those at the beginning of the twentieth century, rode the crest of a wave breaking in Europe, one they helped create; the musical championing of Harlem Renaissance writers by Zemlinsky, Weill, and other émigrés in flight from the Nazis came when Langston Hughes and Jean Toomer were at best minor exotica to all but the most discerning Americans. Samuel Coleridge-Taylor was among the first artists, black or white, to fully embrace W. E. B. DuBois as an aesthetic as well as political visionary. Europeans were also prescient about American art music: Gershwin is now routinely touted as the great American composer, but he was taken seriously much earlier by Ravel, Weill, Krenek, Schoenberg, and other Europeans than by many of the tastemakers in his own country, including Virgil Thomson and Paul Rosenfeld.

This story is full of twists and crossovers rather than neat historical patterns. Some sources of inspiration are deep and lasting, others brilliant but sporadic. Although the power of American landscape has declined as the prairie has become the mall, American literature, jazz, and spirituals continue to exert a strong influence. Dramatic moments stand out, including the Paris jazz bar scene of the 1920s, the creation of Hollywood music in the 1930s, the Broadway musical boom of the 1930s and 1940s, and the presidency of Franklin Roosevelt, which inspired New World Symphonies large and small, including Stravinsky's elegant orchestration of the "Star-Spangled Banner." Sent by the composer to the president as a July Fourth treat in a gold-embossed binding, this gem, like larger examples of European Americana, defies hierarchies and barriers; although the material is robustly American, the chords and coloring are thoroughly Stravinskian. The transnational historical ironies of the piece are also typical: as a foreigner, Stravinsky watched helplessly as major scores were lifted by Disney and other commercial interests; as a patriotic citizen, he saw his "Star Spangled Banner" confiscated by police in 1944 following a Boston Symphony performance, in accordance with a Massachusetts law forbidding tampering with national property.

In this book I do attempt not to be comprehensive but to cover a representative and illuminating sample of New World Symphonists and what most moved them. Looking for patterns in New World Symphonies — a metaphor used here to include all forms of music — is tricky, because not all the influences are easily classifiable as American and some had only temporary impact. The most striking examples are Henry James and T. S. Eliot. Ambiguously American to begin with, they were influential in dramatic but highly idiosyncratic instances. Benjamin Britten's settings of James's ghost stories, *The Turn of the Screw* and *Owen Wingrave*, have an extraordinary sensitivity to the texts and an overpowering sense of the sinister, with spooky parallels to Poe's deeper influence on Debussy and Ravel, but they do not point toward any consistent Anglo-American Gothicism. Nor is there a strong musical legacy in Eliot, though his verse is supremely musical. In addition to its severe beauty, Stravinsky's "The Dove Descending" is of considerable interest as his only Eliot setting and his first serial work. The realization of Stravinsky's long intention to set Eliot, whom he intensely admired, did not, unfortunately, lead to other Eliot pieces. Sophia Gubaidulina, another Russian devotee of Eliot, composed a single, mystically charged chamber setting of *Four Quartets*, called *Hommage à T. S. Eliot*, the fruit of a "shattering" encounter with Eliot's poetry in pre-perestroika darkness. Eliot's combination of high modernism and post-"Wasteland" religiosity suited the needs of both composers admirably, but otherwise the pieces have little to do with each other. Like the Britten-James works, they are ambiguous, isolated, and transnational rather than part of a tradition.

Because America is a nation of immigrants, Europe's discovery of the New World, in music as in anything else, is really a rediscovery of itself in mysterious, half-recognizable forms. The British composer Elizabeth Liddle, who is "obsessed" with Melville and (frightening thought) has read *Moby Dick* "hundreds of times," regards the "sound of Melville's prose" as so "Shakespearean" in its iambic pentameter, so powerfully close to hymns and other forms of old music, that Melville becomes a new form of the Old World "transmitted from the other side of the Atlantic."[12] The crosscurrents take many forms and go in many directions. The split explored in this book between the innocence and calculation that Berlioz discovered in Gottschalk, or Weill in jazz, is partly a self-revelation, the Old World embedded in the New. These composers embody the opposite of the "Wasteland" phenomenon, whereby alienated Americans travel abroad and find only more restlessness. Here Europeans travel to America and experience real epiphanies that erupt from the culture. Dvořák and Delius, the initial voyagers, experienced revelations from encounters with American settings and peoples. For the gregarious Dvořák, who visited a Czech immigrant village in Iowa to get in touch with his own roots, this became a reaffirmation of his Europeanness as well as an encounter with foreignness. For the aloof Delius, who had little use for Europe, Florida and black spirituals became internalized as lonely, ecstatic muses. In some cases, the pattern is a circle rather than a twist: Ravel regarded Poe as a "great American"; yet Poe himself hated America, which he viewed as despotic and vulgar, preferring to see himself as a European in disguise, an Old World exile trapped in the New.

These works excavate the dark side of the New World as lovingly as the bright, Poe's darkness as well as Whitman's optimism. Mysterious parallels emerge as well as influences: for example, Melville's unsettling suspicion that the vastness of American space may be a terrifying void runs through composers as different as Puccini, Delius, Varèse, and Milhaud. On the other hand, European settings of Melville such as Britten's *Billy Budd,* sailing straight into Melvillian blankness, and Elizabeth Liddle's *Whale Rant,* envisioning holiness and damnation in a single white flash, are rare.

Although this is a book about art music, it takes in folk and commercial influences as well, including those of Hollywood, Broadway, and Tin Pan Alley. Europeans were adept at bridging elite and vernacular cultures, of fulfilling the Emerson and Whitman ideal of art serving the people, but they paid a severe price in terms of artistic stature. To this day, intellectuals have trouble taking seriously the Hollywood and Broadway Americana of canonical European composers who "lowered" themselves to American popular culture. The educated public, on the other hand, has an altogether different attitude.

That this book focuses on the love affair between European composers and American culture does not mean I believe Americans have neglected their own reality. Deborah Drattell, George Crumb, and others continue to set Poe; Ned Rorem, Michael Tilson Thomas, John Adams, and Gordon Cyr helped create a remarkable musical revival of Whitman's Civil War poems; André Previn has written an operatic version of Tennessee Williams's *A Streetcar Named Desire* and a Guitar Concerto that reflects his affinity for American dance music; Donald Martino, who began his career as a jazz musician in the 1950s, periodically and lovingly returns to his jazz roots. Numerous other examples of Americans celebrating America could be cited. But when Europeans fall for American culture, they do so with a special obsessiveness, a sense of discovery, spontaneity, and the exotic. And in several cases, notably the works of Poe and the spirituals of black America, Europeans made the discovery first. As they were doing so, Americans, much as Emerson feared, gazed longingly across the Atlantic for something European that would give them high-culture cachet. Some are still doing so.

Europeans have been extraordinarily articulate about their American discoveries. Indeed, it is the composers themselves who make the most passionate case for the New World as a shaping force, and I have included as many of their voices as possible. As fresh as their music, their words on the New World show how America, from Dvořák's *New World* Symphony to the spread of rock and roll, has transformed the musical scene on a global scale.

CHAPTER ONE

The Legacy of the Sorrow Songs

The future music of this country must be founded upon what are called the
negro melodies. . . . These are the folk songs of America.
—Antonin Dvořák

S HORTLY after arriving in America in 1892, Antonin Dvořák declared that the most distinctive
folk music in the United States
came from black America: only through a recognition of this fundamental
fact, said Dvořák, could America realize itself musically.[1] Now a commonplace argument in the post-jazz, post-rock era, this assertion was hugely
provocative in its time. That it was articulated by a white European made
it more so. That the gospel of black music then spread to other Old World
composers before it took root in America seems equally odd—but perfectly in tune with Europe's embrace of subversives such as Poe, Whitman, and Melville before America could deal with them.

It was not only the music of black Americans that attracted these
composers but their literature—their narratives, lyrics, and poems. Their
story of dispossession, isolation, and ultimate endurance became the basis
for a complex musical art that was both invigorating and nostalgic, optimistic and despairing, an art that would eventually bridge popular and
elite culture. The plight of Native Americans was often linked to the black
experience in the imaginations of these artists, becoming part of the musical mix in much the same way "Black Indian" Mardi Gras music did in
New Orleans.

Dvořák composed his most popular symphony in 1892 in New York City, with a copy of Longfellow's poetry on his music stand and the soulful sounds of black folks, sung by his most gifted student, ringing in his ears. Dubbing it "From the New World," he invented a new genre, one peculiarly literary and multicultural, bursting with energy yet drenched in nostalgia. Scholars would squabble throughout the next century—and still do—over the extent to which, if any, this revolutionary work was American and whether it influenced American music; meanwhile, the more powerful, largely unnoticed legacy would be "New World" experiments by other Europeans.

Dvořák's new symphony fanned some of the ugliest flames in American racial politics, changing forever the way we think about classical music. Yet, painfully shy to the point of self-deprecation, he meant only to accomplish two modest goals: to sketch musical impressions of a country he found endlessly fascinating and to encourage Americans—as Emerson had already done in "The American Scholar" and as he himself had done in Bohemia—to be themselves and, as Emerson advised, to stop listening to the "courtly muses" and start listening to the "ballad in the street."[2] Dvořák was searching for what he called an American voice.[3] Like Emerson, he was a peculiarly realistic Romantic, one who rejected a search for "the great, the remote, the romantic," instead discovering the unifying design of those very things in the everyday. Dvořák was interested in all of America, from the lonely plains of Iowa to the "push of the streets" in New York.[4]

In a remarkable coincidence, the British composer Frederick Delius was experimenting with his own New World Symphonies at almost exactly the same time as Dvořák, giving them such names as "Florida," "Hiawatha," and "Appalachia." But Delius was still an unknown, whereas Dvořák—as Henry Krehbiel, James Huneker, and other exponents of the classical age of New York criticism asserted—was the most renowned and popular composer of his day.

He was certainly a coup for Mrs. Jeanette Thurber, a wealthy patron (and the wife of a grocer), who talked Dvořák (the son of a butcher) into chairing her newly founded National Conservatory of Music, in New York City. Every word Dvořák said and every note he composed were eagerly listened to during his two-year tenure in the United States. The words, it turned out, were few—only a handful of articles and interviews appeared—but they were written in passionate, precise English. The notes, however, were many—some dozen symphonic, chamber, and vocal works.

Dvořák was the perfect luminary to head a new conservatory in a country still radically insecure about its musical identity: he was famous and a foreigner. Similarly, Mrs. Thurber was of German lineage, as was her conservatory; the American music she championed would therefore have an Austrian-Germanic pedigree. Best of all, Dvořák was a peasant who had made good, in the best American tradition of the self-made man. Not that his experience had been altogether happy. H. L. Mencken pointed out that despite his popularity, Dvořák suffered from ugly classist subcurrents directed toward him and "was commonly regarded as a sort of inspired clodhopper"; even Hans von Bülow, his greatest champion, "almost cooked Dvořák's goose by calling him 'Der Bauer im Frack' ('the peasant in a dress coat'). This apt and yet unfortunate label has stuck to him ever since."[5] Dvořák had great hopes that America, with its egalitarian traditions, would be more hospitable.

At first, things went more or less according to script. Dvořák launched two large-scale New World pieces for Mrs. Thurber even before his journey to America. In the summer of 1892, he began sketches for a cantata eventually called *The American Flag*; this grandiose *entrata* was to herald both his arrival in the New World and the four hundredth anniversary of Columbus's discovery of it. But Mrs. Thurber was late sending Dvořák the text—a clunky patriotic poem by Joseph Rodman Drake—so Dvořák first composed another calling card, a vigorous *Te Deum*. Despite its Latin text, this initial entry in Dvořák's American period projected a cheerful primitivism forecasting the New World Symphony, with its driving tom-tom rhythms and unpredictable open harmonies.

The American Flag is a genuine oddity. Completed two days before Dvořák began the *New World* Symphony, this forgotten work has been cursed since its inception. Dvořák never got to hear it, for the American premiere occurred just days after he returned to Europe. Possibly because of its tub-thumping American patriotism, the composition did not make its way back across the Atlantic until the 1970s, when it was performed in London by Michael Tilson Thomas. It continues to be denigrated by critics for being totally uncharacteristic and peculiar without being interesting, the only clinker from Dvořák's American period. Its "skyborn glories" and "canon mouthings loud" are viewed as bombs in more ways than one.[6]

With its snare drums and martial aura, *The American Flag* is the Dvořák equivalent of the *1812 Overture* and *Wellington's Victory*. It is a surprisingly agreeable work, and an important one. With the exception of a Stephen Foster transcription, it is Dvořák's only published setting in English, the text of which is clearly projected in three-part harmony. It is also his only work to be initially published by an American company, a function of its belligerent patriotism. The poem is indeed dreadful, a crude piece of imperialism pronouncing the American flag "the guard and glory of the world!" But music is full of bad poems shedding their verbal weight and taking flight when set by a Bach or a Schubert. Dvořák was clearly searching for a new style to announce his American arrival, and Drake's simple, hyperbolic couplets provided a useful vehicle precisely because their mediocrity made them unobtrusive even as they provided the requisite patriotic sentiment.

What resulted was a series of bracing experiments in sound. From the opening fanfares, which never go where the listener expects, to the chromatic fireworks in the "Apotheosis," the piece is full of imaginative modulations and bold colors held together by Dvořák's instinctive gift for melody. The listener must, it is true, work rather actively to ignore the text. Drake's obsession with patriotic gore becomes unintentionally sinister, as when "shoots of flame" and "gory sabres" are personified as "that lovely messenger of death," a line made creepier by being clothed, without irony, in some of Dvořák's' most seductive string writing. Yet this text is no more dated or reactionary than numerous others used by composers from Handel to Wagner and was not, of course, deemed at all offensive in Dvořák's America. This was standard patriotic puff, and Dvořák, eager to prove his enthusiasms for America, latched onto it. In any case, by the time he left America he had demonstrated a far more influential political liberalism.

Indeed, it is significant that this cantata was sketched before Dvořák came to America and heard black spirituals. (There is no evidence he changed his initial outline once he arrived.) *The American Flag* is his prefolkloric vision of America: it doesn't sound like any other Dvořák, and it makes a wonderful racket. If some of the harmony is Wagnerian, as critics complain, that only enhances its New World aspirations: one of Wagner's earliest works, it should be remembered, was a *Columbus Overture*.

Dvořák's ambitions concerning Columbus were large. With his *Te Deum* he had already undertaken one ambitious project for the commemoration of the discovery of America. In November 1892 he agreed on another, one far more grandiose. In collaboration with his National Conservatory colleague Victor Herbert, another European in the New World, he undertook to write music for a massive theatrical project called "The Great Discovery." Dvořák and Herbert had a relationship of mutual adulation: Dvořák admired Herbert for his lyrical gift and because he sought to dissolve distinctions between popular and highbrow art; Herbert regarded Dvořák as a "master musician" and loved being in the presence of his "childlike simplicity and naturalness."[7] With this kind of chemistry between its creators, "The Great Discovery" had great potential.

Conceived by the legendary theater manager Steele MacKaye for the Chicago World's Fair of 1893, this event was to be the inauguration of a new genre called a "Spectatorio," a series of elaborate pantomime and stage effects enacted on a giant stage called a "Spectatorium." A quintessentially American combination of kitsch and grandiosity, brilliance and quackery, the "Spectatorio" was canceled for lack of funds, but it moved Dvořák into a certain epic frame of mind—the American habit of thinking big—just two months before he began his *New World* Symphony. It also firmed up the friendship between Dvořák and Herbert, a connection that ultimately resulted in Dvořák's Cello Concerto, one of the glories of his American period.

Dvořák was excited about the notion of developing a National Conservatory, even though he dreaded leaving his native Bohemia. But when he arrived in New York in the fall of 1892, he discovered there was nothing national to conserve. Astonished to find that Edward MacDowell and other members of the American musical order were—with the exception of a few token "Indian" pieces—slavishly imitating European models, Dvořák quickly resolved to do in America what he had already done in Europe: to mine a folk vernacular and convert it into art that would be both formal and accessible.

That is precisely what he did in composing his epic Ninth Symphony, which turned out to be not only his own most popular work but the most beloved symphony in American history. This is a classic case of the public, which has always adored the *New World* Symphony in a thoroughly uncomplicated way, being more sensible than the critics. Always an awkward public personality, Dvořák was flattered but also embarrassed at the 1893 premiere: "The papers say that no composer ever had such a triumph," he wrote Simrock; "people applauded so much that I had to

take the bow and thank them from my box just as if I were some king! . . .
I rather like to avoid similar ovations."[8] Hired to produce democratic art
but treated like a king: that was to be Dvořák's paradoxical fate throughout
his American stay.

Dvořák's audience had every reason to cheer his new symphony. So
many complicated controversies have swirled around the *New World*
since its Carnegie Hall premiere that the simple spontaneity and exuberance of the piece have all but been buried. Whatever the ultimate sources
of the symphony — and as we shall see they are many — it has a powerful
immediacy, an instantly apprehendible unity of emotion and sensibility.
The sense of open spaces and New World freshness are palpably present,
even if the literal sources are hard to pin down. That the work indeed
opened up a New World was not for a moment doubted by the audience
or the New York Philharmonic. The president of the Philharmonic spoke
for audience and players when he called the occasion "epoch-making"
and spoke of the "justness of the title."[9]

The musical intelligentsia, however, had a far more ambivalent reaction. Their quarrel was not with the music itself — although by the mid-
twentieth century they were carping about that too — but with what
Dvořák said about it, especially his insistence on calling it a New World
symphony. In culture wars, words are always more important than results,
at least for the warriors, and this was no exception. Dvořák's difficulty was
not his use of American folk music but his insistence that this folk vernacular was black — that slave songs offered the best vehicle for building a
New World tradition.

He voiced this politically incorrect discovery in typically blunt, enthusiastic language full of *musts* rather than *maybes*: "I am now satisfied
that the future music of this country must be founded upon what are
called the negro melodies," he told the *New York Herald* in May 1893.
"This must be the real foundation of any serious and original school of
composition to be developed in the United States. When I first came here
last year I was impressed with this idea, and it has developed into a settled
conviction." Dvořák pronounced Negro melodies to be the "folk songs of
America"; rather than merely encouraging American composers to incorporate these melodies, he declared that "they must turn to them. All the
great musicians have borrowed from the songs of the common people.
Beethoven's most charming scherzo is based upon what might now be
considered a skillfully handled negro melody. . . . The aptitude of the col-

REAL VALUE OF NEGRO MELODIES.

Dr. Dvorak Finds In Them the Basis for an American School of Music.

RICH IN UNDEVELOPED THEMES.

American Composers Urged to Study Plantation Songs and Build Upon Them.

USES OF NEGRO MINSTRELSY.

Colored Students To Be Admitted to the National Conservatory — Prizes to Encourage Americans.

T was Rubinstein who bitterly said that the world would make no more progress in music until the controlling influence of Wagner, Berlioz and Liszt had passed away. Right on the heels of this anathema Dr. Antonin Dvorak, the foremost figure among living composers, came to America, the acknowledged leader of the dramatic school and the chosen target for the arrows of the lyric school.

Dvořák's manifesto proclaiming African-American music to be the "folk songs of America." (*New York Herald*, May 21, 1893)

ored race for music, vocal and instrumental, has long been recognized, but no definite steps have hitherto been taken to develop it."[10]

After hearing Native American music during a summer sojourn in Spillville, Iowa, Dvořák broadened his assertion about American folk music to include Indian chants; these, he said, influenced the two inner movements of the *New World* Symphony, with Longfellow's *Hiawatha* as a poetic backdrop. But he never accorded Indian music the central importance he ascribed to black plantation songs. His advocacy was passionate and unstinting. In addition to a new harmonic freedom and rhythmic audacity, African-American songs had what he regarded as unlimited emotional range, indeed "all that is needed for a great and noble school of music. They are pathetic, tender, passionate, melancholy, solemn, religious, bold, merry, gay or what you will. It is music that suits itself to any mood or any purpose."[11] The syncopated rhythm and moody harmony of black hymns were a bracing alternative to both Brahms and Wagner. Dvořák was not the first white artist to be stirred by black music; he was, however, the first important composer since Louis Gottschalk—whose music was taken much more seriously in Europe than in America — to take in the full measure of this music and to understand its significance.

Dvořák had personal as well as aesthetic reasons for his love of black music. What attracted him was its representation of struggle against discrimination and oppression — the same struggle that attracted other Old World Americanists such as Delius, Weill, and Korngold. "It is to the poor that I turn for musical greatness," he said; he himself was "the son of poor parents and was reared in an atmosphere of struggle."[12] Given his love of folklore and his lifelong fight against second-class citizenship, it is not surprising that he was deeply touched by the art of Harry T. Burleigh, who was attending the conservatory, and Mrs. Thurber's other African-American scholarship students. The elegant curve and soulful sensibility of their singing imprinted his musical language for the rest of his life.

Dvořák's assertions, as Henry Krehbiel noted in the *New York Daily Tribune* in 1894, caused "much consternation."[13] They were not only radical but premature, coming a decade before the manifesto on black folk music in W. E. B. DuBois's *The Souls of Black Folk*. Suddenly a loud, ugly noise rose forth from the New York and Boston press, ranging from the "laughter of the skeptics," who claimed there was nothing American in the symphony, to a grudging admission that an insignificant scrap or two of black or Indian music might lie buried in the work. The subtext of both reactions was a horror over even the possibility of such music inspiring a major symphony of such extraordinary popularity.

The permutations of these arguments were endless. Some (such as Anton Seidl, the visionary Wagnerian who premiered the *New World*) claimed that the work contained "pure Indian music";[14] others (such as William Foster Anthorp) wrote that it contained actual black plantation tunes; Victor Herbert, another Thurber student, claimed it was based on melodies sung to Dvořák by Burleigh and Dvořák's other black pupils at the conservatory. The latter conjecture was validated by Dvořák himself, who confirmed that much of his research into African-American music was delightfully firsthand.

The loudest group denied any Americanness. Most vehement was the distinguished music and art critic James Huneker: "Dvořák's is an American symphony: is it? Themes from negro melodies; composed by a Bohemian; conducted by a Hungarian and played by Germans in a hall built by a Scotchman. About one third of the audience were Americans and so were the critics. All the rest of it was anything but American — and that is just as it should be."[15] By mid-twentieth century, as H. L. Mencken pointed out, the group claiming that the *New World* was just another Czech work was in the ascendancy. And it has remained so. Music-appreciation books are adamant on the subject: *Beethoven or Bust* denounces the idea of Americanness in the symphony as nonsense; the *Vintage Guide to Classical Music* argues that the symphony is "one of the greatest manifestations of the Czech/Bohemian spirit."[16]

To a remarkable extent, the terms of the current debate remain what they were in late nineteenth century, with scholars such as Michael Beckerman and David Beveridge weighing in on the American side, or at least on the side of the *New World* representing *something* new. A recent controversy focuses on Dvořák's increasing use of pentatonic scales, drone basses, and other open sounds during his American period. Are these harmonies black? Are they Indian? Or are they, as markers of the exotic, simply recycled Bohemianisms?

What is odd about these tortuous questions and dissections is that Dvořák clarified the entire matter from the beginning, in admirably clear language. As early as 1892, after his revelatory summer in Spillville among Czech immigrants and Kickapoo Indians, he told the *Chicago Tribune* that his method was to study black, Creole, and other indigenous melodies until he became "thoroughly imbued with their characteristics" and was "able to make a musical picture in keeping with and partaking of those characteristics." The ultimate goal was to "grasp the essence and vitality of the subject" and re-create that essence in his own themes.[17]

Just to be sure no one missed the point, he told the *New York Herald* on December 15, 1893, the day before the *New World* premiered, that he composed only in the spirit of black and Indian music: "I have not actually used any of the melodies. I have simply written original themes embodying the peculiarities of the music."[18] Dvořák became understandably irritated that his many statements on the subject were misread or ignored. With uncharacteristic grumpiness, he stated that the whole notion of his using authentic quoted material was "nonsense" and "a lie."[19]

Dvořák's own words therefore render much of the debate irrelevant. Clearly, the music from his experiences in New York and Iowa was not meant to be authentically American (whatever that means), or even an approximation thereof. It was music "imbued" by the spirit and essence of American folk art; it was a poetic vision of the New World, much like his vision of East European folk music, which also captured the spirit of folk music but eschewed actual quotation. Dvořák—like Delius and unlike Smetana and Ives—created his own folk sounds; he was a late Romantic in search of new inspiration, not an ethnomusicologist or a collagist.

In fact, the entire question of authenticity was irrelevant to Dvořák. In his vigorous article for *Harper's* in February 1895, his final say on the subject, he expressed great puzzlement not only over the obsession with American authenticity but over wranglings about whether Negro music originated in Africa or America. He made his own antiliteralism impulses perfectly clear: "Whether the original songs which must have inspired the composers came from Africa or originated on the plantations matters as little as whether Shakespeare invented his own plots or borrowed them from others. The thing to rejoice over is that such lovely songs exist and are sung at the present day. I, for one, am delighted by them."[20]

But rejoicing was the last thing on the minds of squabbling Americanists; the question of who invented the plots was very much the issue. (In academic quarrels, plot displaces poetry every time.) The debate over the Americanness or lack thereof in Dvořák—and the need to keep the debate alive—clearly says more about Americans' precarious sense of identity than it does about Dvořák. The analogy of Shakespeare and his sources demonstrates that Dvořák understood precisely what his art was about: like Shakespeare, he borrowed the bare bones of older plots—the songs of black folk—and re-created them with his own poetry.

Dvořák and his critics raised the question still being asked: Just what is American music? As a European more interested in imaginative art than in ethnomusicology (though he probably knew more about the latter than his adversaries), Dvořák had the luxury of not needing to provide an answer. He did, however, change the nature of the debate, one that continues to have a peculiarly ugly tone. A recent example is Richard Taruskin's 1993 claim in the *New York Times* that Dvořák generated an "ersatz" nationalism that led to such unfortunate things as the "ingratiating white-bread-of-the-prairie idiom" of Aaron Copland—a "left-leaning homosexual Jew from Brooklyn." Worse, Dvořák inaugurated a "critical ethnic cleansing by which the legitimacy of American composers who do not choose to don a Stetson or grow an Afro can be impugned."[21]

In fact, as the *Harper's* article makes clear, Dvořák had an affinity for black songs, but he championed all folk music, whatever the hair or hat style; he embraced "all the races that are commingled in this great country," including the "plaintive ditties of the homesick German or Norwegian."[22] Nonetheless, the Taruskin diatribe is instructive as the latest, most unpleasant example of an ideology that views Dvořák as a corrupter of American culture who forced the music of lowlifes and ruffians down America's throat.

From the beginning, finicky arguments about authenticity barely concealed this larger anxiety and outrage over Dvořák's embrace of African-American music. James Creelman, writing in 1894, found Dvořák's enthusiasm for black music "almost pathetic. I fear that he does not yet appreciate the limitations of the negro race. . . . It will take many generations of culture to develop their intellects to the point of appreciating the higher and larger forms of music. Meanwhile they may serve as hewers of wood and carriers of water to the white race."[23] The viciousness of these white supremacist attacks was matched only by their incoherence. Huneker, for example, ridiculed as false the entire notion of American influences in the symphony, whether black or otherwise — then went on to denounce the African-American influence anyway: "If we are to have true American music it will not stem from 'darky' roots, especially as the most original music of that kind thus far written is by Stephen Foster, a white man. The influence of Dvořák's American music has been evil; ragtime is the popular pabulum now. I hardly need add that the negro is not the original race of our country. And ragtime is only rhythmic motion, not music."[24]

These rantings, which came from two of Dvořák's admirers, typified defenders of the symphonic status quo desperate to discredit the basis, if not the actual music, of Dvořák's symphony. His challenge was a threat precisely because he was a European. It was to European models, after all, that Americans turned for their musical guidance, in part to avoid the "evil" influence of genres such as ragtime (always the most demonized form of black music) — but then along came a European opening the gates and letting in the savages. Dvořák's brief on behalf of black music anticipated DuBois's and Gershwin's and was infinitely more shocking. DuBois, after all, was black, and Gershwin was a Jew (and, like Copland, a left-leaning one at that). But Dvořák should have known better. Most threatening of all to white supremacists was Dvořák's fame. He was the most celebrated composer of his time, a point we tend to forget, but one that was all too clear to Creelman & Co.: "It is not too much to say," wrote Creelman, "that Dvořák is the foremost living composer, and that his word carries more authority than that of any contemporary."[25]

Dvořák's earnestness and naiveté were ironic attributes in this incendiary situation. For better or worse, he is the most nonironic of the great composers, a straight talker, with none of the irony or scathing wit of a Berlioz or a Copland. He fell in love with black spirituals immediately upon hearing "Swing Low Sweet Chariot" and other hymns sung by Harry Burleigh and could not understand the hysteria caused by his promotion of them. When he spoke on the record of his discoveries, he was exuberant and to the point, which drove his critics to increasing extremes of nit-picking hostility. To this day scholars insist that Dvořák, in the words of Adrienne Fried Block, "changed his story about the sources of inspiration for the *New World*," asserting first that they were black, then that they were Indian as well, and, finally, in *Harper's* "tacitly" admitting that America contained commingled folk sources.[26] But Dvořák's statements are by no means mutually exclusive; his sense of folk sources evolved, as one would expect, in a gradual process of discovery. And nowhere in the *Harper's* piece does he take back his judgment about the primacy of black music. Indeed, he reasserts it.

Again, this was always an aesthetic verdict: Dvořák never said that black music was the only folk tradition, only that, to his heart and mind, it was the most beautiful, noble, and fruitful. In a revealing grace note, he added that "plantation songs are indeed the most striking and appealing melodies that have yet been found on this side of the Atlantic. . . . This seems to be recognized, though often unconsciously, by most Americans."[27] This is Dvořák at his most cheerfully blunt: Americans really know their best music is black, they just don't want to admit it.

Dvořák himself did not want to admit the tragic centrality of race in American culture and politics. As Leon Botstein points out, he admired America because of its lack of a common culture: in America everyone was exotic.[28] For once, it made no difference that he was a Bohemian because everybody was "the other." That, at least, was the myth. The special hatred reserved for black people was something he had not seen firsthand.

This is not to say that all the consternation Dvořák caused is attributable to racism alone. The disturbance was much broader. Genteel America was insecure and befuddled not only about the incursions of black music but about musical identity in general, a phenomenon unintentionally summarized by tastemaker James Huneker's characterization, without irony, of Edward MacDowell as "our most truly native composer."[29] Despite all the passionate manifestos by Emerson, Thoreau, Twain, and other writers about the need for nonimitative American art, the best that the musical intelligentsia could come up with was MacDowell.

Like anyone else, Americans wanted to define their own culture, and they resented a foreigner doing it for them. The resentment is still there, as reflected in the statement of a commentator in 1991 that Dvořák was "unfamiliar with the substantial number of talented American composers who had been getting along quite well—and even anticipating his approaches years before his music was known here."[30] The subtext is clear: we Americans were doing quite well until this overrated foreigner came along. This was an issue Dvořák understood: his bold assertions about the mortifying lack of true American music (the bland banalities of MacDowell, Chadwick, and others notwithstanding) indicate that this was one land mine he was prepared to walk into.

As it turned out, the establishment had a great deal to be anxious about. The Dvořák revolution was spectacularly successful, not only with the American public but with American music in general. Numerous music historians (including hostile ones like Taruskin) credit him with starting a line that led to the respectability of jazz and the American idioms of Gershwin and Copland. Dvořák, after all, taught Rubin Goldmark, who in turn taught Gershwin, Ellington, and Copland. Burleigh and Will Marion Cook, two of Dvořák's black students, were directly influenced by him, as he was by them; the next generation of black composers drew on his theories of the centrality of African-American music as well. Indeed, the more scholars celebrating the 1993 Dvořák centennial looked into the matter, the more they discovered just how long his "long American reach" really is.

Anxiety about American musical identity has therefore resulted in a strange ambivalence: Dvořák is credited with everything and nothing. There is nothing American about the *New World* Symphony, yet everything can be traced to it. What is overlooked, ironically, is that Dvořák was profoundly influenced by America in the first place. The depth of this influence is a testament to the power of American culture, not its fragility, no matter how difficult that chaotic culture is to pin down or define. As we shall see in this book, the cultural and literary energies that inspired Dvořák were destined to transform other Europeans as well.

Dvořák himself was clear about the American influence. Writing a Czech friend during his composition of the *New World*, he asserted that "I should never have written the symphony 'just so' if I hadn't seen America."[31] He defined the symphony as "an endeavor to portray characteristics, such as are distinctly American."[32] Once we clear away the debris of racial politics and anxieties about identity, we see that his initial immersion in black American music had a broadening, humanizing effect, opening a subjective stream of impressions: the "penetrating quality" of New York newsboys selling papers on the streets;[33] the "American color" and serene atmosphere of Spillville and Minnehaha Falls, where Dvořák took his visiting family;[34] the "capacity for enthusiasm of most Americans" that mirrored his own upbeat spirits.[35] We shall see the same phenomenon in the black-inspired music of Delius: the emotional power of black music was a catalyst that opened the composer to other American stimuli.

American critics, who initially praised the symphony while quarreling over its sources, eventually began attacking it precisely because of this unruly mulitfariousness. Writing in the *Baltimore Sun* in the 1920s, H. L. Mencken remarked that "a fashion of sniffing at it has grown up among the musical pundits." And the sniffing continued throughout most of the century. Parallel to all the caveats about authenticity emerged complaints about the symphony's artistic status. Irritated by the work's immense and continuing popularity, compared to what they regard as the more tightly written Seventh and Eighth Symphonies, highbrow critics as well as music-appreciation middlebrows pronounced the *New World* to be structurally inferior, its popularity undeserved. But the sprawling, episodic structure of the piece, its themes spilling over from one movement to another, perfectly embodies the uncontainable exuberance and melodic richness of the material. As Mencken points out in his passionate defense of the symphony, enjoyment of the *New World* necessitates submission of its "rush of sounds," its atmosphere of "frank savagery"—a surrender "platitudinous" critics are incapable of. As for the allegedly deficient structure, the first movement offers three subjects that "for all their barbaric color are still somewhat terse and austere—that is, for Dvořák—and their working out is carried on with a relentlessness that he seldom shows anywhere else." Mencken asserted that this symphony actually showed "better discipline" than Dvořák's earlier ones. Its illusion of black-inspired spontaneity, its "barbarous synco-pated" emotionality, hides its artfulness: "The thing goes with a rush that conceals its ingenuity of design and execution."[36]

That Mencken, hardly a paragon of racial tolerance, was one of the strongest defenders of the symphony among American intellectuals is a revealing and pathetic commentary. As usual, racism was more a personal flaw than a professional behavior: in this article, he asserts that the work is, paradoxically, a real "American symphony" by "a Bohemian of the Bohemians" and that virtually all of it can be traced to the Jubilee Songs and the "wailing spirit of Negro music."[37] Indeed, Mencken went overboard in his sightings from the Jubilee Songs, but he was one of the first Americans to get it right about the essential quality and signif-icance of the symphony.

The frankness, openness, ecstatic rush, and "unbroken clarity" cited by Mencken—all set against wailing melancholy—characterized not only this symphony but eventually the America-inspired works of Dvořák's European colleagues. Mencken apparently did not know about the *Hiawatha* influence on the symphony, but he pinned down its mix-ture of exuberance and nostalgia. Among other things, it is this emo-tional complexity, this excitement about the New World tempered by nostalgia for the Old, that gives the *New World* Symphony its unique tension. The most famous case in point is the big tune for English horn in the Largo: this haunting melody, based on the spirit and shape of black hymnody, became a spiritual called "Goin' Home," a perfect metaphor for Dvořák's nostalgia for his homeland.[38] Dvořák thus bor-rowed from black music and gave back to it in equal measure, creating a new folk music. He invented his own New World as he absorbed the one around him.

These characteristics defined most of Dvořák's other American works as well, including the charming Violin-Piano Sonata written for his children when they visited him in New York, its second movement a tone painting of Minnehaha Falls; the justly famous *American* String Quartet, with its open, uncluttered string sonorities, composed at Spill-ville in a three-day burst of inspiration; the peculiarly neglected E-flat Quintet, also from the Spillville summer, with its magical bird and in-sect sounds and its "musical picture," in the composer's words, of plan-tation and Creole tunes;[39] the Suite and Humoresques for piano, with their exotic pentatonic harmonies and unpredictable melodic turns; the heartrending *Biblical Songs*, written in a triple conjunction of grief over the deaths of Dvořák's friend Tchaikovsky, his champion Hans von Bü-low, and his father, news of whose terminal illness he received after launching the cycle. Despite their Czech text, even the *Songs* have strong overtones of the black spiritual. Rarities from Dvořák's American period continue to be revived, including the orchestral version of the Suite and an homage to Stephen Foster in the form of a choral setting of "Old Folks at Home," a work exemplifying Dvořák's keen interest in every aspect of American folk song.

Aside from the symphony, the most epic piece from Dvořák's American period is the Cello Concerto. Because this magnificent work has no American label and was written at the end of his New York sojourn, it is often deemed the most un-American of Dvořák's Ameri-cana. Yet it was composed in New York and directly influenced by another New World European: the Irish-born, German-trained Victor Herbert, a Thurber protégé who eventually headed the conservatory. Dvořák's concerto has an openness, expansiveness, and distinctive nar-rative quality reminiscent of the Ninth Symphony. It also has a cyclic structure similar to both the symphony and Herbert's cello concerto. That it eschews pentatonicisms and other primitive markers matters lit-tle: Dvořák's style had changed internally by the time he wrote the concerto; he no longer needed overt musical symbols from spirituals or what he called the sadness of prairies.[40]

The genesis of the concerto was direct, its composition swift. Dvořák heard Herbert's Cello Concerto no. 2 at Carnegie Hall in a Philharmonic concert conducted by Anton Seidl and was so moved by it that he rushed backstage after the performance and embraced its com-poser. Directly inspired by Herbert's concerto, Dvořák wrote his own Cello Concerto in only three months. It is not surprising that he would have been taken by Herbert's concerto. Like Dvořák, Herbert was a European composer with a seemingly inexhaustible lyric gift, and he, too, loved American culture and was determined to make the most of it. His famous operettas were still before him, but he had composed an orchestral *Vision of Columbus* the year before the concerto, his coun-terpart to Dvořák's *American Flag*.

These New World Concertos have striking similarities, at least on the surface. Both begin with somber motifs that seem to signify their

Old World origins, but they soon shed their weight. The slow movement of Herbert's concerto has an enchanted New World airiness and innocence far removed from his Teutonic training; the remarkable delicacy of Dvořák's slow movement may well have been inspired by its example. In both works, the traditional heaviness of the cello disappears, allowing the instrument to soar into the open air. By the end of the Herbert, the cello has taken on a feathery lightness that makes it sound like a wind instrument. Dvořák's scoring is equally transparent, but his slow movement carries a personal burden of sadness: it was written as a musical love letter to his sister-in-law, Josephina, the secret love of his life, who sent him a letter describing her rapidly disintegrating health just before he began the movement. Dvořák's concerto certainly cuts deeper than Herbert's, but it shares its open-air exuberance, its emotional directness, and its feeling of spontaneity.

When Dvořák returned to Prague in 1894, he carried at least the ghost of his new American sensibility with him. In the symphonic poem "The Wild Dove," for example, the dreamlike conclusion recalls the Largo of the Ninth Symphony. On one occasion, the New World was revisited in a literal way: Dvořák composed a new, more expansive ending to the Cello Concerto upon hearing of Josephina's death in 1895, one that again invoked the *New World* Symphony in its cyclical nostalgia and epic grandeur.

It is this interaction between two worlds that defines New World music. Much of the output of Dvořák's American disciples who followed his lead and mined black spirituals—Goldmark, Loomis, and Cook, for example—is oddly literal-minded by comparison. But the double perspective of a European in the New World created a uniquely productive tension and complexity, that of New World energy combined with Old World sophistication, of jauntiness mingled with homesickness.

Dvořák's experience in America continues to have a powerful resonance for East European musicians who find themselves in America. When Kurt Masur came to New York to take over the Philharmonic, he immediately programmed and recorded the *New World* Symphony, remarking on the difference "between the feeling of Dvořák here and Dvořák at home—here there is the homesickness in the piece, that comes out very clearly."[41] New York in particular evokes homesickness for the old country and an eager embrace of the new. When the Czech conductor Zdenek Macal moved to New York in 1993, the year of the

Dvořák centenary, he felt a parallel between his experience and Dvořák's: "New York always brings excitement, and it did for Dvořák too," he told me after he arrived on the Upper West Side. New York offers an infinite "possibility to explore." Macal regards the paradox of a pastoral *New World* Symphony composed in a big city as a perfectly comprehensible subjective phenomenon; the Largo was "something completely new" coming from "spirituals and Indian songs in the back of Dvořák's mind." Even the *Slavonic Dances* did not emerge "in the form he heard on the street. The greatness of composers is that they are inspired by new songs or cultures, and then they transform them their own way. The New World brought Dvořák a new kind of inspiration."[42]

While Dvořák was forging a New World aesthetic in New York, another European, the English composer Frederick Delius, was engaged in a remarkably similar venture based on his stay in Solano Grove, Florida. Like Dvořák's New World sound, Delius's was based in large part on the spirit and shape of African-American slave songs and, to a lesser degree, on Native American motifs. In another striking parallel, Delius's sound world was strongly influenced by American literature, including Longfellow's *Hiawatha*.

Delius's New World experience is the inversion of Dvořák's. The latter was internationally famous when he wrote his *New World* Symphony; his American period was the culmination of a career spent reinventing folk music. Delius's saturation in American culture came at the beginning, when he was only twenty-two. It was the great formative experience of his life, carrying over into virtually everything he wrote for the next forty-seven years.

Their expropriation of American culture led them in radically different directions. Dvořák's charging rhythms and blazing fanfares could never be confused with Delius's sultry meanderings and regressions; even in its gentlest moments, Dvořák's New World offers constant, unstoppable progression, conforming to the American myth of progress and conquest; Delius offers static calm, a hedonist's celebration of transience that makes moot the whole idea of progress. Still, the two aesthetics have in common an unmistakable soulfulness and freedom deriving from their nonwhite sources—the same qualities that the restless white heroes of nineteenth-century American writers such as Cooper, Twain, and Melville assimilate from people of color. These composers also share another New World quality, a seemingly bottomless nostalgia and sense of exile: for Dvořák, this was a lonely but temporary expatriatism; for Delius, it became something more basic, a permanent sense of disconnection from lost youth and innocence.

Delius's American odyssey began in 1884, when he was sent to Solano Grove to grow oranges on a plantation where his father, Julian, had exercised a business option. What blossomed instead was a submerged musical genius, erupting in total isolation from the musical establishment. Aside from Thomas Ward, an organist from Brooklyn who became Delius's musical tutor (one of the few professionals he claimed taught him anything important), his music lessons came in the form of black plantation workers singing at night in four-part harmony on the St. Johns River, making a sound that changed his life.

Describing these sounds to his disciple Eric Fenby, Delius noted that they had revealed "a truly wonderful sense of musicianship and harmonic resource in the instinctive way in which they treated a melody, and hearing their singing in such romantic surroundings, it was then that I first felt the urge to express myself in music."[43] The New World therefore imprinted not only Delius's musical thinking from the beginning but his very decision to become a composer. Delius's approach to art, more so than even most American artists', was distinctly Emersonian and Thoreauvian; for him, life experienced immediately and ecstatically in nature was the source of art. Artistic creation had nothing to do with anything academic or theoretical, let alone European.

Delius probably had not read these particular transcendentalists, although later, as we shall see, he eagerly imbibed Whitman, reinforcing a non-Christian pantheism forged in America long before his championing of Friedrich Nietzsche and Ernest Dowson. Delius was Emersonian and Whitmanian in his insistence that the highest art was based on the lowliest common people. His admiration of the "instinctive way" black people "treated a melody," eschewing all established rules and expectations, became the mark of his own style, as did his endless evocation of the romantic surroundings where he first heard these haunting sounds.

Dvořák had a similar attitude toward black music, but he rendered it with characteristic robustness, constructing an emotional world less constricted but also less mysterious. According to the music historian

Cecil Gray—normally a wry and skeptical observer—Delius's music is an example of "that which is known to the mystics as 'the state of illumination' . . . a kind of ecstatic revelation which may only last a split second of time, but which he who has known it spends the rest of his life trying to recapture." Delius told Gray exactly when that revelatory moment occurred: "The occasion was one summer night, when he was sitting out on the veranda of his house on his orange grove in Florida, and the sound came to him from the distance of the voices of negroes in the plantation, singing in chorus. It is the rapture of that moment that Delius is perpetually seeking to communicate in all his characteristic work."[44]

What is remarkable about this epiphany is its continuity. Delius is famous for a certain romantic haziness, but the source of his art is unexpectedly clear and permanent. The Joycean or Yeatsian "moment," which the Delian illumination anticipates, is a powerful insight or obsession, blindingly intense but ephemeral, an instant in which things come together in the mind but not necessarily the life. Indeed, the great moment (as in Joyce's "The Dead" or Woolf's *Mrs. Dalloway*) is often ambiguous or negative. But Delius's ecstatic memories of blacks singing on the river were entirely nonironic, life-changing, and positive, though the tunes themselves often told of privation and suffering. The Delian moment was also curiously real, the re-rendering of an actual physical sound, giving the music its ghostlike solidity.

Delius came at the beginning of a tradition of New World illumination. Ives was soon to begin a process of mystical reminiscence with Protestant hymns and marching bands; Varèse was to use noisy whistles and foghorns as vehicles of transcendence. And the jazz epiphanies of Ravel, Milhaud, and others were a phenomenon unto themselves. America provided fertile ground for musical revelation.

Unlike the childhood moments "recollected in tranquillity" by Romantics and post-Romantic moderns (for as Perry Meisel argues in *The Myth of the Modern*, modernism is really a new Romanticism), Delius's revelation had immediate utility: Delius left Solano Grove in 1885 but within a year began working on the suite *Florida*, his first orchestral work, based entirely on his Solano experiences. In the finale, distant horn calls "At Night" evoke Delius's first memories of black spirituals floating up the river. This enchanted nocturne from the New World fades blissfully away at the end, the first of many works by him to do so. As Sir Thomas

Beecham pointed out in his memoirs, Delius meant this signature fade-out to approximate the state of nature; it is not conventional closure but rather the silence and darkness before the next sunrise.

Florida is considerably underrated in its significance; the African-American dances "La Calinda" and the plantation dance in "Sunset–Near the Plantation," with their tambourines and swingy syncopations, pick up where Gottschalk left off forty years earlier yet come well before Joplin, Gershwin, Max Steiner, or anyone else who dealt with this material. Underplaying the originality of early Delius, critics point to the influence of Grieg, but the methodology of the two was profoundly different. Grieg's folk sources were derived from publications of Norwegian folk songs; Delius's came directly from nature, from what he saw, heard, and remembered. And he continued to remember long after he left America. In 1889 he wrote *Idylle de printemps*, a rarely performed orchestral piece, even more deliciously sensuous than *Florida*; within a year he had composed *La Quadroöne* (alternately title *Rapsodie floridienne*) and Scherzo, both part of an orchestral suite d'orchestre. The Scherzo has a Mendelssohnian delicacy—Puck camping out in the Everglades—but with none of the frailty of late Delius. *Idylle* and *La Quadroöne* have the swelling lyricism of Delius's early experiments with black music, first in Florida, later in Danville, Virgina, where he lived briefly in 1886 after abandoning his plantation in Solano Grove, attempting to make it on his own as a Virginia musician until his father allowed him to study music at the Leipzig Conservatory in the summer of 1886.

Ultimately, Delius blended black singing and its romantic surroundings into the same ecstasy, making them nearly inseparable. The focus on one or the other became a matter of choice and emphasis. His next major New World work, the opera *The Magic Fountain* (1893–95), focused on the surroundings, namely the mysterious beauties of the Everglades (as we see in "Beyond the Frontier" in this volume). In it, he also experimented with Native-American motifs, as Dvořák did in the *New World* Symphony.

Delius's personal synthesis of Indian and African-American motifs was similar to Dvořák's, although the spare, pentatonic intervals in act 2, scene 1, and the dramatic war dance are among the few overtly Indian sounds in the opera. Delius had a clear scheme in mind for these operas, at least as far as the libretti were concerned. *The Magic Fountain* was to be a Native-American work, whereas *Koanga* was to be African-American. (A third opera, on gypsy themes, never materialized.)

Koanga, which was completed the year after *The Magic Fountain*, has received a bit more attention but is still remarkably obscure for such an original, and often beautiful, work. Dealing with such juicy themes as Louisiana voodoo and interracial love, the opera may be a bit too racy. Its most controversial elements are rarely mentioned in print, though these may explain its difficulty in getting produced. (The *La Calinda* dance sequence was banned in the state of Louisiana.)

Politically incorrect in a variety of ways, *Koanga* has something to offend just about everybody. In flashback, an old servant, Uncle Joe, depicts plantation life in a long-ago romantic haze that initially seems to present happy slaves preparing their masters' meals and weddings in bucolic sunlight. (Delius was certainly not the first European to admire southern ideology or to romanticize plantation life.) But once the hero is presented, everything changes, even though the initial romantic images are never really retracted: the hero of the piece is Koanga, a proud African voodoo prince sold into slavery who refuses to work for his new white masters, prophesying the bloody liberation and just revenge of his people.

Delius then goes a step further by creating a more elaborate and subversive version of novelist George Washington Cable's original voodoo-versus-Christianity showdown. In the opera, the former unambiguously—indeed, triumphantly—wins. Enraged by the plantation manager separating him from Palmyra, his mulatto lover, Koanga calls down a spectacular, and peculiarly nonselective, voodoo curse that virtually wipes out the plantation—blacks and whites alike. "We shall be free, never more to slave!" he shouts, as he reigns down his "triple curse on land, on air, and flood." In the grim finale, the white plantation owners torture Koanga to death after he has killed his white tormentor with a spear, though the voodoo hex prevails. "His curse will remain with you," gloats Palmyra.[45]

Steeped in the pantheism that Delius continued to develop in his mature work, *Koanga* not only describes but passionately participates in voodoo paganism as the logical alternative to a Christianity that condones slavery. Far from being sinister, the major voodoo scene in the middle of the opera, framed by an austere unison woodwind passage and delicate harp figurations, contains some of Delius's most seductive impressionist effects. Here he conjures music that is literally a magic spell, culminating in Palmyra's faraway voice drifting over Koanga's prayer to the morning star. At the end, Palmyra, a devout Christian, angrily converts to voodoo, renouncing Christianity as she commits suicide so that her spirit can join her "beloved Prince and Prophet... you who gave me my belief and showed me Voodoo's mighty power."[46] As for "La Renaissance," Cable's idyllic Louisiana plantation, it is reduced by Koanga's curse to the "land of the living death." Neither the composer nor his African hero appears to have any regrets.

The opera therefore goes full circle, ostensibly celebrating a white supremacist view of plantation life, then wiping it out. Conventional criticism of the libretto, on the grounds that it is confusing and inconsistent, misses the point: the work is more potent and shocking precisely because it turns on itself. *Koanga* does not merely deconstruct the myth of the Old South; it constructs, then demolishes it. Delius was clearly attracted to the romance and exoticism of southern life, as he was to any lost cause or vanishing way of life. (His tone poem *Hiawatha*, discussed in Chapter 2 of this book, is from the same period.) But Delius's sympathies were more deeply embedded in the black culture that was oppressed and enslaved. The haunting originality of *Koanga* reflects a painful ambivalence in the composer: Delius was notoriously elitist and aristocratic, but he also loved the musical culture and African heritage of black America. *Koanga* is a document of double exile, the work of an outsider not only in the New World but in the Old as well. It avoids all the patterns, and conventions, of both nineteenth-century opera and black life as treated by white artists.

Despite his aristocratic predilections, Delius was more deeply empathetic with his African-American sources—spiritually as well as aesthetically—than Dvořák. Born of peasant stock and a natural friend of the oppressed, Dvořák was also a pious Catholic whose worship of nature was of a decidedly safe variety. Delius, on the other hand, was temperamentally subversive, a radical from the beginning; his idyllic experiences in Florida resulted in a powerful bond with black people, to whom he owed the soul of his aesthetic. This sympathy was neither condescending nor ideological, but profoundly personal: as Christopher Palmer points out, Delius connected with the sorrow and isolation of African Americans, for they reflected his own.

The most potent demonstration of this bond was *Koanga*, which is thoroughly on the side of the African prince and his gods. This perspective gives Delius's New World music a special pagan authenticity, a quality not found in Dvořák, Coleridge-Taylor, or other New World Europeans, and certainly not in the music of Americans such as MacDowell and Beach. His source was George Washington Cable's popular novel *The Grandissimes*, which had appeared five years earlier, after being serialized in *Scribner's*. Cable was a hot author in 1880s America, and Delius was tuned into American literary trends. He loved and imbibed American literature throughout his career. To him, Longfellow, Cable, Whitman, and Twain represented a rich and fresh source of inspiration. As far as he was concerned, Europeans "went on stolidly creating dead works."[47] With the exception of Scandinavia (which became his deep-freeze replacement for sunny Florida), America and its literature represented the best alternative to this stolidity and deadness, much as it did for Poe-lovers Debussy and Ravel and the Whitmanians Gustav Holst and Vaughan Williams. The few critics who have addressed the *Koanga* libretto criticize Cable as an unlikely and problematic choice for an opera. Nevertheless, Cable's novel suited Delius's complicated purposes, despite the challenges it presented in tone, texture, and Creole dialect. An early "new South" liberal from New Orleans, Cable presented slavery as a decadent, destructive institution: the mutilated hero adapted by Delius is Mioko-Koanga (in French, Bras-Coupé, or "Arm Cut Off"), who "made himself into a type of all Slavery, turning into flesh and blood the truth that all Slavery is maiming." A "solemn, exalted" African noble, Koanga refuses to be turned into a commodity. Cable depicts the brutality of slavery in unflinching detail, building to an explicit torture scene that depicts the "mutilated but unconquered" Koanga, "his ears shorn from his head, and the tendons behind his knees severed," a scene rejected by *Scribner's* as "unmitigatedly distressful."[48]

But the novel also has a gushy, late-Victorian side, especially evident in its arch, pseudopoetic dialogue. This jarring combination of violence and unctuousness is turned to surprisingly expressive purposes in Delius's opera: it is refined and glossed over (in the best sense) by the seductiveness of the music, but it also provides the tension between the mythmaking of the opening scenes and its demolition in the rest. Like the novel, the opera takes us by surprise.

The libretto maintains the spicy gumbo flavor of Cable's novel. Its history is a mixed-up affair as well, beginning with a treatment of Cable's story by Charles Keary (a friend of Delius's wife-to-be, Jelka Rosen) that was subsequently embellished by Frederick and Jelka, translated by Jelka into German for the Eberfield premiere in 1904 (after the original English version failed to get produced), translated back into English by Jelka for the 1933 London premiere, and finally "reconstructed" in 1973 by Douglas Craig and Andrew Page.

In the notes to their excellent reconstruction (which does indeed re-create the "feeling of Cable's novel"), the Craig-Page team makes the odd statement that after 1904 "a new element of Christianity versus Voodoo was extraneously introduced" into Cable's original by the Deliuses.[49] In fact, the conflict between the two religions does exist in Cable's novel, though in a less elaborate form. Koanga's curse on the plantation, unlike the version in the opera, is trenchant and in French, but just as deadly; Cable has his African prince invoke only a single voodoo deity, but one that does the job.

Delius made his voodoo sympathies clear in the libretto, whereas for Cable, voodoo was a motif to keep the plot going. Koanga's ecstatic prayer to the morning star, for example, the most overtly pantheistic outpouring in all of Delius, does not appear in "The Story of Bras-Coupé," the chapter of *The Grandissimes* loosely excerpted for the opera, nor does Palmyra's anti-Christian diatribe. *Koanga* is not so much an opera about voodoo as a white man's attempt to write a voodoo opera. On the other hand, Cable's novel, in addition to its greater balance and objectivity, has touches of grotesque humor missing in the opera; in Cable's wedding scene, for example, Koanga gets drunk for the first time in his life and calls his slave owner "white trash."

Koanga brought everything together for Delius; as would be the case with his discovery of Whitman, a literary work became a catalyst for memory. In Florida, he had heard tales of voodoo and slavery from black people who had made their way from Louisiana; these became the seeds that blossomed when he read Cable's vividly sensational novel. Unlike Wagner, who had to invent his own non-Christian mythology to express his outsider status, Delius found one ready-made in the New World.

For all its convoluted exoticism—a Louisiana voodoo opera written by a native of Yorkshire living in Paris as a way of reinvoking Florida—it is surprising how consistent and integrated the work sounds. *The Magic Fountain* has wilder, more unpredictable orchestral music but is still bound by operatic conventions in its separation of scenes, ensembles, and arias. *Koanga*, however, seems to invent its own form as it goes along. The vocal writing is more delicate than the heavy breathing in *The Magic Fountain*, its sources in black folk culture clearly evident even in Delius's sumptuous harmonies. *Koanga* is therefore exactly the kind of American opera advocated by Dvořák and Anton Seidl, the erotic electricity in the Koanga-Palmyra love story adding multicultural spice.

Lacking conventional separation between aria, ensemble, and other traditional operatic devices, *Koanga* has what Delius called flow, his term for aesthetic bliss. This is not Wagnerian continuity, although Delius admired Wagner more than he did most other composers. The music is too concise to be Wagnerian. The main device involves free variations on a Delian re-creation of an old slave tune—the same structure Delius was later to use in the revised *Appalachia*. This hymnlike melody (one Delius picked up in Danville, Virginia) opens the opera and hauntingly suffuses it from beginning to end. The blazing sunrise scene in the epilogue, one of Delius's rare fortissimo endings, brings the curtain down on his American operas.

The better-known *Appalachia*, originally sketched at the same time as *Koanga* but revised six years later in Delius's mature style, is thoroughly steeped in the opera's experiments. Again, Delius reinvents a form, in this case the tone poem, and again uses variations on black melody transformed by Delian harmonies. *Appalachia* (the title refers to the Native American name for North America) is a further refinement of the aesthetic inaugurated in *Koanga* and *The Magic Fountain*. The offstage choruses in the two operas, which progressively dominate each work, become subliminal night sounds here, until they coalesce into a cappella renditions of two texts, the black spiritual "After Night Comes the Day" and a tragic narrative of a black family separated by slavery, "Oh Honey, I Am Going Down the River." Together these summarize what Delius was trying to say in both the human and natural realms, the first intoning the eternal renewal of nature despite the loss described in the second.

Cunningly shorn of Christian references, this newly created "spiritual" compactly articulates Delius's view of the world:

> After night has gone comes the day.
> The dark shadows will fade away
> t'ords the morning lift a voice
> let the scented woods rejoice
> and echoes swell across the mighty stream.

The scented sounds of nature lift a voice, even as echoes swell to slow them down, prolonging the promised cadence in a way that suggests infinity. The harmony itself embodies nature's infinite regeneration in the face of the tragedy depicted in the second text.

According to Christopher Palmer, the chorus captures "within the context in which it was experienced" the exact moment Delius heard echoes of black music swelling "across the mighty stream."[50] But this double vision appears earlier in Delius's New World operas. "After night"—the doom suffered by both sets of racially mixed couples—"comes the day": the "rosy hues of dawn" in *The Magic Fountain*, the "sun-kissed world" awakening in the peroration of *Koanga*. *Appalachia* gains its greatest power when experienced in the context of the two Appalachian operas, authenticating with African-American Sorrow Songs what Delius had intuited in his own *Magic Fountain* libretto and his black-voodoo version of Cable's white-genteel novel.

Appalachia is the culmination of a New World aesthetic that begins with *Florida*. The more dense harmonic language of *Appalachia*, meandering into infinity, has its beginnings in the straighter lines but exotic atmosphere of *Florida*, as well as in the gradually expanding harmonic sophistication of the *Idylle*, Suite, and operas. Early Delius is more vital and important than is commonly supposed. The innocence and openness of *Florida* and the *Idylle*—the vigorous rhythms, the clear sense that the harmonies are going somewhere—are actually closer to the spirit of its prejazz folk sources than the more static, "advanced" Delius (the latter anticipates progressive jazz harmony, something dramatically different from prejazz spirituals); and the operas, neither as linear as *Florida* nor as voluptuous as *Appalachia*, embody the best elements of both.

Constant Lambert speculated in *Music Ho!* that Delius provided the link between jazz and art music. But Delius's rhythms, limpid to the point of mystical stasis, are far removed from the electric pulse of jazz. What he more clearly hooked up to concert music were the harmonies, cadences, and deep spirituality of black hymns. This achievement he was to share with the far more popular Dvořák and with the briefly popular Samuel Coleridge-Taylor. The former has remained extraordinarily prominent; the latter has fallen into an obscurity as deep as Delius's when he was living in the Flordia Marshland.

In 1904, the British composer Samuel Coleridge-Taylor, the "black Mahler," declared that reading W. E. B. DuBois's *The Souls of Black Folk* had changed his life. This was a year after the book's publication; two years later DuBois was to launch the Niagra Movement, and in another two the National Association for the Advancement of Colored People (NAACP). Coleridge-Taylor was already an avid follower of American literature, especially that of Longfellow and Whitman, but DuBois's masterpiece was a more life-changing epiphany. Calling it "the greatest book I have ever read," he immersed himself in its radical politics and its evocation of African-American slave songs.[51]

Coleridge-Taylor had already made his reputation with *Hiawatha*, his astonishingly popular cantata; for the remainder of his short life, he would concentrate on the African Americana inspired by DuBois. Like Dvořák, his "first love," he based his New World music on a precise configuration of American poetry—including, in the case of *Hiawatha*, the same poem—and on black spirituals. But in his case the transmission was more direct: Coleridge-Taylor was a black composer himself, and *The Souls of Black Folk* was a declaration of independence for black music.

Coleridge-Taylor's rapid rise to fame was without parallel in the history of black classical composers; had he been American, his dramatic ascent as a musical celebrity would have been dubbed an American success story. Born into a racially mixed family—his father was a doctor from Sierra Leone, his mother a white Englishwoman—Coleridge-Taylor prevailed over formidable racial obstacles to receive the imprimatur of Stanford, Elgar, Joachim, and virtually everyone else in the Victorian musical order, composing for the Royal College of Music at the young age of sixteen. Every stage of his career, including all three installments of *Hiawatha*, was met with huge acclaim, demonstrating that an aspiring black musician could make it in the highest levels of Anglo culture.

Or so the mythology goes. The real story, at least in London, seems to have been harsher, although no one has pieced it together in its entirety. Coleridge-Taylor's life was a constant struggle against poverty, even the *Hiawatha* phase, which earned him critical success but little money. His relationship with his white wife, a young singer from Croydon who studied with him, was clouded from the beginning by racial insults from his wife's family. Even Coleridge-Taylor's most fervent supporters had trouble with this aspect of his life: his early biographer W. C. Berwick Sayers, in an ostensibly positive account, wrote that the wife's white parents regarded Coleridge-Taylor as a low form of life, but that they were, after all, "honourable, kindly people, who desired the best for their girl." Because blacks were seen as belonging "to a lower stage of development," what else should one expect from the poor girl's kindly parents? Coleridge-Taylor's father eventually returned to Africa, because he could no longer tolerate racial bigotry, but his son had to fight it constantly. The most trivial aspects of genteel London life were fraught with trouble: on one occasion a clergyman who came to tea casually asked the composer, "Do you actually drink tea and eat bread-and-butter like other people?"[52]

As a consequence, Coleridge-Taylor was more than ready for the cleansing anger of DuBois. But DuBois was not the first African-American writer to influence his life. In 1896, the American poet Paul Laurence Dunbar toured London and became Coleridge-Taylor's friend and colleague. Together they delivered remarkable joint recitals, with Dunbar reading new poems and Coleridge-Taylor performing his new settings of them (*African Romances, Dream Lovers*) as both pianist and choral conductor. Dunbar, a celebrated singer as well as poet, was often a soloist.

The great sweetness and sincerity of Dunbar's verse, so disarmingly combined with its extraordinary technical brilliance, was an ideal match for Coleridge-Taylor's music. Numerous extramusical parallels exist as well. Both men rose with meteoric swiftness as pioneer black artists, then died just as quickly within ten years of each other, Dunbar of tuberculosis at thirty-three, Coleridge-Taylor of pneumonia at thirty-seven. Both wrote in an essentially Romantic idiom yet were genuine vanguard figures in anticipating the Harlem Renaissance. Both had the official approval of the most stuffily influential elder white artists in their fields: for Coleridge-Taylor, it was Sir Edward Elgar, who pronounced him the best composer of his generation; for Dunbar, it was William Dean Howells, who introduced Dunbar's *Lyrics of Lowly Life* by stating that Dunbar's "divinations" of black life offered "for the first time in our tongue, literary interpretations of a very artistic completeness." Unlike Elgar, whose praise was clean, Howells peppered his accolades with racist asides, including the comment that Dunbar had a "finely ironical perception of the negro's limitations."[53]

Above all, both men were lyricists who envisioned music as subjective and therapeutic. Pioneers in the struggle for black equality, they were Romantic artists first. Coleridge-Taylor, like his model Dvořák, completely reinvisioned his folk sources, investing the lowliest "Bamboula" with Tchaikovskian plushness, the saddest funeral scene with his indomitable optimism. Authenticity was distinctly less important than imagination. The son of slaves, Dunbar has been criticized for romanticizing plantation life, but he too reimagined reality aesthetically, viewing music as the great transformer and comforter. In "Over the Hills," which appears in an all-Dunbar set by Coleridge-Taylor called *African Romances*, the poet declares, "Singing, I roam afar"; in a world of sorrow,

> Life is the night with its dream-visions teeming,
> Death is the waking at day.

Like Whitman in *The Sleepers*, the Dunbar persona links erotic love with subjective vision as the source of meaning:

> Daytime or night-time, I constantly roving,—
> Dearest one, thou art my star.

Coleridge-Taylor also fused dream visions with love lyrics, collaborating with Dunbar on *Dream Lovers*, a compact opera in which a racially mixed couple meets first in a dream.[54]

The nearly total disappearance of the Dunbar–Coleridge-Taylor collaborations from the repertory is sad and perplexing, especially in a musical culture that thrives on revivals of forgotten Romantic works. With its Dunbar libretto and Coleridge-Taylor music, *Dream Lovers* is a landmark in the history of black art, and the *African Romances* are musical treatments of some of the most ravishing lyrics by America's first major African-American poet. Black music has become so completely identified with American pop idioms that a classical composer like Coleridge-Taylor is simply off the cultural radar screen.

One exception to this neglect is "Danse Nègre," an orchestral work named after and inspired by a Dunbar poem. This piece does occasionally find its way onto programs devoted to black material (thereby being ghettoized even as it is revived). Originally the finale from the 1898 *African Suite*, the "Danse" was later orchestrated by the composer as a separate entity. As a European work inspired by an American literary text and imbued with the spirit of African-American folk music, it stands as a notable example of the New World genre initiated by Dvořák. The flute melody that dominates the piece is an invention, not a quotation; it breathes an air of freshness and spontaneity, though its composer was a master of calculation.

Coleridge-Taylor's connection with Dunbar was aesthetic and personal. DuBois added a new political dimension. Coleridge-Taylor happened to read DuBois the same year he set sail for Boston on the first of three American tours. He was particularly moved by the final essay in the book, "Of the Sorrow Songs," on African-American music and its significance. In this somber and searing manifesto, a prose poem in the form of music criticism, DuBois declares these songs to be the "articulate message of the slave to the world. . . . They are the music of an unhappy people, of the children of disappointment; they tell of death and sufferings and unvoiced longing toward a truer world of misty wanderings and hidden ways." This music is "distinctly sorrowful . . . music of trouble and exile," yet it also breathes hope and "a faith in the ultimate justice of things. The minor cadences of despair often change to triumph and calm confidence. Sometimes it is a faith in life, sometimes a faith in death."[55]

Calm confidence exactly describes Coleridge-Taylor's African-American settings. He must have been particularly struck by DuBois's experience—identical to his own—with the Fisk Jubilee Singers: according to DuBois, the sounds of the Fisk Jubilee Singers awoke in him a powerful awareness of the struggles, tragedies, and unique musical achievements of his black ancestors. Coleridge-Taylor was stirred too: when he heard the Fisk Jubilee Singers for the first time in London in the late 1890s, he credited them with revealing to him for the first time the "beautiful folk music of my race." [56]

"Of the Sorrow Songs" is a critical document in the literature of New World Symphonies. It offers a gloss not only on Coleridge-Taylor but on other Europeans enraptured by African-American material. De-

The Fisk Jubilee Singers, whose tours inspired a new sense of African-American musical identity. (Beinecke Rare Book and Manuscript Library, Yale University)

lius was moved most by what DuBois called the sense of exile in spirituals, the "unvoiced longing" that finds its expression in "misty wanderings"—an apt description of Delius's art. Later Europeans such as Lambert and Korngold would also wander in these mists. Coleridge-Taylor focused on endurance and hope, on "minor cadences of despair" changing to "triumph and calm confidence." With its lucid lines and bold resolutions, Coleridge-Taylor's music is never wandering or misty.

The most startling connection between *The Souls of Black Folk* and the literature of New World music is the uncanny resemblance of key phrases to Dvořák's statements on black melody. DuBois called spirituals "the sole American music" and "the most beautiful expression of human experience, born this side [of] the seas";[57] more than a decade earlier, Dvořák, in an 1892 article in the *New York Times* on the centrality of black plantation songs, had called them the "folk songs of America," and in his 1895 piece for *Harper's* he had revered them as "the most striking and appealing melodies that have yet been found on this side of the Atlantic."[58] Again, it is hard to underestimate the importance of Dvořák, naive and childlike as he may have seemed, as a sophisticated and prescient observer of the American scene. And again, we see the emergence of a remarkably unified New World musical aesthetic, as composers and writers of different races and ethnicities on both sides of the Atlantic echoed one another. The configurations are everywhere similar: like Dvořák and Delius, Coleridge-Taylor was influenced by a combination of literature and, more directly, black spirituals. As the composer of *Hiawatha*, Coleridge-Taylor resembled both composers by mingling the motifs of Native Americans—the other "other"—with those of African Americans.

On the surface, Coleridge-Taylor's mission appears more straightforward than that of Dvořák or Delius. His sources, DuBois and Dunbar, had immediate resonance; they were black men speaking in eloquent poetry and prose to someone who was determined to make the music of his race accessible to the world. A black European, for a change, was working with African-American music.

Yet these progressive literary voices created a curious paradox for Coleridge-Taylor, for they were in tension with his musical conservatism. (His dilemma was the inverse of many modernists', whose political conservatism clashed with artistic radicalism.) For a young composer, Coleridge-Taylor's musical vocabulary was stolidly diatonic and conventional; it was his imaginative manipulation of a waning language that was distinctive, not the language itself. He deplored "modern music" (which he invidiously compared with the "genuine simplicity" of Dvořák).[59] His advocacy of black music, however, did not emphasize the rhythmic swing and harmonic inventiveness that would later be called jazz—and become an important marker of modernism.

Like Dvořák and Delius, he was interested in the long lines and swelling cadences of spirituals. The music of these composers constitutes a prelude and a parallel tradition to symphonic jazz but is not really part of it. Rhythmic snap and syncopation did interest Coleridge-Taylor, as illustrated in his bracing piano setting of "Run, Mary, Run," but rhythmic innovation was never his main focus. The latter setting is one of the most charming of the *Twenty-Four Negro Melodies* for piano, Coleridge-Taylor's major achievement in an idiom that became the forerunner of Copland's *Old American Songs* and Percy Grainger's transcriptions of Gershwin. Composed in 1904, the year of his first American tour and his reading of DuBois, these variations on African and African-American tunes, including several Sorrow Songs discussed in *The Souls of Black Folk*, strip away Coleridge-Taylor's usual Victorianisms for a new American directness, even as they retain a rich strain of his Romantic voice.

This ambitious work is based on African-American melodies from the Jubilee Songs and, to a lesser extent, on *Les Chants et les contes des Ba-Ronga*, a South African set. Sixteen of the pieces are African-American, including "Deep River," "I Was Way Down A-Yonder," "Steal Away," and "Sometimes I Feel Like a Motherless Child." The *Melodies* continued to pop up in Coleridge-Taylor's later music: "I'm Troubled in Mind" became the theme for the fourteen *Symphonic Variations on an African Air* (one of the first Coleridge-Taylor orchestral works to appear on compact disc); and "Deep River" became a violin solo, "Slow Movement on a Negro Melody, Deep River."

Coleridge-Taylor chose only six tunes from Africa, the rest from African America. His imagination was increasingly drawn to the New World, a tendency that began with his Longfellow phase and culminated in his American tours. DuBois regarded music as the art that most piquantly conveyed the black experience in America, both its horrors and triumphs. In the *Melodies*, Coleridge-Taylor explored what DuBois called America's spiritual heritage, from the most primitive tribal sounds to "music of a singular sweetness," although he was decidedly more compatible with the latter.[60]

In his foreword to *Twenty-Four Negro Melodies*, Coleridge-Taylor stated that "what Brahms has done for the Hungarian folk music, Dvořák for the Bohemian, and Grieg for the Norwegian, I have tried to do for these Negro Melodies." These were not so much transcriptions as free variations: "The Negro Melodies in this volume are not merely arranged—on the contrary they have been amplified, harmonized and altered in other respects to suit the purposes of the book. However beautiful the actual melodies are in themselves, there can be no doubt that much of their value is lost on account of their extreme brevity and unsuitability for the ordinary amateur. . . . The actual melody has in every case been inserted at the head of each piece as a motto. . . . Therefore my share in the matter can be clearly traced, and must not be confounded with any idea of 'improving' the original material any more than Brahms's *Variations on a Theme of Handel* improved that."[61]

These words reveal a late nineteenth-century predilection for embroidery over actuality, amplification over authenticity. Like Anton Rubenstein before him, who created a virtuoso version of "Yankee Doodle" for his American tour, Coleridge-Taylor was a major concert pianist, a performer who needed something more than material that was merely beautiful and of "extreme brevity." Still, he managed to create something with real substance and inventiveness. These are not just showpieces. In now-familiar songs such as "Sometimes I Feel like a Motherless Child" and "Deep River," the basic melody is instantly recognizable but profoundly altered by a rich accretion of rolled chords, embellishments, and surprise modulations, some sounding like early barbershop, others like early Debussy, most like nothing else in music. By the end, the melody has taken on a new profile, its loneliness soothed into a feeling of relaxed benevolence—the emotion usually produced by this sunny composer's music.

These transcriptions are some of Coleridge-Taylor's most original pieces. Having been written long before Gershwin, they constitute an extraordinary example of multiculturalism, an Anglo-Negro hybrid unlike anything in modern culture. In Coleridge-Taylor's earlier work, only the Anglican part of the equation received full voice; the combination of DuBois and the Fisk Jubilee Singers now released the "heritage of [his] race" in full voice.

Booker T. Washington credited this music with reviving an appetite for black folk music at the very moment "when interest in the plantation songs seems to be dying out with the generation that gave them birth."[62] The importance of the *Melodies* is incalculable, yet they are rarely mentioned in histories of African-American music or in analyses of how America and Europe nourished each other musically. In his concept of a "Black Atlantic," for example, Paul Gilroy discusses such noisy phenomena as rap and hip-hop as "the latest export from black America to have found favor in black Britain," its success "built on transnational structures of circulation and intercultural exchange established long ago."[63] Although Coleridge-Taylor's name typically never appears in this discussion, the evidence cited by Gilroy for an early black Atlantic "intercultural exchange" is the music kept alive by the Fisk Jubilee Singers in their Victorian tours—the music protected from later oblivion (if Washington is correct) by Coleridge-Taylor.

Coleridge-Taylor himself was aware of his blurred image and complex identity. When invited by a group of black singers to tour America, he assured them that his life was "not spent entirely in drawing rooms and concert halls, but among some of the roughest people in world."[64] (He was referring here to an earlier tour through the Welsh hinterlands.) He made this somewhat defensive statement eight months after reading *The Souls of Black Folk*; from then on, he wanted to be thought of as a black man aware of his heritage, not merely as a genteel inhabitant of drawing rooms. Even his own racial mixture began to trouble him: on his death bed, he worried that he would be remembered as a Creole rather than as a black.

What was so impressive and poignant about Coleridge-Taylor was his deft ability to negotiate both worlds, Dunbar-DuBois as well as Stanford-Elgar. The *Negro Melodies* are richer and stranger precisely because their creator had one foot in each reality, his imagination set in the cotton field, his experience in the drawing room. The tension between the two created a vitality and freedom from formula that are the essence of Coleridge-Taylor's best work.

Even Coleridge-Taylor's advocacy of American black intellectuals was peculiarly complicated. He expressed equal admiration for DuBois and Booker T. Washington, although the former gradually won his deeper sympathies. Coleridge-Taylor's popularity was based on *Hiawatha*, a work with an adventurous program composed in a conservative musical idiom—Indian touches such as drone basses notwithstanding. Prior to his commitment to black folk music, this was the quintessential Coleridge-Taylor production, with an admiring introduction by Washington adding the requisite imprimatur. After 1904, however, Coleridge-Taylor embraced DuBois's more radical vision, creating a split in himself between the composer who shrewdly catered to the white musical establishment and the restless thinker who made it cater to him.

Well before his American tours, Coleridge-Taylor was regarded by African Americans as a role model for black achievement in a hostile white world. The premiere of *Hiawatha* at the turn of the century had made the twenty-five-year-old composer famous on both sides of the Atlantic. Washington called him "the most cultivated musician of his race," and as early as 1901 a Samuel Taylor-Coleridge Society was formed in Washington, D.C.[65] By the time he actually toured America, he was ready to wholly embrace DuBois's advocacy of black music as the ancient basis for a New World art.

In one important respect, Coleridge-Taylor's vision of black music differed dramatically from DuBois's. The Sorrow Songs were, in DuBois's view, fundamental and self-sustaining, though music was but one aspect of DuBois's revolutionary perspective on black culture. "Your country?" he asks white America: "How came it yours? Before the Pilgrims landed we were here. We have brought our three gifts and mingled them with yours: a gift of story and song . . . the gift of sweat and brawn to beat back the wilderness, conquer the soil, and lay the foundations of this vast economic empire two hundred years before your weak hands could have done it."[66]

In contrast to this stinging rhetoric, Coleridge-Taylor, a black but also a European trying on New World clothes, continued to evaluate black music in terms of its equality with the white European tradition. The latter remained his measuring stick, as the foreword to the *Melodies* makes clear: "One of the most striking points regarding this music is, in the author's opinion, its likeness to that of the Caucasian race. . . . Primitive as it is, it nevertheless has all the elements of the European folk-song and it is remarkable that no alterations have had to be made before treating the Melodies."[67]

This assessment of black music in relation to what, by the 1980s, came to be known as the art of dead white males has surely been a factor in Coleridge-Taylor's frequent exclusion from African-American studies. Coleridge-Taylor's attitude was consistent with his scathing denunciation of Scott Joplin and ragtime. Like many of his black contemporaries, notably Washington, Coleridge-Taylor regarded ragtime as the lowest form of "coon music," a genre barely distinguishable from minstrel music, associated with brothels and saloons, mingling the worst aspects of black and white life. Now, of course, Joplin is regarded as a cultural hero who suffered all manner of racial insult and abuse to forge a new minority art; his former detractors are regarded as reactionaries and as enemies of jazz and all things multicultural. That Coleridge-Taylor was himself black only makes matters worse, especially since he managed to accommodate himself to an elite white establishment. What is sometimes forgotten is that even DuBois largely regarded "contemporary 'coon' songs" as debasements and imitations of real black music.[68]

Like Gershwin, Coleridge-Taylor was a unifier, a figure who bridged genres and ideologies. He was as comfortable with Washington as with DuBois, with Victorian musical values as with black slave music, with the post-Romantic longueurs of Tennyson (in his musical *Idyll*) as with the cotton fields of Dunbar. He learned to survive and prosper in all these worlds. Fiercely proud of his race, he was, nonetheless, neither a separatist nor a nationalist, musically or politically.

Coleridge-Taylor's attitude toward folk music was similar to that of Grainger, Dvořák, and Bartók. He believed all folk songs to be the great proof of humanity's common roots, not merely a series of markers for separate ethnicities. When Grainger enthusiastically wrote Coleridge-Taylor that he had found Irish motifs in the *Negro Melodies*, this was regarded by both as an affirmation of racial and national connectedness. They simply assumed Irish and black folk music bounced off each other in the New World: that was an essential, ennobling aspect of the American immigrant experience. The precise manner in which European and black folk motifs impregnated each other, the subject of so much academic debate, was of limited interest to Coleridge-Taylor and his circle. The *fact* of the exchange was the significant point, and an altogether positive one. It was this context that allowed Coleridge-Taylor to regard DuBois and Washington as kindred spirits. The militance of the one and ecumenicism of the other were not mutually exclusive but equally valuable in the quest for racial justice.

Like Dvořák, Coleridge-Taylor had, before his American tour, visited the New World many times in his imagination, in the works of Longfellow, Whitman, Dunbar, and DuBois. Nevertheless, the actual visits were even more spectacular than he had anticipated. The first tour, in 1904, came about at the invitation of the Samuel Coleridge-Taylor Society, which, three years after its establishment, boasted some two hundred members. The society had made certain that the young composer would be a household name among black intellectuals as the first black artist to achieve the status of a great composer.

"My American affair," Coleridge-Taylor said in 1910, after his final tour, "has been the greatest delight of my life." On these tours, he was wildly cheered and feted by racially mixed audiences in New York, Washington, Baltimore, and Chicago, as well as by black audiences in venues such as Howard University. On his second visit to Norfolk, Virginia, according to Carl Stoekel, "he was given the rising salute by two thousand people who made great applause. . . . Then we had a truly magnificent performance of his work."[69] Wherever he went, he appeared onstage with icons of the period—at the Norfolk concert he was joined by Fritz Kreisler, Alma Gluck (who performed Minnehaha in his *Hiawatha*), Horatio Parker, and Thomas Chadwick—though he was always the star of the show.

Hiawatha provided the launching pad, but important new works were written and performed as well, including the *Negro Melodies*, commissioned by Coleridge-Taylor's new Boston publisher during his 1904 tour. Reading DuBois provided not only a new sense of mission but the impetus to dispute Washington's contention that black people should limit themselves educationally to practical rather than artistic pursuits. Coleridge-Taylor passionately agreed with DuBois that blacks should be as limitless in their ambitions as whites. In America, he was beginning to reap the benefits of that liberating point of view. Unlike his critically successful but pathetically underpaid gigs in England, his American performances netted real money as well as first-class travel accommodations.

The most dramatic product of Coleridge-Taylor's American tours was his big, splashy *Bamboula* for large orchestra. It was in 1910 at Carnegie Hall rehearsals of this "Rhapsodic Dance" that New York Philharmonic musicians named him the "African Mahler." Mahler himself presided over the Philharmonic during this period, and the label really has more to do with Coleridge-Taylor as maestro than as composer. Still, the piece almost supports it, especially when we compare this *Bamboula* with the earlier, more famous one by Gottschalk, which is sultry, snappy, and to the point. Even Coleridge-Taylor's piano *Bamboula* is relatively straightforward, despite its basic pulse being teased, slowed, and speeded up with his usual alterations.

The orchestral version, however, is something else altogether. Despite Coleridge-Taylor's bland statement that it is "merely a series of evolutions" of the dance motif, this is a gaudy extravaganza, a European reinvention of black folk music full of rich string tremolos, huge brass climaxes, and a lyrical clarinet-oboe interlude that renders the original motif barely recognizable—a *Bamboula* in Technicolor.[70]

The final, triumphant cymbal crash of *Bamboula* was an appropriate finale to Coleridge-Taylor's "American affair." His sudden, tragic death left undiminished a rare encounter with the New World in which reality matched mythology. In his case, the myth of the New World delivered in full its promise of egalitarianism, generosity, tolerance, and creative energy. He was fully prepared for the worst, as were his promoters. The Coleridge-Taylor Society warned him in 1904 to expect racist taunts, and the composer was acutely aware of America's post-Reconstruction race problems. "I can assure you," he wrote the society, "that no one will be able to stop me from paying you my long deferred visit. As for prejudice, I am well prepared for it. Surely that which you and many others have lived in for so many years will not quite kill me."[71]

What did kill him, two years after his third tour, was pneumonia, but the anticipated racial insults apparently did not materialize. Nor is there any indication that he was feted out of tokenism, Uncle Tomism, exoticism, or any other condescending motive. He was hailed as a serious, successful black artist, with no caveats or noxious qualifications of the sort endured by Dunbar in the guise of praise from William Dean Howells. It may well be that his love of America was a function of his touring rather than of living in it; nevertheless, America became his favorite artistic environment, his new Eden. His early death at least ensured that this New World innocence would never be tarnished.

Coleridge-Taylor's triumph in America fulfilled the faith proclaimed in *The Souls of Black Folk*, perfectly timed to launch Coleridge-Taylor's first American tour. "Through all the sorrow of the Sorrow Songs," wrote DuBois, "there breathes a hope—a faith in the ultimate justice of things. . . . The meaning is always clear: that sometime, somewhere, men will judge men by their souls and not by their skin." Of course, DuBois is merely voicing a hope, a faith, and he concludes with the obvious question: "Is such a hope justified?"[72] In the case of Coleridge-Taylor, the answer, for once, was a rousing yes. Music was the vehicle of this hope, and Coleridge-Taylor became, during three sensational visits to the New World, its personification. Like the promise of racial harmony he embodied, he has fallen into obscurity and is long overdue for revival.

The legacy of black spirituals in European music continued long after the breakthrough trio of Dvořák, Delius, and Coleridge-Taylor. The most poignant continuity is in the work of Entartete Musik ("Degenerate Music") composers, Jews and other "degenerates" persecuted by the Nazis in tandem with their war against "degenerate" painting. Degenerate composers and their supporters found in the Sorrow Songs a source of courage and endurance in the face of suffering and horror. The attraction had partly to do with the texts of the spirituals and with references to the struggles of biblical Jews, but it was also the music itself,

the soaring melodies and open harmonies, that seemed to promise redemption — what Coleridge-Taylor had called an intrinsic tenderness set
against bitterness and suffering,.

These qualities found their way into mid-century European music,
often in ways strikingly similar to the model of Dvořák's *New World*
Symphony. An example is Erich Korngold's String Quartet no. 1, composed in the early 1930s shortly after Korngold arrived in the New World
to escape Hilter's *Anschluss*; the composition is filled with melodies and
cadences that sound like old spirituals but are entirely new creations.
The nostalgia for the Old World echoes Dvořák's and, like his, finds an
emotional release in African-American hymns. Korngold follows Dvořák's lead in making specific references to Old World forms, in this case,
fragments of Viennese dances quoted in the finale. This is a Viennese
version of Dvořák's lost Bohemia, with a dreamlike glow unique to Korngold. In this quartet, the juxtaposition of Viennese dance fragments with
the swelling cadences of black spirituals leaves a haunting impression.
This neglected work belies the cliché that Korngold was unchanged by
America, that he simply imposed a Viennese tradition on everything he
wrote in the New World, including his fabled music for Hollywood.

An entirely different kind of "spiritual" was created by Alexander
Zemlinsky in his Symphonic Songs and in the Harlem Renaissance
settings from his Lieder op. 27. The texts are poems by Langston
Hughes, Jean Toomer, Countee Cullen, and Frank Home, many of
whom were themselves influenced by spirituals. As we see in Chapter
7, the Harlem Renaissance played a dramatic role in the Entartete story,
contributing a new idiom and sensibility to composers who suddenly
found themselves in a desperate situation. Like Korngold, Zemlinsky
was driven from his native Vienna by the Nazis; unlike his Hollywood-
bound colleague, he died four years later in total obscurity (in Larch-
mont, New York), as much an exile as the heartbroken protagonists in
the poems of Toomer and Hughes.

These settings of largely leftist black poems by a Jewish composer
represented everything abhorrent to the Nazis; they were "Jewish nigger
filth" writ large.[73] Except for a broadcast on Radio Brno in 1935, they
remained unperformed until 1964, when they were revived in Baltimore.
Zemlinsky selected his texts from the remarkable anthology *Afrika singt*,
a large collection of black American poetry translated into German by
Maurice Wright that circulated through artistic circles in Germany and

Austria in the late 1920s. (Langston Hughes turned out to be the most important musical figure, later providing the libretto for Weill's *Street Scene* and the inspiration for songs by Elie Siegmeister and other late twentieth-century composers.) At its worst, this phenomenon represented, in the words of Alex Ross, "the manipulation of dimly understood African-American imagery in behalf of shallow exotic atmosphere";[74] at its most eloquent, as in Zemlinsky's songs, it resulted in works of desolating power.

Although confronting Langston Hughes in German may seem a bit of a stretch to some listeners, especially with such titles as "Lied aus Dixieland," that peculiarity becomes part of the strange power of these songs. The harshness of the German lends itself to the dark, sometimes snarling sounds conjured by Zemlinsky, especially in the orchestral songs; more important, it contributes an atmosphere of threat and trauma. Hearing these sad, frightening poems in German makes them instantly seem like Holocaust pieces.

As a maestro, Zemlinsky's New World credentials were formidable: he conducted the premieres of both Ernst Krenek's *Jonny spielt auf*, the first jazz opera, and Weill's *Mahagonny*, which launched a revolution in musical theater. His musical idiom here is one of a complete outsider; unlike Weill, Krenek, and Erwin Schulhoff, Zemlinsky had no feel for jazz and made no attempt to jazz his work up. The musical style of these songs resembles a modern set of spirituals, with a clear melodic line complicated by harmonies that blur the distinction between major and minor thirds, between despair and hope, much like DuBois's descriptions of the Sorrow Songs. Despite the elaborate crossovers—a Viennese Jew setting black-American poems translated into German—the music feels surprisingly basic and authentic. Indeed, it is actually closer to the text, especially to the bleak conciseness of Hughes, than many treatments of black art by whites. Intensely passionate, it has not a wasted note nor a trace of sentimentality.

The Symphonic Songs open and close violently with poems depicting lynchings and their aftermath. The quietly ominous "Lied aus Dixieland," a setting of Hughes's "Song for a Dark Girl," leaves the victim in the hands of a "white Lord Jesus," an ambivalent deliverance at best. The D minor of this opening song becomes major by the final "Arabesque," a bitterly ironic gesture given the final image of a "Nigger hangin' from a tree." Like other spirituals, the Symphonic Songs invoke divine intervention as a final alternative to oppression, but they are only cautiously hopeful about its efficacy, and sometimes sarcastically dismissive. In the spirit of Huckleberry Finn, Langston Hughes's "Bad Man" says

> I'm goin' to de devil an'
> I wouldn't go to heaben if I could.

Zemlinsky is sometimes accused of being timid and indecisive, never sure whether to invoke the legacy of Mahler or Schoenberg. In these defiant settings he invokes neither but creates an idiom of New World Songs. The music is spare and stinging; open, American sounds are invoked, but with an oddly claustrophobic effect. Jean Toomer's "Cotton Song," for example, features barren octaves and clanking percussion to suggest the shackles of slavery. Equally austere is Countee Cullen's "A Brown Girl Dead," depicting a black mother who must pawn her wedding ring to pay for her daughter's funeral—so she can "lay her out in white." The cutting irony of this poem is conveyed with powerful restraint. By contrast, the pounding timpani in Hughes's "Danse Africaine" and "Bad Man" sound like a lethal sneer. Sometimes Zemlinsky achieves a cool tenderness, especially in "Misery," from the piano Lied, the most frequently performed of these songs.

In these songs, Zemlinsky stripped away the elaborate post-Romanticism and expressionism of his earlier style. What is left is the lonely English horn solo—the same instrument Dvořák used in the most famous "spiritual" in his *New World* Symphony—singing mournfully over open harmonies in Hughes's "Disillusion." As woodwinds and woodblocks mysteriously whisper good-bye to the "great dark city" of Harlem, Zemlinsky seems to bid a lonely farewell to the great cities of Europe.[75]

The remarkable range of European music influenced by spirituals can be quickly grasped by comparing Zemlinsky's songs with those of Wilhelm Grosz, also a Viennese Entartete émigré in the United States who became entranced by *Afrika singt* in the 1920s. Grosz's Afrika Songs, premiered on Radio Breslau in 1930, use three of the same poems chosen by Zemlinsky plus five others, but in his version they are utterly purged of angst. Even Jean Toomer's grim "Cotton Song" and Frank Home's image of a lynching in "Arabesque" have a lilting sweetness more akin to pop than to concert music. Touches of late Romanticism caress the harmonies, but Grosz stays close to the melodic shape of spirituals. Accompanied by bluesy trumpets, fruity alto saxophones, and atmospheric banjo-piano continuo, the Afrika Songs have a cabaret atmosphere that suggests Kurt Weill, but the music lacks Weill's irony and darkness. Grosz's version of the Harlem Renaissance offers instant therapy, a quick deliverance from the suffering and anxiety it ostensibly depicts. Depending on one's point of view, his aesthetic is either astonishingly shallow of shrewdly prescient in forecasting the late twentieth-century triumph of American pop and European neo-Romanticism in concert music.

In Europe, the spiritual continued to emerge in unexpected places, inspiring emotional catharsis and formal ingenuity. One of the most unusual settings was A Child of Our Time, a 1939 oratorio by the British composer Michael Tippett. This highly personal response to the Holocaust was first conceived when Tippett read of the imprisonment of a young Polish Jew by the Nazis and the pogrom that followed the boy's killing of a minor Nazi official as a response to the persecution of his parents. Tippett's innovation was the incorporation of black spirituals into a huge oratorio modeled on Handel's Messiah.

The idea was as simple as it was brilliant. "The spirituals themselves have turned and twisted Bible language into a modern dialect," Tippett explained. "The stories they tell of the Bible Jews are used to comfort Negroes in the bitterness of oppression, and I use these Negro spirituals to symbolize the agony of modern Jews in Hitler's Europe. It makes a powerful, condensed poetic image."[76] Used in place of the traditional congregational hymns, spirituals thus provided not only texts, musical interludes, and harmonic structures but a "condensed image" of horror and heroism played out on different stages of history. Again, black spirituals proved to have international resonance in a time of great trouble.

Tippett's original, if convoluted, libretto speaks at the beginning of "pogroms in the east, lynchings in the west," linking the plight of black Americans at the hands of white supremacists with that of Jews during the most savage Nazi pogrom launched up to that time. (Tippett had approached T. S. Eliot to write the libretto, but Eliot correctly encouraged Tippett to create his own.) The spirituals themselves provided the most eloquent linkage. Tippett modestly asserted that he quoted these in the most simplified form possible, so much so that harmony itself nearly disappears, yet the trans-harmonic purity of his treatment of spirituals—a release from modernist angst and complexity—is not as simple as it seems. "Go Down, Moses," "O, By and By," and "Steal Away" are not Victorianized in the manner of Coleridge-Tayor, but they are subtly transformed in ways that gradually imprint the rest of the piece, as if Tippett's voice and that of the spirituals are consoling each other in the face of unspeakable horror.

"O, By and By," for example, curves around elegant woodwind figurations and a fluttering chorus that brighten its "dark despair" and lighten its "heavy load"; the resulting consolation momentarily warms the "icy waters" and abates the "dark forces" in the grim Holocaust scenes surrounding the song. Similarly, the lilting syncopations in Tippett's version of "Nobody Knows the Trouble I See, Lord" makes more bearable the "dread terror" in the central narrative of the Polish child. Even the despairing anger of "Go Down, Moses," here a direct commentary on the "terrible vengeance" of the pogrom, is soothed by rich brass elongations and cadences. Throughout, the spirituals are deftly placed so they mitigate the bleakness of what they all too briefly interrupt.

For Tippett, Negro spirituals were therapeutic and cathartic, oases in a traumatized world. He first heard them on the radio, after becoming obsessed with recordings of Bessie Smith's blues in the 1920s. He allowed spirituals to gradually permeate the entire oratorio, not only in the continual outlining of major and minor thirds but in an increasingly lyrical discourse reaching its climax in the penultimate "I would know my shadow and my light," the philosophical centerpiece. Here Tippett's European modernism attains a lyrical rapture that the spirituals naturally exhibit, allowing the piece to come movingly to rest in "Deep River." It is the ultimate testament to the final European number—surely the most beautiful thing Tippett has written—that "Deep River" does not completely upstage it but seems to follow naturally. The complex harmonies and polyphonic textures in the composed sections are given a new soul and melodic momentum; by the end they are able to "cross over into camp-ground."

Tippett's agnostic, pacifist message does not easily fit the worldview of the spirituals. Tippett's pacifism was deeply felt: it is a philosophy for which he was imprisoned. When the boy shoots the Nazi, he kills the "dark brother," the Nazi in us all; he kills a part of himself. Most commentary on the piece focuses on Tippett's vision of shadow and light within all people, the need for confronting our own capacity for evil, a view eloquently articulated in the last two European sections. But admirably rational as these sentiments may be, they are at odds with the Sorrow Songs, which recognize innate human depravity but nonetheless locate evil in the outer world and in monstrous people and which do at times embrace vengeance—indeed, explicitly so in "Go Down, Moses." They also speak of an afterlife that has little place in Tippett's worldview. But Tippett's treatment is so musical and dignified that we scarcely notice the incongruity. The piece maintains a mysterious tension. Tippett seems an unlikely composer for this composition, yet it is one of the most compelling settings of spirituals in the literature. His advocacy of nonviolence even in the face of the Nazi beast is in the tradition of Martin Luther King, invoked in Tippett's Third Symphony, who also chose to see in spirituals a resistance to all violence.

A *Child of Our Time* bears a structural and philosophical resemblance to Britten's *War Requiem*, which it anticipates by thirty years: Tippett's use of spirituals in an oratorio about World War II parallels Britten's use of Wilfred Owen in a requiem mass mourning the horrors of World War I. Indeed, Britten was one of the early enthusiasts of the piece, which premiered (with Britten's partner Peter Pears in the tenor role) in 1944, just after Britten's own American period. Britten had gotten over his infatuation with Americana; Tippett's, as we see in our final chapter, was just beginning.

Spirituals also had an impact on Tippett's instrumental pieces. The early Concerto for Double String Orchestra begins as a bustling exercise in British neoclassicism, but a spiritual sails in at the end, bringing a transcendence subtly forecast in the slow movement. The parallel with Dvořák is striking; the spiritual that disrupts the densely layered polyphony is one created by the composer, not a quotation, yet it seems real, so thoroughly has the composer entered its world.

Delius was inspired by spirituals in a state of wild nature; Tippett heard his on the radio. Dvořák and Coleridge-Taylor heard live singers, but professionals, not folk singers. One could make a case that nature had the greatest resonance: Delius spent his entire life in an exquisite, despairing Proustian effort to reenter campground, to recapture the moment of ecstasy on the St. Johns River that would redeem time. The others reconjured spirituals in glorious episodes of their careers. For all these composers, the legacy of the Sorrow Songs was large and permanent. "Deep River" continued flowing through their work.

CHAPTER TWO

Hiawatha Fever:
The Legacy of Longfellow

The music is only justified if it speaks in the language of the poem.
— Samuel Coleridge-Taylor on the importance of
Longfellow in his cantata Hiawatha

IKE the great Iroquois tribes whose vanishment it chronicles, Longfellow's *Song of Hiawatha,* once one of the most beloved Romantic poems in any language, has sunk into virtual oblivion. At its publication in 1855, *Hiawatha* was a best-seller, widely translated and admired by both intellectuals and the larger public. It influenced music as well as poetry, becoming the vehicle for a cantata by Samuel Coleridge-Taylor that, with the exception of Handel's *Messiah,* was the most popular choral work in England. W. C. Berwick Sayers, Coleridge-Taylor's biographer, wrote, "As is usual with young people for whom poetry has any attraction at all, [Coleridge-Taylor] fell under the influence of Longfellow, who is the acknowledged poet of youth, and the introduction to all other poets."[1]

Now, of course, all that has changed. In a climate that insists on authentic Native American voices rather than invented ones, *Hiawatha* is considered hopelessly dated and retrograde. The 1995 edition of the *Heath Anthology of American Literature,* the Bible of political correctness, calls it "a sitting target for parody";[2] even Edward Wagenknect, a Longfellow partisan, admits that it is "the most parodied poem in the

English language."[3] Numerous spoofs, of course, usually indicate that
the object of mirth was once regarded seriously. And Europe has never
completely gotten over *Hiawatha*; schoolchildren there are still required
to recite it on occasion. Americans, however, are most likely to encounter *Hiawatha* in an unlikely source, one they are not apt to recognize:
Dvořák's *New World* Symphony, an orchestral narrative of two scenes
from Longfellow's poem. Indeed, Dvořák's symphonic reading is now
virtually all that is left of the Longfellow musical legacy.

The intriguing question of why *Hiawatha* became such a potent
musical vehicle even as its literary reputation was beginning to deteri-
orate goes back to its inception. Most mid-nineteenth-century reviewers
endorsed the poem enthusiastically, as did the public, but from the
beginning there was an undercurrent of controversy in the poetry world,
especially in Europe. Many critics saw the poem as simultaneously primitive and slick; its unrhymed trochees were viewed as outré but also a
bit tedious. Some accused Longfellow of singsong silliness and monotony. A few went so far as to claim he had plagiarized the Finnish epic
the *Kalevala* (printed for the first time in 1835), although, ironically, the
resemblance of *Hiawatha* to the *Kalevala* became one of its great at-
tractions to musicians.

The basic complaint was that the poem was superficial, concerned
with sound rather than sense. Longfellow himself probably contributed
to this assessment in his own statements about his art; he said, for example, that he wrote not for "the few who think but the many who
feel," forgetting that the thinkers may have been few but were the ones
who wrote criticism. Longfellow's cult of feeling, a foreshadowing of all
manner of neoprimitivisms in modern culture, sometimes seemed to
exclude thought and complexity altogether. He ridiculed these qualities
in his betters, panning Coleridge for his "cumbrous phraseology" and
Browning for his obscurity.[4] (Superficiality and excessive euphony were,
as we shall see, the charges leveled against Poe—and the very qualities
that turned so many composers into Poe enthusiasts—but Poe regarded
himself as an elite, not one of the Longfellow "feeling" crowd.) Mrs.
Longfellow expected trouble from the beginning: "Its rhymeless rhythm
will puzzle the critics," she worried, "and I suppose it will be abundantly
abused."[5] She was right. *Blackwood's*, in one of the kinder pans, stated,
"We are interested, pleased, attracted, yet perfectly indifferent. The measure haunts the ear, but not the matter."[6]

It was the French who, more than any other European readers, originally identified this haunting of the ear as the poem's strength. As the *Revue des deux mondes* put it, "Two or three notes comprise the whole music of the poem, melodious and limited as the song of a bird." The review went on to pinpoint Longfellow's "exquisite art" as being "rapid and monotonous, like the song of Nature, which never fatigues us repeating the same sound."[7] Converting tedium into virtue, this clever review suggests why Hiawatha was congenial to certain composers: from Beethoven to Copland, the idea of small motifs ("two or three notes") generating the "whole music" has been an ideal. In an uncanny way, the review connects Longfellow to his musical transcribers: both Dvořák and Coleridge-Taylor specialized in an art that was "melodious and limited as the song of a bird." The sound world of both composers is songful and birdlike, "limited" and repetitive in the best sense. The matchup between poet and musician is ideal.

Dvořák was not the first European to set *Hiawatha*. As usual, the young Frederick Delius was there before him, if only by a few years. His tone poem *Hiawatha* was written in 1888, five years before the *New World* Symphony and four years after his own *Florida* Suite. *Hiawatha* has become the rarest of Delius's large-scale pieces. He never went back to revise it, as he did *Florida*, and it seems to have received only a single performance: like *Florida*, it was played in a Leipzig beer hall by a loopy band of players paid off with a barrel of beer. The only person in the audience besides Delius was his mentor, Edvard Grieg.

With such a colorful and bizarre history, one might think that this *Hiawatha* would attain cult status among both the dwindling subculture of Longfellow enthusiasts and the growing ranks of Delians. But such has not been the case. (The two major biographies of Delius ignore the piece altogether, in index as well as in text.) One damaging factor among the cognoscenti was the assessment of Sir Thomas Beecham, who in his memoirs described the work with lofty condescension as "a budding and not wholly unsuccessful attempt to capture the atmosphere of wild woodland life. . . . Its chief weakness is an unequal and sketchy scheme of instrumentation suggesting that Frederick was as yet only experimenting with that grand vehicle of sound, the full orchestra."[8]

Beecham's statement does show that *Hiawatha* was an important work in Delius's development, an experiment that enabled him to create more successful large-scale orchestral works. It is not surprising that Delius would take to Longfellow's poem (although he does not mention it in his writings): Longfellow's Romantic primitivism and his preoccupation with American Indians as heroic outsiders would automatically have gained Delius's sympathies. The slaughter, displacement, and vanishing of the Iroquois was a ready-made emblem for his lifelong obsession with transience and displacement.

Unfortunately, *Hiawatha* proved transient as well, but it did pop up in one glorious place, where it can still be enjoyed. Eric Fenby first pointed out that *Hiawatha*'s main melody, one of the most unabashedly Romantic Delius ever wrote, erupts in a lush viola version in the middle of the 1899 tone poem *Paris*, where it lingers luxuriously until it upstages the piece. Delius obviously thought highly of this music, enough (as Bach and Handel did in recycling their favored themes) to revive it in another work.

Dvořák's version of *Hiawatha* was also an abstract orchestral work rather than a literal setting. Like Delius, he was interested in the poem as a Romantic depiction of a vanishing race, but his version delivers the poem's earthy vigor as well as its melancholy. Like Mahler in his concept of a symphony, Dvořák regarded his *New World* as encompassing all the world. The use of Longfellow's poem as a literary backdrop rather than a vocal text fit perfectly with Dvořák's embrace of the imagination. His idea of a *New World* Symphony was a poetic conceit consisting of subjective impressions. Eschewing literalism, he instructed his black students such as Burleigh and Will Marion Cook to avoid imitation and quotation, even of black motifs (advice they apparently ignored). Only through the imagination could the artist discover the fundamental spirit or vitality of the subject at hand.

It is thus not surprising that the oldest influence on the *New World* Symphony, one going back some thirty years, was also the most poetic and subjective, a work of literature rather than a musical source. Dvořák himself announced the influence of *Hiawatha* in the December *New York Herald* interview, stating that the slow movement was "in reality a study or sketch for a longer work, either a cantata or an opera which I purpose [*sic*] writing, and which will be based on Longfellow's *Hiawatha*." The Longfellow opera referred to here was a project of Mrs. Thurber's, which Dvořák never completed. Nonetheless, the *Hiawatha* music made its way extensively into the new symphony, in the Scherzo as well as the slow movement: "The Scherzo of the symphony was suggested by the scene at the feast in *Hiawatha* where the Indians dance and is also an essay I made in the direction of imparting local color of Indian music."[9]

In the same interview, Dvořák made the remarkable statement that he had been hooked on *Hiawatha* for decades and had been meaning to set it since the beginning of his career: "I first became acquainted with it about thirty years ago through the medium of a Bohemian translation. It appealed very strongly to my imagination at that time, and the impression has only been strengthened by my residence here." Like African-American slave songs, *Hiawatha* thus created a powerful impression that coalesced into musical sound when Dvořák experienced America as a physical reality.

Speaking in 1993 at the "Dvořák in America" Centennial in New York, Leon Botstein dryly commented on Dvořák's reading of *Hiawatha* in Czech as "an unenviable experience."[10] Many feel the same about reading it in English. Longfellow's unrelenting trochees, repetitious rhetoric, and "purple vapours" have not worn well. The poem nonetheless stirred Dvořák's deepest sympathies. Its frank primitivism was precisely what he was striving for in New World art—the savage atmosphere admired by Mencken. The poem also suited Dvořák's pastoral impulses; as a Czech, he loved Longfellow's depiction of "vast and vacant" landscapes and forests. Most important, he was moved by Longfellow's portrayal of the dispersion and decay of American Indians, the ancient nations "Sweeping westward, wild and woeful . . . Like the withered leaves of Autumn." Dvořák's Bohemian sympathies for the plight of the poor and dispossessed made him an easy candidate for *Hiawatha* worship.

It should be remembered that by the 1890s, once noble tribes like the Iroquois were, as depicted in the poem, "scattered" and "wasted," wrenched from their native lands, confined to reservations, and reduced to disease and poverty, much as Longfellow had prophesied through the voice of Hiawatha. The exuberance of Longfellow's invented Indian voice, as in

> All the air was full of freshness
> All the earth was bright and joyous

is juxtaposed with "a darker vision" of dispossession and exile, a clash that carries undeniable power. The problem for modern readers is that this tension is often slackened by bland, feel-good rhetoric coming from

the mouths of a people in the process of being destroyed, as in Hiawatha's pleas to his tribe, just before he departs for the Hereafter, to be
nice to the white missionaries.

In any case, the poem suited Dvořák's needs admirably, and his
translation of it into a symphonic narrative is a remarkable literary-
musical crossover. The celebrated Largo, one of the most frequently
quoted classical pieces in popular culture, evokes the "deep and dark-
some" forest in the Minnehaha funeral scene, from the haunting chord
progression that opens the movement to the "wailing" and "moaning"
of the central funeral march. In the spectacular climax of the middle
section, ecstatic birdsong announces dawn on the prairie. Birds return
during the Scherzo following the mystic dances of Pau-Puk-Keewis. The
dizzying rhythm of the Scherzo irresistibly delivers the poem's "whirling,
spinning" energy.[11]

Dvořák specifically tied *Hiawatha* to the inner movements, but
given the cyclical structure and unified atmosphere of the symphony, it
is reasonable to conclude that it influenced the outer ones as well. Longfellow's juxtapositions of ecstasy and longing set against a primitive backdrop infuse the entire symphony, which recycles and rearranges themes
and colors throughout its four movements. Pau-Puk-Keewis's mystic
dances animate not only the Scherzo but the Allegro con fuoco. The
celebrated English horn melody in the Largo, later transformed into the
spiritual "Goin' Home," becomes in the finale a linking device for a
grand reminiscence of the symphony's themes. The poetic unity of the
New World, combining literary images with newly conceived folk music,
is eloquently summarized in the multiple uses of this melody, which
began with Longfellow and ended as a black spiritual.

Dvořák's announcement of the *Hiawatha* connection was soon
eclipsed by the controversy over whether he had used authentic Indian
motifs; the usual suspects lined up, pro and con—Krehbiel versus Huneker in Dvořák's time, John Clapham versus Otakar Sourek a century
later—with the opinions of a newly emerging Indianist movement
thrown in for good measure. Critics have frequently derided Dvořák for
professing to find a link between black and Indian music in their common use of pentatonic scales. This device, they say, is actually infre-
quent in real Indian music, and in any case it also crops up in Dvořák's
earlier Czech motifs. Again, the dispute is curious, since Dvořák himself
never made any claims about authenticity but clearly stated that he was

interested only in the color and character of Indian music, much as he was moved by the spirit of black plantation songs.[12] Pentatonicisms are not the point here; as Michael Beckerman points out, Dvořák's use of pentatonic scales and minor-key drones as a symbol of the exotic is in the well-worn tradition of Saint-Saëns, Rimsky-Korsakov, and many other composers. In any case, "for good or ill," Beckerman reminds us, "most of us don't know any more about Native-American music than Dvořák did, perhaps even less, and we would not be likely to recognize the genuine article even if we tripped over it."[13]

Like Bartók, Grainger, and other musicians who came immediately after him, Dvořák was far more interested in the commonalities of folk music from different cultures than he was in dissecting their differences. These were artists first, musicologists second. Dvořák's New World aesthetic involved the re-creation of America and its folk music from the peculiarly intense perspective of an enraptured European. As far as he was concerned, the American influence was real and palpable; that it was poetic rather than literal, literary rather than musicological, made it more potent, not less. If pentatonic scales—which have a more consistent use in Dvořák's American works than in his earlier ones—created new space and freedom, that was enough for Dvořák, even if they only occasionally occurred in real black or Indian music. As we have seen, Dvořák saw his New World aesthetic as a commingling of divergent American folk traditions with personal experiences of locations, people, and poetry.

Dvořák was not the last European to take on *Hiawatha*. The Anglo-Negro composer Samuel Coleridge-Taylor had Hiawatha ambitions for a Hiawatha work as grandiose as Dvořák's original opera. What is more, he achieved them in his early twenties, setting the entire poem in a remarkable fin-de-siècle extravaganza that ultimately turned into one of the most inspiring and heartbreaking musical success stories of the new century. (Coleridge-Taylor's contemporary Frederick Cowen set "Onaway! Awake, Beloved," but it has faded from the repertory.)

Unlike Dvořák, who botched *Hiawatha* as an opera, then sneaked it into a symphony, Coleridge-Taylor envisioned an appropriate form for the poem from the beginning: a gigantic cantata, lucidly orchestrated, the text entrusted to a chorus that rarely rests. The choral focus gives the work a chantlike ambiance that better fits these "tales of strange adventure" than the more formal format of grand opera. The vocal so-

Samuel Coleridge-Taylor, whose cantata *Hiawatha* was more popular at the turn of the century than Handel's *Messiah*. (Hulton-Getty/Tony Stone Images)

los—the passionate baritone love song "Onaway! Awake, Beloved!," the tenor "Farewell" soaring toward the Hereafter, the haunting solos depicting "waste and pathless" desolation—are all the more striking for being so scant.

As mentioned in Chapter 1, Coleridge-Taylor was a significant figure in the history of black music, regardless of the sad fact that his *Negro Melodies, African Suite,* and other important pieces are rarely performed today. *Hiawatha,* by far his best-known work, provided him with a ticket to respectability and eventual success. According to Stanley Crouch, Dvořák gave African-American composers license to use their own music.[14] But by embodying a self-made success story, Coleridge-Taylor created his own license, especially in America, which doted on stories of the self-made individual. After *Hiawatha,* Coleridge-Taylor could do anything.

Scenes from the Song of Hiawatha is a mammoth trilogy. Each scene was composed and performed separately, "Hiawatha's Wedding Feast" in 1898, "The Death of Minnehaha" in 1899, and "Hiawatha's

Departure" in 1900. Two of the three scenes are thus the same ones that had already made their way into Dvořák's symphonic narrative, but here they are real rather than imagined settings of Longfellow's text. As such, they had considerable cachet as exotic novelties, especially since they were composed by a black. The Dvořák version feels like poetry, whereas *Scenes from the Song of Hiawatha*, with its literalness, straightforward harmony, and avoidance of mystery, seems like epic prose.

"Hiawatha's Wedding Feast," the showiest and most dramatic piece in the set, premiered at the Royal College of Music, under the direction of Sir Charles Stanford. Its opening tom-toms and Indian drone basses heralded a huge success. (Michael Beckerman perceptively notes that the opening may have its origins in the splashy opening of Dvořák's *Te Deum*, which announced his entry into the New World.)[15] Exceptionally good-natured, Coleridge-Taylor became a canny musical politician behind the scenes; he had already received Elgar's imprimatur as being "far and away the cleverest fellow among the younger men" in English music—no small accolade.[16] Elgar provided the twenty-three-year-old composer with a major opportunity by turning down a commission from the Three Choirs Festival the same year the festival commissioned "Hiawatha's Wedding Feast," and Coleridge-Taylor made the most of it.

Students at the college kept the work they were rehearsing secret, but not surprisingly, word leaked to the music community that something unusual, and even wondrous, was about to be unveiled. A gravely ill Sir Arthur Sullivan told Coleridge-Taylor that he "would come to this concert even if I have to be carried into the room." (He sat alone in a chair at the front of the sold-out hall.)[17] Like Coleridge-Taylor, Sullivan was a Longfellow fan. His own larger-than-life Longfellow cantata, *The Golden Legend*, had enjoyed a glorious premiere in 1886; the *Times*, concurring with what it called an unprecedented public reception, called Sullivan the English Mozart; the *Leeds Mercury* compared Sullivan and his new cantata to a conquering Roman army. Relishing an acclaim that cemented his reputation as the premier Victorian composer, Sullivan was relieved at not having to share the limelight with W. S. Gilbert. (The truth was that Gilbert and Sullivan needed each other: Gilbert's cutting, diamondlike prose and his cynicism and unpleasantness were softened by the melifluousness of Sullivan's music, just as the latter was given a refreshing spice and dissonance by Gilbert's lyrics.) Sullivan quickly pronounced *The Golden Legend* to be his finest work. What he didn't know was that after seventeen performances in its premiere season, this choral-orchestral extravaganza would quickly fall into an eclipse as depressingly dramatic as that of *Hiawatha*, which *The Golden Legend* anticipated in its high-Victorian pomp and instant popularity. Indeed, Sullivan's fall was dizzier, for although *Hiawatha* continued to be played through World War II and is occasionally revived, *The Golden Legend* was in decline by the Edwardian-Elgar period and has now virtually vanished from the repertory. Longfellow seems to confer upon his musical admirers a kind of lost Romanticism, a glamorous but highly temporary cult status.

The premiere of *Hiawatha* was even more dramatic than that of *The Golden Legend*. Writing in the *Times* just after the composer's death, Sir Hubert Parry called it "one of the most remarkable events in modern English musical history." A feverish anticipation was in the air, and "expectation was not disappointed."[18] Like Dvořák in his shy public persona, Coleridge-Taylor was embarrassed by the noisy acclaim for this New World Cantata; he tried to hide offstage and had to be hunted down by Parry himself to acknowledge the lusty applause.

More dramatic yet was the premiere of the complete trilogy at Royal Albert Hall, which catapulted Coleridge-Taylor to fame that buoyed him the remainder of his short life. The event itself, quite apart from its musical value, was remarkable: a twenty-five-year-old black man having a long evening devoted to a single gigantic work, conducted by himself in the largest concert hall in the British Empire, with over one thousand performers. According to the *Times*, this premiere was "probably without precedent in the history of music," especially since it was "brought out by the most conservative society in existence."[19]

In its basic style and harmonic vocabulary, the work itself is conservative, posing little threat to a late-Victorian audience that expected, and received, hearty diatonic chords and cadences with exotic trappings. For this reason, perhaps more than any other, *Hiawatha* has not been taken seriously in recent years by the musical community. Commentators lament (although not overtly) that there are no connections to black folk music or culture in this first major concert success by a black composer and that even the Indian aspects are slighted; the tragedy of American genocide against Native Americans, wrote Richard Wilson in 1993, "is not reflected in Coleridge-Taylor's tuneful, mellifluous, optimistic setting."[20] Between the lines is an objection to Coleridge-Taylor's tasteful optimism. Black composers at the turn of the century were not supposed to be optimistic, especially about matters as distressing as those recounted in *Hiawatha*. Optimism is a definitive element in the New World musical aesthetic. Dvořák too had trouble with the label of naive optimism (he once said that his "tragic" Seventh Symphony was a bid for respectability); even today his sunniness is held against him by some musical intellectuals. But his problem is not as severe as Coleridge-Taylor's, whose work is rarely darkened or complicated by genuinely tragic elements. Even Longfellow's "long and dreary winter" in "The Death of Minnehaha" sounds like summer in Coleridge-Taylor's tuneful setting. Like many late nineteenth-century English artists and intellectuals, Coleridge-Taylor was drawn to the plight of the Sioux and Iroquois—perhaps more than most because of being black—but he was temperamentally incapable of sustained grimness. This music focuses on the nobility and endurance of American Indians, not on the horror of their genocide.

What was most important to Coleridge-Taylor was the absolute primacy of Longfellow's text. According to standard commentary, Coleridge-Taylor was interested in the poem only because of its euphony and the exoticism of the odd names Longfellow gave his Indians. But the poem clearly meant more to Coleridge-Taylor than that. His admiration for Longfellow was consistent and lifelong. He set Longfellow throughout his career, from student efforts performed at his first public concert through forgotten settings such as the *Southern Love Songs* and the *Five Choral Ballads*.

The latter work, based on Longfellow's *Poems of Slavery*, provided the aesthetic link between his identification with the struggles of African and Native Americans. It also provided a transition between his literary interest in African-American material and his more direct, folkloric explorations. Composed in 1904, the *Choral Ballads* came the same year as Coleridge-Taylor's revelatory reading of DuBois's *The Souls of Black Folk* and his first tour of the New World. In this work he set texts such as Longfellow's "The Quadroon Girl," "Lord He Sang the Psalm of David," and "In Dark Fens of the Dismal Swamp"; within a year he would create his "Six Sorrow Songs" and *Twenty-Four Negro Melodies*.

Longfellow's work was therefore a powerful influence. As for the poem *Hiawatha*, Coleridge-Taylor loved its great beauty as well as its

"naive simplicity, its unaffected expression, its unforced idealism." This
could be a description of Coleridge-Taylor's own music: naive in the
best sense, it too has an unforced, unaffected idealism. Coleridge-
Taylor's commitment to this poem bordered on a kind of benign fanat-
icism. He committed the entirety of *Hiawatha* to memory, living and
breathing the poem as he translated it into sound. He declared the
primacy of the text to be absolute: "I take it to be an artistic crime in
the musical treatment of a poem to make it subordinate to orchestral
effect. The music is only justified if it speaks in the language of the
poem."[21] Here Coleridge-Taylor reveals himself to be the most literal of
literary composers. Artists as different as Dvořák, Debussy, Rachmaninoff, and Delius—indeed all the New World Europeans covered in this
book—use a text freely for its atmosphere, theme, or underlying aesthetic philosophy, so that words and sounds interpenetrate one another.
For Coleridge-Taylor, the words came first; tampering with the text or
making it in any way subordinate was an "artistic crime."

Composers usually find the writer to match their aesthetic, and
this one was no exception. Longfellow's prosody, with its trochaic meter
and dronelike repetitions, is precisely the language of Coleridge-Taylor,
who made a virtue of repetition. Sometimes criticized for lack of counterpoint and sonata-form development, his symphonic discourse is based
almost entirely on constant, fluid variations on a few themes. In its
limited range and clear focus, Longfellow's verse is similar. Coleridge-
Taylor is the ideal tone poet for Longfellow, just as Delius was the great
musical mouthpiece for Whitman.

Critics of the time understood this, pointing out that Coleridge-
Taylor managed to avoid the potential monotony of Longfellow's trochees. As Booker T. Washington, one of the earliest and most astute
admirers of Coleridge-Taylor, put it, the work holds the attention
through its "haunting melodic phrases, bold harmonic scheme, and
vivid orchestration."[22] For better or worse, the poem is simply *there*, all
of it, clearly enunciated, its purple sunsets and perfumed primitivism
rendered without irony or condescension. There is no polyphony in this
consistently homophonic music to obscure text. There is none in the
poem either: this is an aesthetic where we get one thing at time, the
opposite of the dizzying juxtapositions of locations and images in Whitman, which allowed Hindemith, for example, to weave some of his most
intricate counterpoint. From the joyous tom-toms in the introduction to

the sumptuous climaxes in "And they said, 'Farewell for ever!' " this music rarely surprises or engages us on the deepest levels, though it does charm and beguile at length.

Coleridge-Taylor's resolutely straight treatment of a poem that is now a "sitting target for parody" helps explain why this ambitious, once-adored work has largely vanished. Charm and pleasure for their own sake are no longer in vogue in a culture where art, particularly by minorities in white societies, is increasingly judged for political content. To be sure, *Hiawatha* had a political resonance for its composer: as a black man in a white musical establishment, he empathized with American Indians as outsiders, much as black Indians and Creoles celebrate what unites them at Mardi Gras. As we have seen, Coleridge-Taylor became a committed spokesperson for black liberation and a passionate champion of DuBois. But it was mainly the poem's romance and naive idealism—qualities he increasingly associated with America—that interested the young Coleridge-Taylor, fueling his optimism and warm personality.

In an increasingly cynical, racially polarized culture, naive optimism and idealism are of little interest, and it is not terribly surprising that the great *Hiawatha* phenomenon of the early twentieth century has crashed. Beginning in 1924, it inspired a kind of British Mardi Gras at Royal Albert Hall, surely one of the more colorful and bizarre spectacles in musical history. In the words of the conductor Kenneth Alwyn, who attempted a *Hiawatha* revival in the 1990s, "For two weeks every summer all roads to the hall were thronged with capacity audiences and close on a thousand 'Red Indian' performers. These 'braves' and 'squaws' came not from 'the Land of the Dakotas' but from the concrete wigwams of Wapping, Tooting, Penge, Cheam, and Coleridge-Taylor's own village of Croydon—in fact from any village that could send singing braves and squaws to the great 'Pow-Wow' in the Albert Hall."[23]

This peculiar pow-wow in Britain was parallel to the spread of jazz in Paris, but it was destined not to last. After the 1930s, the Hiawatha cult collapsed, although according to Alwyn, "those who remember [the Hiawatha gatherings] speak of them with affection."[24] By the end of the twentieth century, such a spectacle seemed silly and passé, just as Alwyn's description sounded hopelessly quaint. The work's supreme exoticism—a setting by an Anglo-Negro of a white American's poem about Indians—was no longer attractive in an academic culture where Julian

Barnes's "necessary exotic" was viewed at best with suspicion, at worst as the root of hegemonic evil.

As Desmond Shawe-Taylor put it in the 1950s, *Hiawatha* "brought a freshness and spontaneity into the stuffy world of English choral composition."[25] For the stuffy moment at least, that New World freshness has departed, and with it a whole line of Longfellow-inspired works. Unlike Poe and Whitman, who continue to fascinate composers across the Atlantic, Longfellow's influence seems confined to a discrete group of composers who were sympathetic to his peculiar brand of sentimental primitivism. At least for now, that spirit lives only invisibly, in Dvořák's *New World* Symphony.

CHAPTER THREE

New Worlds of Terror:
The Legacy of Poe

It is in Music, perhaps, that the soul most nearly attains that great end for which,
when inspired by the poetic sentiment, it struggles—the creation of supernal Beauty.
It may be, indeed, that here this sublime end is, now and again, attained in *fact*. We
are often made to feel, with a shivering delight, that from an earthly harp are stricken
notes which *cannot* have been unfamiliar to the angels.
—Edgar Allan Poe, "The Poetic Principle"

My teacher was Edgar Allan Poe.
—Maurice Ravel

I spend my existence in the House of Usher.
—Claude Debussy

THE profound influence of Edgar Allan Poe on Claude Debussy, Maurice Ravel, and other European composers is one of the most fascinating instances of one art nourishing another in modern culture. It involves not just musical settings of literary texts but a literary philosophy shaping a musical one—something far more intricate and mysterious.

European composers revered Poe in a way that his fellow Americans, whether writers, musicians, or critics, never did. Ignored in his own short lifetime and vilified immediately afterward, Poe is treated by many contemporary American scholars and artists (Harold Bloom and Thomas Disch, to name two recent examples) with attitudes ranging from condescension to contempt. Beginning with Baudelaire, however, European artists, especially in France and Russia, have sustained an entirely different attitude toward this darkest of Romantics. To them Poe is a force of inspiration akin to the "Lyre within the sky" in "Israfel," his spellbinding poem about the god of music.

What stirred these composers' imaginations was not only Poe's poetry and tales but also his literary theory. Edward Said, in his *Musical Elaborations*, points out that current literary intellectuals are often ignorant of even the most basic musical ideas and trends. The same could easily be said about musicians in regard to literature. Yet as recently as the nineteenth and early twentieth centuries, musical intellectuals imbibed essays on literature as avidly as literary thinkers discussed musical issues. Poe's contributions to literature—the unity of mood and economy of means he advocated in his theoretical essays and bequeathed to the modern poem and short story—are well known. In music, we see him shaping another art as well, in ways continually elegant and surprising.

As far-fetched as this literary-musical crossover may seem, it is clearly documented. Claude Debussy and Maurice Ravel are both on record saying they were more influenced by Poe than by any composer. Ravel, who once told the *New York Times* that his "greatest teacher in composition was Edgar Allan Poe," based all his music on Poe's literary theories;[1] as the composer and Ravel authority Ned Rorem put it, Ravel was "blinded by Poe, whose essay, 'The Philosophy of Composition' influenced him (he claimed) more than any music."[2] As for Debussy, Marcel Dietschy points out that he was not so much influenced as "obsessed," identifying himself repeatedly with Poe's most morbidly isolated hero, with whom he felt a terrible empathy and spiritual kinship.[3] *The Fall of the House of Usher*, Debussy's final, incomplete work, which consumed a significant part of his creative life, meant more to him than perhaps any other single project.

This is more than just another case of the celebrated French taste for the shunned, the eccentric, the avant-garde. The inspiration is real and palpable. One need only listen to the music—to almost anything— to hear it. Arbie Orenstein called it Poe's "spiritual imprint," this subtle sense of the sinister that, as Poe himself would have put it, is all the more powerful for being mysterious and "indefinite."[4] We hear it in the creepy bitonalities of Debussy's "Brouillards," in the demonic scamperings of Ravel's "Scarbo the Dwarf" and the hallucinatory violence of his *La Valse*, in the mists and distant tolling bells of Debussy's "Feuilles mortes" and Ravel's "Le Gibet" and "La Vallée des cloches."

The impact of Poe on these composers is part of a larger Old World fascination with Poe, not only in France but all over Europe, especially in England and Russia. European artists have always been attracted to American eccentrics and (as literary critics put it) "redskins," to what D. H. Lawrence called white aboriginals, and to the black inaugurators of jazz. The attraction occurs at the extremes, and it scarcely matters whether the artistic vision is affirmative or nihilistic. As we shall see, Whitman's lusty yes! to life was attractive to a certain type of European artist. But Poe's resounding no! had a wider and earlier currency.

Poe's appeal had two, seemingly contradictory aspects. Europeans were attracted to his adolescent New World naiveté. His predilection for the unknown and the fantastic fit nicely with stereotypical European notions about America as a dangerous, mysterious place; his innovations in Gothic horror were admired and imitated by Baudelaire, Arthur Machen, Algernon Blackwood, E. F. Benson, Walter de la Mare, and many other literary figures. "There are terrible spirits, ghosts, in the air of America," said D. H. Lawrence, and Poe was their most magisterial conjurer.[5] But beneath the exotic atmosphere and verbal music, the childlike fantasy so innocent of adult concerns, is the most basic concern of all, the unrelenting struggle against mortality. As embodied in the doomed children of "Annabel Lee," Poe combines a New World innocence and childishness—an irresistible draw for Old World artists— with the oldest conflict, the struggle between life and death, converting humanity's terror of mortality into an unflinching poetry of disintegration and resuscitation.

There is a basicness about Poe, a willingness to plunge into fundamental issues of life and death, that European artists similarly inclined—Yeats, Lawrence, Rachmaninoff, Alexander Blok, and so many others—admired, no matter how much Poe was derided by Henry James, T. S. Eliot, Ezra Pound, and his other distinguished detractors (who, as this list indicates, were often Americans who relocated abroad, rejecting as gauche and passé what European artists found refreshing and liberating). Poe was "an adventurer," said D. H. Lawrence, "into horrible underground passages of the human soul," and as far as Europeans were concerned, he pushed further in that dark adventure than anyone ever had.[6]

Poe articulated an aesthetic creed particularly attractive to European composers: the notion that artifice and music are the way into and out of the mortal struggle he so relentlessly documents. The elaborate depiction of life's fragility through a verbal texture alive with musical sounds and images was, for Poe, the very definition of beauty in art— and art itself became the only antidote to that fragility. This desperate aestheticism, characterized by a constant absorption in the details of technique, was central to numerous European artists, but especially to Debussy, Ravel, Rachmaninoff, and other composers who admired Poe. It had wide currency throughout the Continent, in everything from the decadence of Baudelaire to the modernism of Yeats.

Poe's most obvious contribution to culture, his innovations in the tale of terror as a distinct genre with genuine literary possibilities, was widely praised and imitated in Europe as well. The cosmic dread projected in such stories as "The Facts in the Case of M. Valdemar" and "MS. Found in a Bottle" influenced virtually everyone who dabbled in spook stories. As Lawrence suggests, the ultimate Poe nightmare, the solipsistic horror of being entombed in one's own mind, developed in such tales as "The Imp of the Perverse" and "The Fall of the House of Usher," haunted many more artists than just specialists in terror. This overseas recognition of Poe's psychological acuity in the Gothic tale came at a time when advocates of Emersonian transcendentalism and nationalism in his own country regarded him as an irrelevant reactionary dabbling in antiquated European forms. Eventually, Poe attained wide influence in America, in everything from the subtle shivers of Shirley Jackson and the shock horror of Stephen King to the "new Gothic" of Joyce Carol Oates and Anne Rice. But Europeans affirmed Poe's creation of beauty from the terrors of the psyche long before Americans did. To Baudelaire, Ravel, Debussy, and other creative minds, Poe's New World was supremely seductive because of its location of the beautiful—not just the chaos of the sublime—in mystery and terror.

There is also a political reason why Europeans found it easy to embrace Poe. Like Cooper, Melville, Mencken, and so many other prominent Americans, Poe was rabidly anti-American, once going so far as to assert that America exhibited "the most odious and insupportable despotism . . . upon the face of the earth."[7] It was therefore politically safe for Europeans to embrace Poe on a Continent where fear and contempt for America vied ambivalently with adulation and envy; artists like Ravel and Rachmaninoff, who purported to admire America, could have it both ways when they championed Poe, for he was hardly a spokesperson for the New World in its ideological battle with the Old. Indeed, with his aristocratic ideals, his frequent European settings, and his pro-southern political views, Poe was the most European of American writers, even though Europeans, as we shall see, often viewed him as quintessentially American in his eccentricity and iconoclasm.

Poe's aestheticism, his contempt for mediocrity, and his resolutely hierarchical view of art were similarly consoling to Europeans, for they exempted him from the Old World's fear of American democracy as a deadly leveling force. C. Vann Woodward, in *The Old World's New World*, elegantly traces this fear among European writers and intellectuals, who tended to see America as a nation of bores, materialists, and philistines spreading a cancer that would ultimately consume Europe. In other words, they viewed America much the way Poe did. Composers, however, tended to idealize certain aspects of America: Debussy and Ravel, in particular, were alienated from nineteenth-century European musical formulas and found the same freshness in American culture as did Dvořák and Delius (although with drastically different results). By embracing Poe, who was American yet superficially European, they could have it both ways.

Consequently, European composers were more likely to be influenced by Poe than were Americans, who were tied to a culture in thrall either to the sunny optimism of Emerson or to the residual Puritanism and didacticism that Poe systematically rejected. The democratic renunciation of hierarchy in art espoused by Whitman and other cultural figures near the end of the nineteenth century made Poe seem even more remote in America, where only Ambrose Bierce, Nathaniel Hawthorne, Charles Brockden Brown, and a few other die-hard Gothicists had practiced the art of literary terror. As for composers, the few authentically American artists, such as Gottschalk and Ives, were busy mining American folklore and had little interest in Poe.

Although Europe was basically hospitable to Poe, the question persists: How could a writer—an American one at that—exert a stronger pull than the musical currents of their time, especially the tidal wave that was Wagner? The question is increasingly important as the stock of these composers continues to rise. Debussy is widely regarded, by composers ranging from Toru Takemitsu to Pierre Boulez, as the founder of musical modernism. Along with Stravinsky (who, as we shall see, was also profoundly influenced by American culture), he is the most important composer of the twentieth century. As for Ravel, he has emerged as one of the most popular, performed, and recorded of serious modern composers.

The issue is also significant because it reveals something palpable about the larger relationship between literature and music, two arts that artists themselves frequently regard as more intimately connected than commonly perceived. Despite T. S. Eliot's declaration of a "dissociation of sensibility" culminating in the early twentieth century, Debussy and Ravel were part of a culture that still valued broad learning and connectedness within the arts. In the spirit of Virginia Woolf's proclaimed affinity with late nineteenth-century French painters, they considered themselves part of a stream of sensibility flowing through all the arts, connecting nationalities, periods, and disciplines.

In the terminology of today's academic discourse, these artists were interdisciplinary. To them, the specialization of the present moment would have seemed puritanical and confining. Indeed, Debussy viewed the "feverish haste to dissert, dissect, and classify"—the beginnings of modern criticism—"the disease of our time." Debussy was one of the first to recognize the early symptoms of this disease, which he feared would be especially destructive to music.[8]

As Margaretha Muller and other critics have pointed out, these composers were heirs—the last ones, as it turns out—to an age in which poets and musicians orbited in an elegant circle: beginning with Gérard de Nerval, Symbolist poets aspired to what Walter Pater called the "condition of music," an approach that deemphasized literal content and emphasized the sensuality of musical sound. Paul Verlaine was directly influenced by Wagner (who, it should not be forgotten, was a powerful literary as well as musical thinker); Stéphane Mallarmé strove to create linguistic arabesques that were purely musical. Debussy in turn was inspired by the Symbolists, especially Verlaine and Mallarmé, whose techniques he regarded as fundamentally musical. His prelude to Mallarmé's *L'Après-Midi d'un faune* (1876), which Boulez calls the awakening of modern music, completed the circle.

As a major music critic—who shared a column with Colette in *Gil Blas*—Debussy had a keen penetration of other art forms, to which he frequently alluded in his remarks on music. He had a profound visual sense, and his musical impressionism (a term he deplored) owed a great deal to the shifting colors and shapes of Monet, Rodin, and especially Manet. His astuteness as a literary critic was equally impressive: he sprinkled his essays and letters with lively, acute observations of Conrad, Chesterton, and other writers who inspired him. That Poe inspired him most is not altogether surprising. Debussy and Poe are an ideal match: Debussy was a distinctly literary composer, just as Poe was the most musical of poets. François Lesure, a coeditor of Debussy's letters, asserts that Debussy was the most literary of all composers: "No other composer has ever been so committed to finding ways of revitalizing music from outside the musical world."⁹

Indeed, Debussy often shunned the company of musicians (the young Stravinsky and Varèse being notable exceptions), whom he considered narrow and provincial, preferring the company of novelists and painters. Describing a "magnificent" Palestrina evening in a letter to the writer André Poniatowski, he wrote: "Needless to say, there were very few musicians there. Perhaps they had the good sense to know they'd be out of place."¹⁰ Once confiding to Paul Dukas that he was "not thinking about music any more, or at least very little," Debussy advised his pupil Raoul Bardac to "forget all about music from time to time."¹¹ Debussy would be even more out of place in today's highly specialized conservatory than he was in his own. He witnessed the beginnings of the great chasm that was to separate classical music from the rest of culture, and it troubled him deeply.

Ravel did not share his colleague's volubility and cantankerousness, but he too was a lively appreciator of the arts. He showed his admiration for Verlaine in his *Un grand sommeil noir*, a setting of Verlaine's verse, and like Debussy was entranced by Mallarmé. He dealt directly with leading artists in other disciplines, including Picasso, Matisse, Cocteau, and Colette (who, though he never met her, did the libretto for his magical mini-opera *L'Enfant et les sortilèges*). He made few public pronouncements, however, about the influence of other artists: his sense of privacy and reserve was as pronounced here as in other aspects of his life and art.

It was Poe, the obscure, long-dead American artist, who cast the most potent spell over both composers, not only for the general reasons cited above but for specifically musical ones. What immediately rang out in their imaginations was Poe's special sound and his obsessive emphasis on sonority. In America, Poe has long been criticized—even by the gentlemanly New Critics from the South, who recognized him as spiritually one of their own—for promoting sound over sense, especially in his poems. But to his musical admirers in Europe he was merely one of the first to recognize, and the first to consistently manifest, the principle that in art sound and sense, form and content, are inseparable. As for the charge that Poe's art is all surface, that too is a strength for composers rather than a liability. Music is the most immediate and sensual of the arts; as Charles Rosen has pointed out, music seems to be the most abstract art only because it is the least representational. In fact, music is "the least abstract in its direct physical assault on the listener's nerves."[12] The all-enveloping sound and texture of Poe's literary surface come closer to the state of music than the work of virtually any other writer.

There is also another, more specific carryover in the case of these particular composers: their fondness for the otherworldly and the fantastic, the realm in which Poe was judged by the French to be the master. Rosen's definition of music as an assault on the nerves resembles the goals of Ann Radcliffe, Matthew Lewis, and other literary Gothicists who founded the tradition within which Poe worked. The idea of music as a pure evocation of terror and the sublime was first articulated by E. T. A. Hoffmann, who in his article on Beethoven defined music in its highest manifestation as "opening up the realm of the monstrous and the immeasurable," setting in motion the "lever of fear, of awe, of horror."[13] Poe's contribution fits this context ideally, for it is not so much fantastic narrative that interested him—and the artists he later influenced—as fantastic atmosphere, a state close to music. (With the exception of "MS. Found in a Bottle," his fiction contains surprisingly few unambiguously supernatural occurrences.)

It is Poe's emphasis on atmosphere, on suggestion over explicit definition, that had such potent musical resonance. What Poe evoked was not the fantastic per se but what he called "an air of the fantastic—approaching as nearly to the ludicrous as was admissible." For Poe, spooks and Gothic machinery were ludicrous, but their psychological and aesthetic uses were profound. He denounced the literal idea of the supernatural even as he embraced its usefulness in conjuring the "pleasurable elevation of the soul" he deemed to be the purpose of art.[14] Poe's notion of the centrality of atmosphere was crucial to the aesthetic of

Debussy and Ravel. With the exception of "Scarbo," "Ondine," *L'Enfant et les sortilèges*, "The Sunken Cathedral," and a few other works, ghosts do not actually appear in their music, though a sense of the ghostly is ever present. Atmosphere, of course, is far easier to transfer from literature to music than elements such as plot or character: no libretto is required, only the witchery of pure sound. Aside from Debussy's teasing operatic fragment *The Fall of the House of Usher*, the Poe legacy with these composers is reflected entirely in instrumental and orchestral music.

An advocate of absolute music as the highest art form, Poe would have liked it that way. "It is in music," he said in "The Poetic Principle," "that the soul most nearly attains the great end for which, when inspired by the Poetic Sentiment, it struggles—the creation of supernal Beauty."[15] Music combined with poetry (what is commonly called "program music") provides "the widest field for poetic development." But pure music—even a deft stroke of a harp—lifts us to the highest levels of beauty: "We are often made to feel, with a shivering delight, that from an earthly harp are stricken notes which *cannot* have been unfamiliar to the angels." Poe thus anticipates Walter Pater's famous 1893 statement that "all art aspires towards the condition of music," but he is more concrete: it is the "shiver"—what Pater more abstractly calls "the perfect identification of matter and form"—that takes us into the realm of the angels. No matter how esoteric Poe's theory of art seems, it is, like his tales, peculiarly physical and visceral. And music, in his judgment, came closest to delivering that sublime physicality in its least diluted form. Poe therefore implies that composers can come closer to attaining his aesthetic ideals than literary artists, and it was perhaps inevitable that musical creators as literary and discerning as Debussy and Ravel would eventually latch on to Poe's theories.

The most important document here is Poe's "The Philosophy of Composition," which both composers devoured in Baudelaire's famous translation. In this 1846 essay, which originally appeared in *Graham's Magazine*, Poe argued for unity and brevity (the latter being a necessary consequence of the former) in poetry and extended the generalization to fiction as well. As Jacques Barzun recently pointed out, Poe endeared himself to French poets forever by laying the justification for the prose poem, which is what "The Fall of the House of Usher" surely is and which Baudelaire and his disciples took up as their main form. Equally important, Poe argued that suggestiveness and complexity were "invariably required" to counteract "a certain hardness or nakedness, which repels the artistic eye." This insistence on complexity, the forerunner of James's argument in "The Art of Fiction," is usually missed or ignored by Poe's critics, who pounce upon the more famous "certain single effect" Poe had argued for in *Graham's* four years earlier—actually an argument that fiction as much as poetry needed a unified design—and accuse him of superficiality and worse. In "The Philosophy of Composition," Poe clarified this effect to mean a particularly rich or subtle emotional charge, not an obvious or one-dimensional gimmick. Indeed, it is the "undercurrent, however indefinite, of meaning" that imparts richness to a work of art: any "excess of the suggested meaning" turns poetry into prose "of the very flattest kind." In a teasing grace note, Poe added that the most potent undercurrent, or "tone," is "one of *sadness*. Beauty of whatever kind, in its supreme development, invariably excites the sensitive soul to tears."[16]

The supreme beauties in art, whatever else they may be, therefore have a unified, overpowering atmosphere and a mysterious undercurrent, one that is suggestive, complex, and usually melancholy. These are precisely the qualities that describe the musical style of Debussy and Ravel. In the morbid sensuality of Ravel's "Le Gibet," the yearning and fantasy of Debussy's "Sirens," and the ecstatic melancholy of Ravel's *Daphnis et Chloé,* and even in many neoclassical works, such as Debussy's ghostly Violin-Piano Sonata, the Poe-like suggestiveness, that indefinite sense of melancholy and the fantastic, creeps up the listener's spine.

In the case of Ravel, one finds a surprisingly exact series of musical principles derived from Poe's "Philosophy," as well as a more general aesthetic inspired by the tales. Scrupulously private and introspective, Ravel did not say nearly as much about the Poe connection as the more voluble Debussy, but clues do exist. Ravel had been moved by Poe in his earliest creative years. Like so many young people, he was obsessed with Poe and his delightful malevolence. According to Ricardo Vines, the boyhood friend who introduced Ravel to Poe, Ravel fervidly admired both the tales and the poetry, especially "The Raven." Ravel, says Vines, produced horrific drawings of Poe's tales of the sea, "MS. Found in a Bottle" and "A Descent into the Maelstrom." It doesn't take much of a stretch to hear in Ravel's own seascapes—the spectral nocturne in

Daphnis et Chloé, the undertow of menace in "Une Barque sur l'océan" — the downward pull of Poe's dark sea.[17]

A sinister subcurrent flows beneath the glitter of even lighter works such as *Tzigane* and *Rapsodie espagnole.* Other pieces conjure a more palpable terror. In "Le Gibet," the repeating bass line, evoking a hanged man swaying in the dying sunlight, has a hypnotic regularity reminiscent of the repetitions in Poe's verse and the fatal tolling bells of the tales. In the Concerto for Left Hand Alone, the gloomy sounds of churning double basses and contrabassoon suggest dark chasms and subterranean vaults. Occasionally, Ravel made these analogies explicit. Using Poe-like language, he described the cataclysmic horror of *La Valse* as "a fantastic and fatefully inescapable whirlpool," a description suggestive of "MS. Found in a Bottle." Some musicians suspect the work to be a rendering of "The Masque of the Red Death," a view supported by the frenzied buildup and sudden collapse of Ravel's ghoulish waltzes.

The most revealing link between Poe and Ravel is the remarkable similarity in their treatment by critics. Both have been accused of being contrivers of superficial, sensual effects, of being more concerned with sound than with sense. Poe collided with nineteenth-century American puritanism just as Ravel offended an equally puritanical musical establishment obsessed with all things "profound" and properly German.

Similarly, both artists were accused of being obsessed with the fantastic and the artificial. Ravel had an amusing rejoinder: "Does it not occur to these people," he said, "that I might be artificial by nature?"[18] Like Poe, Ravel regarded art and artifice as superior to nature and the natural, just as he followed Poe's lead in regarding beauty as superior to truth. Ravel thoroughly embraced Poe's rejection of didacticism. Poe was perhaps the first major literary artist to reject the notion that art, particularly fiction, had an obligation to teach moral truth. Given the didactic impulse of mid-nineteenth-century American culture, this renunciation was more subversive than any of Poe's other innovations. In "The Poetic Principle," Poe declared that the creation of beauty, the sole purpose of art, "has no concern whatever with Duty or Truth." Only a blind observer could fail to see the "radical and chasmal differences between the truthful and poetical modes." In making this argument, Poe saw himself not as an arcane theorist but as a supremely practical writer who was merely describing how art works. Only someone who is "theory-mad beyond redemption," he wrote, "still persists in at-

tempting to reconcile the obstinate oils and waters of Poetry and Truth."
Unlike ideological theorists of today, Poe was a genuine radical who
believed that art should not inculcate any received truth, whether conservative or progressive. "Excitement of the soul" achieved through hard
work and refined technique defined what art is about.[19]

This credo describes what Ravel was about as well. In his repudiation of didacticism, he was praised and attacked in much the same
ways as Poe. His first opera, *L'Heure espagnole*, was denounced for amo-
rality; his second, *L'Enfant et les sortilèges*, for immaturity. Ravel has
frequently sustained the charge—even by otherwise admiring critics
such as Robert Craft—of being a childlike or adolescent artist, one shel-
tered from adult concerns and interested only in fantasy. Only after
being championed by Boulez, Bernstein, and other influential maestros
did Ravel gain grudging acceptance among the musical intelligentsia.
In everything from minimalism (*Boléro*) to the preoccupation with fantasy and mystical atmosphere, Ravel anticipated musical trends. Similarly, Poe was vilified in nineteenth-century America, then regarded as
vaguely suspect in the twentieth, until Leslie Fiedler and his disciples
declared him to be the quintessential American artist precisely because
his artistic adolescence was the prototype of Melville, Twain, Heming-
way, and other lonely outsiders estranged from American middle-class
culture.

According to Marguerite Long, Arbie Orenstein, and other writers,
Ravel was most directly influenced by Poe's emphasis on brevity and
conciseness and his concomitant obsession with technique. Beginning
with Baudelaire, French artists were much taken with Poe's insistence
on short forms, and Ravel was no exception. To Poe, the awesome
"shiver" produced by art was by nature transient and could not "be
sustained through a composition of any great length." In his still-
controversial caveat regarding Milton's *Paradise Lost*, Poe declared that
even "the best epic under the sun" was a "nullity" unless separated into
self-contained fragments. Ravel too deplored large forms; almost everything he wrote is short and intensely unified, exactly as advocated by
Poe. Even his operas—the musical equivalent of epics—are short, barely
taking up a single compact disc; and his one larger-than-life work, *Daphnis et Chloé*, is less than an hour long. "In the whole composition," Poe
wrote, "there should be no word written of which the tendency, direct

or indirect, is not to the one pre-established design." Substitute *note* for *word* and you have Ravel's philosophy of composition.[20]

Anti-Romantic in their exacting attitude toward form, both Poe and Ravel are nonetheless regarded by many critics as Romantics, at least in their championing of mystery and childlike states of consciousness. If so, their Romanticism is similar to that of Yeats, who was fond of saying that art promotes the illusion of freedom and spontaneity even though it is supremely calculated. Ironically, this emphasis on what Poe called rigid precision is the prototype not only of Ravel's art but of the obsession with objectivity manifested by Stravinsky and the neoclassicists of the 1920s and 1930s. Ravel, however, like his mentor, was seeking a highly controlled but unabashed sensuality, an aesthetic far removed from Stravinsky's ideal of the hard, classical, and objective. The paradox for Poe and Ravel was the same: the Romantic ideal of inspiration could be achieved only through uninspiring, arduous work.

The most fetching statement on Ravel's lifelong enchantment with Poe was made by the composer himself, in a brief but powerful speech delivered in Houston, Texas, on April 7, 1928. Unlike Debussy, who was aggressively verbal to the point of crankiness, Ravel was private and even secretive, rarely speaking on the record about his art. Poe, however, was important enough for him to make an exception. Weary of constantly being compared to Debussy, he declared, looking back over his life and work, that "the aesthetic of Edgar Allan Poe, your great American, has been of singular importance to me." Like Mallarmé, Ravel's other great love, Poe inspired him with "illimitable vision but of precise design," one "enclosed in a mystery of somber abstraction." His was "an art where all the elements are so intimately linked among themselves that one cannot analyze the effects but only perceive them."[21]

This combination of the precise and the indefinite—clarity of design linked with visionary content—served Ravel throughout his career. The somber and mesmerizing mystery cited here suffuses all of Ravel's art, the elements of which "are so intimately linked" that the seeming effects produced by technical wizardry become much more than that, ultimately eluding analysis.[22] What we are left with is the sustained shiver—so astonishingly consistent with this composer—that Poe declared to be the goal of art.

In Debussy's case, the influence of Poe was equally decisive, but the emphasis was different. Debussy was more attracted to the visionary and the fantastic in Poe than to the artificial and the calculated. Ravel was more fixated on the means, the technique, Debussy on the end. Similarly, Debussy was drawn to the tales, whereas Ravel saturated himself in the theoretical essays, especially "The Philosophy of Composition" and its explication of "The Raven" as a model for technique. A sophisticated literary critic, Debussy understood that Poe meant the tales to be as poetic—as unencumbered by didacticism and realism—as poetry. Above all, Debussy apprehended that although Poe advocated calculation, he also, in practice, embraced risk and daring, a headlong leap into the unknown. As Poe's "The Oval Portrait" implies, art was a life-or-death enterprise.

Debussy was always astonished that no American composer had ever taken an interest in Poe. He spoke of being entranced by "the secret atmosphere, the feelings, the tensions and the emotions contained in the tales of Poe," which "had never been translated into music." He intended to do so.[23] Debussy's music does indeed seem to harbor a secret atmosphere, a complex code of tensions and emotions in a state of incomplete translation between literature and music. From the distant wordless chorus in the early nocturne *Sirens* to the ghostly violin melody in the late Violin-Piano Sonata, Debussy's sound world has an aura of sublime mystery closer to the tales of Poe than to the music of other composers.

As early as 1893, Debussy was looking for ways to infuse his music with Poe's spectral magic. In a letter to Romain Rolland, André Suarès speaks of a projected Debussy symphony "on psychologically developed themes for which the idea comes from many a Poe tale, and in particular, 'The Fall of the House of Usher.' " Debussy never wrote the Poe symphony—at least not in name. But Poe's psychologically developed themes and secret atmosphere found their way into his work nonetheless.[24]

For Debussy, who struggled continually with depression and anxiety, Poe had a deeply personal as well as aesthetic resonance, so much so that it is hard to separate the two. Debussy's letters, especially in their outpouring of self-doubt, are full of Poe references. In 1893, Debussy wrote to Ernest Chausson (another neurotically perfectionistic French artist addicted to self-doubt) that his "days are dark and soundless, like

"Open Here I Flung the Shutter," Edouard Manet's unpublished illustration of "The Raven" for Charles Baudelaire's translation of Poe, a work that profoundly influenced French music. (Baltimore Museum of Art, George A. Lucas Collection, BMA 1996.48. 18047)

those of a hero from Edgar Allan Poe. . . . The bell has tolled now to mark my thirty-first year, and I'm still not confident that my musical attributes are right."[25]

The reality was that Debussy's attributes were more than routinely right. He was deeply into the composition of the sinister and seductive *Pelléas et Mélisande*, an opera that would revolutionize the form—and one that already manifested the imprint of Poe. Maurice Maeterlinck, whose play provided Debussy with a libretto, was himself an admirer of Poe, having credited the American poet with "the birth in my work of a sense of mystery and the passion for the beyond."[26] These are the qualities that impregnate Debussy's *Pelléas*, an anti-opera that rejected both conventional aria-recitative structures and the continuous melody of Wagner. The music seems to well up from the subterranean vaults of the story's castle, especially the shivery whole-tone passages in the orchestral interludes. As for the Poe-like scenario, it includes a hyper-neurotic hero and a beautiful, wraithlike heroine with whom he is incestuously involved and who suffers a mysterious death. With *Pelléas*, Debussy was already warming up for his tortured attempts to set "The Fall of the House of Usher."

Throughout his career, Debussy continued a pattern of comparing his fits of depression, his terrible struggles with self-confidence, to the hypersensitivity of Poe's characters. (Ravel suffered similar depressions and feelings of worthlessness about his work, but they occurred mainly toward the end of his life, and without documented reference to Poe.) Near the end of his life, when he was diagnosed with cancer, he was still making the comparison, more grimly and obsessively than ever. Isolated from the musical establishment and saddened by increasing sickness and death around him (especially the illness of his daughter, Chouchou, and the loss of his first wife, Lilly Texier), he compared his life to Roderick Usher's, even to the point of envisioning himself trapped in Usher's doomed house. To his friend Robert Godet, he wrote that his life was "an awful nightmare" and that his "house has some current points of resemblance to the House of Usher. . . . Even if I haven't got Usher's cerebral disorders, we share a certain hypersensitivity."[27] The same year he wrote Paul Dukas that "it is possible 'The Fall of the House of Usher' will also be the 'fall' of Claude Debussy."[28]

Debussy's identification with Poe's story presents a complicated pattern of projection. Among many other things, the story is about the workings of chronic depression, recording a sad process in which a man projects his suffering onto his house, indeed onto "all objects of the moral and physical universe," until inner darkness becomes inseparable from outer reality. Debussy identified himself with Usher, then transferred the Usher identification to his own house, his own reality. His goal was to merge as fully as possible with his dark mentor, both artistically and spiritually, through a story that is about the dissolution of boundaries and the merging of personalities—Usher with the increasingly spooked narrator, as well as with his twin sister, Madeline, and his spectacularly gloomy house. There was nothing unconscious about this process: Debussy did it deliberately, with elaborate self-consciousness.

But "The House of Usher" provided more than a spiritual analogue to Debussy's life. This multilayered narrative was also a specific project for his art, one he returned to continually. Debussy looked to Poe for a new aesthetic, and one place he may have found it was in the text of "The Fall of the House of Usher." To an eerie, exacting degree, Debussy's music mirrors aesthetic theories described in extravagant detail in the story, most of them advanced by Usher and explicated by the narrator.

This parallel, oddly ignored by scholars, is too striking to be coincidental. An amateur composer, Usher is described as the creator of short, intensely atmospheric pieces based on psychological or pictorial subjects. The narrator calls them *impromptus,* "wild fantasias" so removed from traditional musical structures as to sound "improvised." Usher's musical theories are inseparable from his theories of visual art; the pattern for his music is the "spirit of abstraction" displayed by his "phantasmagoric conceptions" on canvas, fictional precursors of impressionism.

These descriptions sound a great deal like Debussy's music, which is equally phantasmagoric and atmospheric and which partakes of the spirit of abstraction that also permeates Manet, Whistler, and other impressionist painters. With their shifting, unpredictable patches of color, Debussy's Nocturnes, Preludes, and other short pieces convey the air of the sinister and the sublime, the otherworldly spirit of abstraction displayed by Usher in his wild improvisations and nonrepresentational paintings. Even the habits of composition are similar. Like Usher, Debussy required "intense mental concentration and collectedness" to counteract acute depression and isolation—the awful nightmare of his personal life—before he could work.

Usher and Debussy also shared an important model: Carl Maria von Weber, who pioneered a musical fairyland that eschewed classical sonata form for a musical discourse based on the phantasmal and the fantastic. Usher admired Weber's "wild air," and composed "improvised dirges" based on "a certain singular perversion and amplification" of a Weber waltz. Debussy was also an intense admirer of Weber, whom he praised in his columns for *Gil Blas,* citing Weber's "dreamy melancholy" and his command of "all the ways music can describe the fantastic."[29]

Above all, Debussy's work is a translation of Usher's theory that art, especially music, is based on implication and undercurrent. The "Usher" narrator declares that his friend's art is based on deliberate mystery, even "vagueness." "I shuddered all the more thrillingly," he says when describing Usher's work, "because I shuddered knowing not why." In the "Usher" universe there is no real distinction between poetry and music, no clear transitions between discussions of either, just as there is no clear distinction between music and painting. This blurring is similar to Debussy's reliance on Poe as a more significant inspiration than other musical artists. Profoundly shaken by Usher's "Haunted Palace," a poem set to a musical "rhapsody" the narrator states that its power is defined by "the under or mystic current of its meaning" rather than by anything obvious or explicit. This is the feeling for which Debussy strove in his art, a haunted music where all obvious melody, rhythm, and harmony are eschewed in favor of mystic insinuation.

Paradoxically, the means of arriving at this sinister vagueness must be anything but vague. It must, in fact, be precise and carefully calculated, the result of "intense mental collectedness and concentration." Here again is Poe's fixation on technique and calculation, echoed in the meticulous precision of Debussy's music, as it is in Ravel's, although Debussy's overall architecture is freer, more seemingly improvised and phantasmal than his French colleague's. It is expressed through a fictional depiction of the quintessential Poe artist rather than in the expository prose of a theoretical essay. Continuing to work even in the throes of acute mental distress, Roderick Usher heroically embodies the principles of "The Philosophy of Composition," particularly the requisite state of sadness and melancholy, even as the narrator articulates them. But "Usher" goes further than the "Philosophy" in dramatizing an art based on the mysterious and the horrific, with music at its center. No wonder Debussy and other Poe-inspired artists (especially Baudelaire) were drawn to this particular Poe tale. For Debussy perhaps more than any of the others, Usher's collectedness as a means of producing a shuddery emotional end became a central enterprise.

To summon this combination of the precise and the mysterious, the poet-composer must possess what the narrator calls a "morbid acuteness of the senses"—the quality Debussy refers to in his letters as the hypersensitivity he shared with Usher. To us, this identification of neurosis or near-madness with creativity may seem a Romantic cliché, but to Debussy, who suffered through the kinds of mental crises depicted in "Usher," it was refreshing and liberating, the source of a strange species of hope. It certainly produced positive musical results. Usher's peculiar state, further defined by the narrator as a "morbid condition of the auditory nerve," renders all coarseness in music intolerable. The singular delicacy and shivery tenuousness of Debussy's music is a precise rendering of this morbid state.

In a related paradox, the narrow limits of Usher's musical art, its restriction to subtlety, indirection, and transparent instrumentation (he prefers muted strings, lutes, and other lithe sounds), give birth to the limitless and the awesome. The fantastic character and the sense of the limitless in Debussy's music are similarly drawn from deliberately refined and narrow sounds — the distant horns in *Fêtes*, the lighter-than-air harp and strings in the *Sacred and Profane Dances*, the claustrophobic organum of "The Sunken Cathedral."

In a sense, Debussy was more faithful to Poe's aesthetic than Poe himself. For all his talk of mysterious undercurrents, Poe frequently indulged in percussive Gothic effects of the most hyperbolic kind — one of the reasons his stories are such fun. That many of these Gothicisms are parodic and savagely funny (as in "The Black Cat" and "The Facts in the Case of M. Valdemar") does not alter their fortissimo character. Debussy may have been innocent of the extremity of Poe's hyperbole, partly because Baudelaire's translation was (as T. S. Eliot was fond of saying) more attenuated than the original and partly because Debussy's favorite Poe tale was "Usher," one of his most sophisticated and spectral works. (The famous opening section alone is pure atmosphere, pure music.) In any case, Debussy's art is consistently, triumphantly refined. Usher would surely have taken pleasure in Debussy's music; it would have appealed to his "morbid acuteness of the senses," his neurotic abhorrence of anything crude or shrill.

The other Poe tale that had a singular impact on Debussy, and that he attempted, unsuccessfully, to turn into an opera, was "The Devil in the Belfry" ("Le Diable dans le beffroi"). Between 1902 and 1910, during which time he worked intermittently on the opera, all he managed to complete was the sketch of a scenario. Yet once again, the tale itself had a strong impact on his musical style.

"The Devil in the Belfry" would seem an odd choice for an opera. It is not only one of Poe's lighter, more whimsical works but also one of his more obscure. It is still left out of most Poe collections and is one of the few tales that is not the subject of intense critical commentary. But Debussy loved obscure and neglected art, and the very qualities that have made critics ignore this tale were the ones he found attractive.

The fairy-tale plot involves the townspeople of a Dutch village who, like so many Poe characters, are fixated on time, extending their gaze upward to the great clock in the belfry every hour. One day just before noon, a "finicky little personage" with a fiddle enters the town out of nowhere, climbs up into the belfry, knocks down the belfry keeper with his instrument, and somehow causes the big clock to strike thirteen after it has struck twelve. All the other clocks in the village do the same and take to "dancing as if bewitched." The narrator flees in terror, appealing for outside help to "all lovers of correct time." With its bright, comic imagery, and just a hint of the supernatural, this tale breaks out of Poe's usual gloom; it even features a character — never mind that he seems to be the devil — who can defeat time, the great enemy in Poe's mortality-haunted world.

The impish *diablerie* of this tale found its way into Debussy's music. "There's something to be got from this tale," he wrote André Messager, "in which reality and fantasy are so happily combined."[30] To Debussy, Poe's devil was not a spirit of evil but the "spirit of contradiction" who "whispers to those who do not think like everybody else." As usual, Debussy was attracted to the nonconformist impulse in Poe; in his "Belfry" opera he was searching for new harmonies combined with a novel and simple style of choral writing that had no trace of tradition or heaviness.[31]

Although he never finished the opera, scholars postulate that "Gigues," the last of the *Images*, contains some of the projected "Belfry" music, as does the later *Jeux* and the chorus in *The Martyrdom of Saint Sebastien*. This hypothesis seems credible, not only because (as Edward Lockspeiser points out in his classic biography) Debussy would have been following the practice of numerous composers who constantly borrowed motifs from unfinished works but because the music itself supports it. After 1902, an increasingly sly and mischievous sense of irony invaded Debussy's work. "Gigues" in particular could very well provide a setting for "Belfry." It scarcely matters that Debussy quotes a Scottish folk song rather than the Irish tunes played by Poe's devil: the point is that the music, like Poe's tale, has a folkloric litheness, a comic spirit of contradiction that continued to suffuse later works. (The moonstruck *grotesquerie* of the Cello-Piano Sonata is a particularly delightful example.) Like Poe's story, "Gigues" ends in irresolution, a quiet collapse that provides even less closure than the fade-outs in Debussy's earlier works.

In the case of both Poe operas, the process of composition had a major effect on Debussy's musical thinking, even though he never completed either project. Debussy's letters are filled with references to these oddly invigorating failures. By striving to translate Poe's fictional world into music, Debussy arrived at a new world of sound in the works he did complete. In 1909, he interrupted the composition of *Images* to resume the "absorbing task" of writing the music and libretto to "Usher." Like the earlier Poe symphony, the work was never completed, but the struggle helped stamp his musical style. As he put it two years later in a letter to Robert Godet, the absorption into Poe's trancelike world revealed an exciting, "mobile" alternative to the "unimpassioned chaos" of Wagner, a new world of "masterly illusion" in sound that Poe had already conjured in words.[32]

To Debussy, Poe represented the "naked flesh of emotion," a nakedness he himself could never quite achieve. The twin Poe projects resulted in new colors and textures being "discovered," then "suppressed," as what had at first seemed novel and fresh turned out to be a gimmick that continued to "smell of the lamp."[33] To succeed in creating a musical equivalent to Poe would involve a total liberation from musical tradition, a freedom Debussy strove for throughout his creative life and at which he invariably judged himself to be a failure. Despite the new ground he broke, he felt "oppressed" and "depressed" by musical traditions he attempted in vain to destroy. Commenting on the Usher music, he noted that "for every bar that has some freedom about it, there are twenty that are stifled by the weight of one particular tradition."

Debussy was out to demolish all traditions, at least in music. He hated the "false profundity" of the Germans — including Wagner, whom he saw as "a beautiful sunset who has been mistaken for a sunrise"[34] — as well as "the hysterical mysticism" of "Gounod & Co."[35] When a critic declared *Pelléas et Mélisande* to be the "negation of everything musical,"

Debussy wore the criticism like a badge, retorting that "negation is very often worth several affirmations." He put Poe in the same rarefied category as the composers he admired—Mussorgsky for his "magical landscapes," the young Stravinsky for his "enlarged" sense of the "permissible," gamelan improvisers for their "percussive charm."[36]

Ultimately, Poe represented the same thing to Debussy that he did to Ravel: the elevation of beauty as the sole ideal in art, rather than one subordinate to tradition, religion, ideology, or anything else. This was the most important revolution, the one with the potential to sweep aside the dead weight of the past. Debussy was emphatic on this point: beauty of sound, he was fond of saying, was the only absolute in music.

The Poe operas therefore promised a complete liberation of technique and sensibility that Debussy tortured himself to achieve, revision after failed revision. He considered it his lifelong duty to wrestle with Poe. During moments of severe depression, he went so far as to declare that the Poe operas were the only antidote to suicide. "If I didn't have the desire as well as the duty to finish the two Poe operas," he told Jacques Durand in 1916, "I'd have done it already."[37] He found reading Poe "an excellent way of strengthening the nerves against any sort of terror."[38]

That these frustrating, perceptually unfinished operas—one of them based on a tale of nihilism and despair—provided Debussy with his raison d'être for living sounds like something right out of Poe. The operas represented what Poe would have called Debussy's "imp of the perverse," a sinister but infinitely seductive obsession. Like Poe, Debussy was an isolated innovator who nursed loneliness and failure. This was more than just fashionable Decadence ennui: it seemed an important spur to creativity. Had Debussy completed the operas, they would not have continued providing their strange life-giving energy.

There is an aesthetic symmetry to these failures as well. Poe's tales derive much of their power from their willful insubstantiality, the terrifying vagueness and indefiniteness that the Usher narrator declares to be the soul of art. Other than Madeline's death and seeming resurrection, remarkably little happens in "Usher." An anonymous narrator visits a friend to help him through a terrible depression but finds he is powerless to do so. That is about all we get in terms of story line, and the minimal narrative moves toward an ambiguous conclusion that has been debated by critics since the beginnings of modern criticism. The tale is mostly atmosphere, mood, psychological projection—the qualities with which Poe altered modern fiction—along with enough disquisition on artistic theory to constitute another "philosophy of composition." Even the horrific staircase scene at the end is probably the double hallucination of Usher and the distraught narrator, but we never know for sure. As for "The Devil in the Belfry," it too has a tenuous, threadbare plot and a suspended, ambiguous ending: at the conclusion, the diabolical clocks are still tolling as the villagers ponder what to do next.

The strange fragment that is the only surviving product of Debussy's lifelong struggles with "Usher"—a shivery orchestral prelude and other stitches of mostly unorchestrated music, plus three versions of the libretto—therefore has a poetic appropriateness. Like Coleridge's "Kubla Khan," it is more enticing because of its ghostly incompleteness. The floating, disembodied music, which kicks away at the moorings of tonality, breathes an atmosphere of decline and decay symptomatic of both Usher and the dying composer, who described his life during his final years as "a meticulous combination of the grotesque and the horrible."[39] Debussy called the Usher score "music that moves stones to tears."[40] In its despair and incompleteness, it is a haunting final testament that sums up the fundamental ambiguity of his art.

It is not surprising that two attempts undertaken in the 1970s to complete "Usher" were both flops, and that neither finished version has entered the repertory. Both orchestrators were criticized for clumsiness, for failing to really sound like Debussy. But it may be that the problem is more basic. Perhaps Debussy never completed the opera because the task was impossible. Opera may well be too literal a form for Poe, whose secret atmosphere was more naturally translated into instrumental works, in which secrecy could be maintained through the mysterious power of abstract sound. Poe's tenuous spirit of abstraction is not easily sustained in the opera house.

Nonetheless, the libretto does offer a fascinating glimpse into Debussy's lifelong view of the artist and his indebtedness to Poe in arriving at it. In Debussy's variation on Poe's story, Madeline wanders about like a ghost, intoning lines from "The Haunted Palace," Usher's allegorical poem that, like the main narrative, depicts a collapsing house as a metaphor for mental disintegration. The extraordinary loneliness of Debussy's musical fragments—a recitative with the scantiest tonal underpinning—

is emphasized by this daring dramatic device: Madeline's lines are strictly monologue; she is utterly isolated from the other characters.

As for those strange others—Roderick, his friend, and a sinister doctor that Debussy created from a few hints in Poe's text—they engage in an argument over Usher's illness that reveals what Debussy considered most important about Poe. In Poe's original, Usher, whom Debussy believed to be a stand-in for his creator, suffers from "an anomalous species of terror," a vicious cycle of anxiety and depression. In the libretto, the doctor (whose veracity is undermined by arrogance and general unpleasantness) claims Usher's madness is hereditary "crankiness." But Roderick's friend eloquently defends Usher as suffering from an infatuation with art and beauty. Incomplete though the music may be, the libretto gives full vent to Debussy's identification with Usher—and with Poe himself—as an artist who was misunderstood by the mob and who martyred himself to beauty.

For Ravel and Debussy, who were attracted to American culture and its artistic possibilities, Poe represented the dark side of the New World. These composers were interested in the sinister and decadent aspects of the same America that inspired Dvořák, Weill, and others with sunshine and optimism. Instead of spontaneity, healthy open spaces, and the freedom of nature, Poe conjured a world of claustrophobic tunnels unearthed through anxiety and artifice. As Camille Paglia succinctly puts it, Poe's "Gothic entombments shut down the American frontier and repeal the idea of progress."[41]

Another way to put it is that Poe discovered a new idea of the frontier, one of the imagination, an underground space where the only meaningful freedom is the freedom to create and the only reward is the shiver of terror and ecstasy that art uniquely delivers. This frontier is decidedly dangerous, leading sometimes to beauty but always to isolation and anxiety, without which beauty cannot be forged. Composers like Delius and Dvořák attempted to mine authentic American folk sources in their versions of New World music, and indeed Ravel and Debussy created a specific set of jazz works that did the same. But for the most part, they took Poe's cue and went in the opposite direction, looking inward rather than outward, using their inner ear as the sole determinant of what was beautiful rather than the harmonic or rhythmic formulas of the musical establishment.

Poe influenced other composers as well, especially Rachmaninoff and Messiaen, but Debussy and Ravel traveled further on this sinister journey than any other musical artists. True to the stereotype of Romantic agony, both paid a severe price: Ravel, like Poe a perfectionist who inevitably produced a limited oeuvre, ended his life in a depression, convinced after so many flops and disappointments that his output was hopelessly small, his life a failure. (Also like Poe, he became sensationally popular following his death.) Debussy ended his life even more isolated and embittered, in his own self-created House of Usher.

The impossible Poe ideal — defined by Ravel as a search for endless mystery in a "precise design" — led to an isolating self-entombment in a fanatical search for technical perfection. But it also led to what Debussy called Poe's "naked flesh of emotion," a dark core of "supernal Beauty" behind the impressionist mist. Poe's influence was fundamental, permeating the most basic aesthetic principles. Unlike the New World defined by the actual — the African-American and Native American folk art uncovered by Dvořák and Delius — this world was based unabashedly on fantasy, on the triumph of subjective, artificial beauty. Like the creations of Roderick Usher's weird psyche, it was not borrowed but *literally* new, created from the frontier of the imagination.

Although Debussy and Ravel were unique in the intensity with which they absorbed the sensibility and aesthetic of Poe, they were by no means the only composers to attempt Poe settings. In America, MacDowell, Sousa, Gottschalk, and Charles Sanford Skilton contributed long-forgotten pieces, as did several marginal composers; in the last three decades of the twentieth century, Leonard Slatkin, George Crumb, Jack Beeson, Deborah Drattell, and other composers wrote scattered Poe pieces. Settings by Europeans are far more numerous, including efforts by John Ireland and Joseph Holbrooke in England; Nikolay Myaskovsky and N. N. Tcherepnin in Russia; and Florent Schmitt, André Caplet, Louis Diemer, and D. E. Inghelbrecht in France.

The only thing more remarkable than the sheer number of these pieces is their lack of distinction. Virtually all have fallen into oblivion or onto the remote edges of the repertory. Two exceptions are André Caplet's *The Masque of the Red Death* (original version, 1908) and Florent Schmitt's *The Haunted Palace* (1904), both of which enjoyed a brief revival in the 1980s. These are certainly interesting works, plumbing as they do the gloom and terror of Poe to register the deep anxiety in

Henri Matisse's drawing of Poe for Stéphane Mallarmé's translation of Poe's works, published in 1931–32. Poe and Mallarmé were inspirations for the music of Debussy and Ravel. (Baltimore Museum of Art, BMA 1950.12.69.XXV)

European culture that would soon explode into World War I. Musically, however, they offer little of the Poe-inspired sublimity found in the music of Caplet's friend and colleague, Debussy. What they do have is plenty of imaginative, sometimes garish color. In the terminology of Poe, they produce the effects without the undercurrent.

It may be that the very musicality of Poe is a trap for some composers, especially those of the second rank. Poe is perhaps too easy a subject, seeming to offer instant thrills, to invoke ready-made morbidity and melancholy. For Debussy and Ravel, tricks and effects were secondary; they were haunted by Poe in a fundamental way, one that evoked what they called "secret atmosphere" and "somber abstraction" — a quiet reach toward the infinite.

One other authentic Poe masterpiece did emerge during the apocalyptic period of the early twentieth century, when Poe settings were so apt and so popular. In 1913, at the same time Debussy was struggling with a vocal work inspired by Poe, Sergei Rachmaninoff was doing the same. Unlike Debussy, Rachmaninoff completed his Poe project, not an opera (which may, as we have seen, be the wrong format for Poe) but a gigantic cantata called *The Bells*. As was the case with Debussy and Ravel, Poe's inspiration was singularly potent: to the end of his life, Rachmaninoff regarded *The Bells* as his best work.

It is easy to see why. For one thing, the subject is unusually felicitous. "The Bells"—a poem that links musical sound with basic experiences and states of mind—is an ideal work for a musical setting. Furthermore, Rachmaninoff was at the height of his powers and was in just the right mood for this work: *The Bells* comes at the end of the same remarkable period during which he produced *The Isle of the Dead*, the minor-key *Etudes tableaux*, and other essays in the sublime and the horrific. The emotional range, echoing that of Poe's poem, is wider than anything Rachmaninoff had ever attempted. His score has all the anxiety and morbidity one could ask for in an invocation of Poe's "alarum bells" and death knells; Rachmaninoff's Russian sensibility was fully compatible with Poe's darkness. But the music also has a surprising charm and subtlety, a freedom from the alleged self-pity and sentimentality that— at least in the early part of the twentieth century—damaged Rachmaninoff's reputation among the intelligentsia.

Like his French contemporaries, Rachmaninoff shared an affinity with Poe that was partly autobiographical. Rachmaninoff suffered a series of breakdowns as spectacularly painful as those of any Poe character. Indeed, much of his art reflects a pattern of collapse and recovery, with exuberant, bell-like affirmations (the finale of the Second Symphony, for example) following passages of sustained moroseness and pessimism. But Rachmaninoff, unlike Poe's depressive personae, did pick himself up, and the process of composing *The Bells* was part of the uplift.

Throughout the late 1890s, Rachmaninoff was plunged into a terrible depression that left him barely able to function. This state was set off by the disastrous premiere of his First Symphony, during which he fled from the hall in horror, later destroying the score. He was devastated by extraordinarily vicious reviews, the most notorious of which was written by the composer César Cui: "If there were a conservatory in Hell, Rachmaninoff would get the first prize for his symphony."[42] To be sure, a Poe-like ennui and lassitude were as fashionable in prerevolutionary

Russia as they were in the rest of Europe at the turn of the century, but Rachmaninoff's decline was clearly more than aesthetic posturing. His friends became so alarmed by his condition that they talked him into seeing Dr. Nikolai Dahl, a pioneer in psychoanalysis and hypnosis as well as an amateur musician. So dramatically successful was Dr. Dahl's therapy that by the summer of 1900 Rachmaninoff found himself besieged by new musical ideas. These became the genesis of the Second Piano Concerto, one of the most popular works in the repertory (with a dedication to Dr. Dahl that is surely the most impressive early advertisement for psychotherapy) and the beginning of a singularly productive period in Rachmaninoff's career that was to last more than a decade.[43]

Buoyed by a successful marriage—like Poe, he wed his first cousin—Rachmaninoff completed his Second Symphony and Third Piano Concerto, two of his most self-confident works. But it was *The Bells*, which he called his Third Symphony, that meant the most to him. Like Ravel, he had been attracted to Poe since childhood. When an admirer casually suggested a setting of "The Bells," he immediately took to the idea. The subject was such a natural one for Rachmaninoff that he finished the score quickly (despite the nerve-wracking hospitalization of his wife and daughter for typhoid), was gratified by the results, and enjoyed a hugely successful premiere, replete with laurel wreaths and bouquets—a welcome relief from his usual pattern of anxiety and self-doubt.

It is often said that Rachmaninoff was drawn to Poe because the two artists shared a fatalistic or deeply depressive temperament, but the larger picture is more complex.[44] The fatalism of the final two movements of *The Bells*, punctuated by quotations from "Dies irae" (a Rachmaninoff trademark), is set against the sleigh and wedding bells of the enchanting opening movements. Like Ravel and Debussy, Rachmaninoff found in Poe's emotional volatility a paradoxical respite from depression and morbidity, a kind of aesthetic shock therapy that inspired a broad range of moods and colors.

Like these composers, Rachmaninoff was affected by Poe in a peculiarly visceral way consistent with Poe's own aesthetic. He was especially taken with Poe's linkage of musical sound with potent emotional states, an association that, as a Russian, he found congenial because of the poem's obsessive emphasis on bells. "Most of my life was lived around the vibrations of the bells of Moscow," Rachmaninoff said in his dictated reminiscences, and contemplating Poe's verses during a stay in Rome set these vibrations ringing again in his imagination. Far from having been written in a depressive mood, *The Bells* was composed "in the drowsy quiet of a Roman afternoon," where Rachmaninoff "heard the bell voices and tried to set down on paper their lovely tones that seemed to express the varying shades of human experience."[45]

From the silvery woodwinds and transparent strings in the opening "Silver Sleigh Bells" through the piquant bitonalities of the "Mellow Wedding Bells" to the shivery fade-out of the "Mournful Iron Bells," Rachmaninoff's score expresses these "shades" with hallucinatory intensity. The violent chromaticism of the scherzo, "Alarum Bells," is a vortex of anxiety, an expression of existential terror unlike anything else in the Rachmaninoff canon. More surprising is the delicacy of orchestration, a frequent characteristic of Poe-inspired music—the spine-tingling woodwind trills and percussion effects in the first movement, for example, and the clarinet climbing over otherworldly strings at the end. The latter, coming after all human words have been silenced by death, is quintessential Rachmaninoff, the most moving ending he ever wrote.

In *The Bells*, Rachmaninoff's embrace of death—suggested in *The Isle of the Dead, Rhapsody on a Theme of Paganini*, and the *Symphonic Dances*—is made explicit by Poe's text. But the ending illustrates again that the most telling Poe-inspired music is often purely orchestral. Darius Milhaud, for example, unleashed his sensational (though, alas, rarely performed) version of *The Bells* as a ballet in 1946; Milhaud's racy rhythms and polytonalities were exactly in tune with the diablerie of the poem. Again, it is what Poe called the undercurrent of mood rather than specific words in a text that translates so potently into music.

Like his French colleagues, Rachmaninoff read Poe in translation, in this case a Russian version of "The Bells" by Constantin Balmont that he received anonymously in the mail. (An avid reader, he was probably conversant with Baudelaire's popular translations of Poe as well.) A heavily Russianized Poe, Balmont's translation is a virtual recomposition that spells out and makes literal what Poe suggests through the verbal tolling of bells. Poe's concluding stanza, for example, is a *danse macabre*, full of grim irony, featuring ghouls dancing to a paean of bells sounding a "happy Runic rhyme." Balmont's version, eschewing Poe's irony and imagery, comments directly on the futility of human endeavor and the attraction of death as an end to all struggle.

In an important sense, the crudity of the Balmont translation is irrelevant. Again, Rachmaninoff was inspired not by Poe's literal words but by his emphasis on atmosphere and the beauty of sound—indeed, by Poe's conviction that music such as the sounds of bells could toll thoughts and feelings more profound than those communicated by words. Paradoxically, it took a master of words to show their limits, to move musicians into a world beyond language, a world to which Poe himself despairingly aspired.

Ultimately, Rachmaninoff's parallels with Poe go beyond a single work, extending into his nonprogrammatic output as well. Rachmaninoff turns out to be a far more interesting figure than was once supposed. Rather than simply a reactionary who resisted the innovations of Stravinsky and Schoenberg, as painted by musical intellectuals for over fifty years, he was an early neo-Romantic, a pioneer in a genre that erupted full force in the closing years of the twentieth century. It is therefore important to look at his musical architecture afresh—which, it turns out, involves the principles advocated by Poe.

Music critics in the late twentieth century pointed out that Rachmaninoff's symphonic style is based not on the dialectic principle of sonata form, with its balanced contrasts, but on unity of atmosphere. The consistent mood in a given movement creates a seamless emotional unity rather than classical balance and contrast; this unity permeates everything, including development sections and transitional passages. This musical style is strikingly similar to the poetic principle advocated by Poe, and Rachmaninoff's description of the technique has a distinctly Poe-like ring: "Each piece is built up around a climax: the whole stream of tones must be so calculated, and the content and force of each so clearly graduated, that the climax seems to be completely natural. . . . It must come as a liberation from the last material obstacle, and overcome the last barrier between truth itself and the means used to express it."[46]

It is unclear whether Rachmaninoff was directly inspired by Poe's aesthetic philosophy or whether his saturation in Poe's work gave him a clear sense of its dynamic. What is clear is that the emphasis on a calculated, graduated unity of design is strikingly close to Poe's advocacy of a single "tone" leading to a "preconceived effect." Like Poe, Rachmaninoff created a despairing emotional world brilliantly contrived and preconceived even though it seems romantically spontaneous. However he absorbed the influence, he was another European composer who found a New World by sailing in the dark waters of Poe.

Since Rachmaninoff's death, the most remarkable Poe music has again come from a European: Olivier Messiaen's *Turangalîla* Symphony, first performed in 1949, one of the most eccentric and important symphonies to be written after World War II. To be sure, the musical legacy of Poe has also continued in the work of American composers— in Leonard Bernstein's vivid setting of "Israfel" from his cycle *Songfest*, for example, and in Philip Glass's opera *The Fall of the House of Usher*. But neither of these works—especially the pallid Glass setting—reaches for an authentic Poe atmosphere. Poe continues to travel more easily across the Atlantic than within his own country, and in Messiaen he found an especially congenial harbor.

Messiaen's greatest secular work, *Turangalîla* represents the sensual, fleshly side of a composer generally known for otherworldly mysticism and convoluted musical theology. With its gigantic orchestra (including a daring exploitation of vibraphone, glockenspiel, and electronic keyboard), unleashed with uninhibited garishness, the work feels more like a hallucination than a piece of music.

Turangalîla was an elaborately postmodern hybrid long before that term obtained currency, a mélange of highly disparate elements, including gamelan drumming, the *Tristan* myth, and the Indian motifs that account for its Sanskrit title. But the core inspiration was Poe: the three sinister movements associated with Poe's tales (called Turangalîla I, II, and III) were composed and performed first, providing a center of gravity for the unabashedly schmaltzy *Tristan* movements.

The "Turangalîla" sections constitute what is surely the most horrific Poe-inspired music ever written. If Debussy, Ravel, and Rachmaninoff mined the more abstract, poetic elements in Poe, Messiaen must be credited with exploiting Poe at his most ghoulish and Gothic. "Turangalîla II," based on Poe's "The Pit and the Pendulum," captures what Poe's narrator calls the "darkness of eternal night." Poe's tale, with its sonorous prose and musical references, is ideal for a musical setting. "And then there stole into my fancy, like a rich musical note, the thought of what sweet rest there must be in the grave," says the narrator near the beginning, registering the pull toward death so central in Poe. In Messiaen's later, more theologically rigorous works, death is inextricably connected with the Resurrection. Here, the Grim Reaper is challenged only by desire, depicted in the erotic energies unleashed by the *Tristan* movements.

In the most startling of Messiaen's funhouse gallery of special effects, an electronic keyboard slithers downward into Poe's fearful pit, with dissonant brass and percussion shrieking and pounding above. The narrator's "long agony" and "deadly nausea" of spirit are captured with an explicitness that goes beyond the symphonic Gothicism of earlier works such as Berlioz's *Symphonie fantastique* and Liszt's *Todtentanz*. The pendulum's "rushing vibrations" are captured by the Ondes Martenot, an electronic keyboard instrument, in musical onomatopoiea; the pit itself, an abyss of physical and mental suffering, is opened up by a chasmal brass motif that begins and concludes the symphony.

With the death of Messiaen in April 1992, Western music lost one of its last genuine mystics. Like Debussy, his chief musical influence, Messiaen repudiated the narrative structure of music passed down by Haydn and Beethoven. In this countertradition, music does not lay out a symmetrical exposition and then develop its themes; rather, the themes are spun out of one another and juxtaposed according to a dominant mood. Edward Said has explained it thus: "Whereas the main Western musical tradition by and large relies upon development, control, inventiveness, and rhythm in the service of logical control, Messiaen's music is consciously at some eccentric distance from these characteristics. Instead his work emphasizes repetition and stasis."[47] The static, hypnotic state induced by Messiaen once again invokes Poe's idea of art as atmosphere, of an overpowering mood being "struck at once," then constantly reinforced by deft repetition and variation. Debussy absorbed this aesthetic through an immersion in Poe. Messiaen picked it up from both Poe and Debussy, the latter his musical mentor.

There is another parallel as well, one that gets at the heart of Poe's contribution to European music. Messiaen often spoke of a state of childlike wonder as a necessary ingredient in the authentic performance of his work. Debussy and Ravel also require this resuscitation of atavistic mystery and terror; Debussy in particular emphasized the "magic landscapes" of childhood as the location of musical revolution. As we have seen, Poe staked out this territory in a consistent way, eliciting both adulation and sneering condescension for his refusal to be adult. This open embrace of the adolescent and the childlike, paradoxically combined with the sophistication and calculatedness of Poe's literary theories, represented what European composers most admired about the New World as an artistic ideal. These composers carried the legacy of Poe forward into music, Poe's favorite art, where the childlike shiver of ecstasy and terror could exist in its purest, most mysterious form.

The legacy has continued, sometimes with striking results, as exemplified by the Danish composer Poul Ruders, whose evocations of American cityscapes and jazz sonorities make him a prominent New World artist of the 1980s and 1990s. For Ruders, Poe was not merely a source of spooky subjects and effects but a broad aesthetic model, as he was to the French impressionists. According to the composer Karl Aage Rasmussen, Ruders had "his imagination set afire" by Poe's poetry and by the "unique way in which Poe merges strict form, symbolic content, and emotional intensity."[48] Ruders was therefore inspired by the same unity of form, content, and feeling that moved his Poe-worshipping predecessors. In a 1996 interview, Ruders told me he was attracted to Poe's "tight form," "dark exuberance," and hatred of all things puritanical and didactic, demonstrating again the remarkable consistency of what attracted Europeans to Poe for well over a century.[49]

Ruders's version of *The Bells*, from 1993, is as profoundly different from Rachmaninoff's as can be imagined, providing an example of the extreme emotional variation a single Poe work can sustain in music. Ruders sets the entire poem, without changes, in English. Scored for chamber ensemble rather than full orchestra, this setting is chillier and creepier than Rachmaninoff's, an effective piece of neo-Gothicism with a remarkable range of subtle, bell-like sounds for both orchestra and singer. The entire ensemble rings and vibrates. Intoning the earlier, more innocent stages of Poe's life cycle, the soprano soloist begins in the highest registers; at the end, she abandons vocalise altogether to growl and shout the ghoulish "groaning of the bells" over repeated poundings on muted piano strings. Strongly attuned to the poem, the music brings the Grim Reaper to garish life with meticulous calculations and effects. Poe's aggressively musical verse seems equally at home in the nontonal expressionism of the opening and the near-medieval tonality and finality of the ending.

In music, Poe can sound oddly contemporary; one forgets the singsong musicality of his rhyme and meter, the repetitive effects for which he is often criticized. This version of *The Bells*, like so many European settings, brings out Poe's deeper musicality. At the end of the twentieth century, Poe was still a resonant sounding board for the European muse, still an igniter of the European imagination set afire.

CHAPTER FOUR

New World Songs:
The Legacy of Whitman

I never got over him, I am glad to say.
—Ralph Vaughan Williams, at age 84, on the influence of Whitman

F OR a poet often accused of being unmusical, Walt Whitman has inspired an enormous amount of music. Whitman settings span both sides of the Atlantic and take in an astonishing variety of musical styles, even though his own musical tastes were peculiarly narrow, confined mainly to Italian opera.[1] From modernist orchestral works such as Carl Ruggles's *Portals* to romantic epics such as Ralph Vaughan Williams's *Sea* Symphony, the catalog of Whitman-inspired pieces is as huge and variegated as Whitman himself; it includes works by Delius, Burleigh, Gustav Holst, Charles Villiers Stanford, Hamilton Harty, Hubert Parry, Elinor Remick Warren, Kurt Weill, Roger Sessions, Roy Harris, Virgil Thomson, Elliott Carter, Stefan Wolpe, Jane Frasier, Ronald Roxbury, and many other composers—not to mention pop settings such as "I Sing the Body Electric" from Alan Parker's *Fame.* With the possible exception of Shakespeare, no other poet has received more musical settings.

Just why Whitman is so attractive to composers is one of the more tantalizing mysteries of American culture. Is it because the flexibility of his free verse, combining fluid outer structures with internal symmetries, makes a musical setting more natural than the relatively rigid verse of traditional poets? Or, to put it negatively, is it because the very "unmusicalness" of Whitman makes a setting less redundant? Not everyone, of course, regards Whitman's verse as nonmusical. Gay Wilson Allen and other mid-century critics used to argue that Whitman's reliance on literal repetition (the very quality that causes his detractors to damn him as unmusical) mimics the process of musical composition, treating words like repeated notes: Could it be that composers picked up on this similarity and mirrored it back?

Perhaps the draw has to do with the voice or theme. Is Whitman's intimate, first-person voice inviting to composers because it imposes no masks or barriers? Or is it the expansiveness and universality of Whitman, celebrating everything from "lusts and appetites" to visions of the Oversoul, from the American "continent of glories" to Russian politics and Eastern religion, that inspires musicians, as it does so many poets?

Each of these possibilities offers a hint of an explanation based on intuitions of eye and ear. Amazingly little has been written on the subject. What is so fascinating about the written evidence that does exist is that the composers most profoundly shaped by Whitman speak of his connection to music as if it was self-evident; when composers write or talk about Whitman, they dwell on political and spiritual issues rather than on musical ones. Clearly, the resonance is basic, direct, and deeply personal, going well beyond technical considerations—like an electric current flowing from one art to another. The exuberant tone of this commentary suggests that certain literary composers found great comfort and uplift in Whitman's New World optimism, just as others (Rachmaninoff, Ravel, Debussy) were fueled by the melancholy of Poe.

Typical is a statement Hubert Parry made in 1883 during an argument over Whitman that raged all evening: one of Parry's colleagues had read several Whitman poems aloud, after which another attempted to demonstrate their "formless bathos" by countering with Shelley. Parry admitted that Whitman belonged "to a totally different order, but I don't give up my sympathy for him all the same. Possibly it is the democratic tinge that fetches me in him, and the way in which he faces our human problems and speaks ruggedly himself—and such a strange, wild, at the same time hopeful self."[2] The issue goes beyond aesthetics: Parry concedes that Whitman is in a "different order" from Shelley and other poets, but he finds Whitmanian qualities such as wildness, strangeness, humanness, egalitarianism, and ruggedness more important, indeed, irresistible. Parry admired not just Whitman's verse but his worldview.[3]

Some composers feel a powerful link with Whitman's method of composition, his gradual accretion of minutiae into a grand design. Frederick Delius and Michael Tippett were particularly attracted to this aspect of Whitman. Tippett attributes his first encounter with America, "my dream country," to his early reading of Whitman in the 1920s, which continued into his old age: "Whitman still fascinates me: and I certainly identify with his habit of carrying everywhere a trunk full of notes and jottings, which he then proceeded to fuse together to create *Leaves of Grass*. My mind is rather like Whitman's trunk."[4]

Performers feel the kinship too. William Stone, the baritone soloist in Robert Shaw's recording of Hindemith's Whitman-based *When Lilacs Last in the Dooryard Bloom'd*, told me that musicians regard Whitman as supremely musical: "His rhythm is free: it's not ta-tum, ta-tum, ta-tum." The pattern is consistent; musicians, far more than literary critics, see Whitman as profoundly musical, largely because of his rhythmic elasticity. Other advantages, according to Stone, are Whitman's tremendous "variety" and "timelessness."[5] The range of Whitman musical settings supports this claim. It is hard to think of another poet who is able to combine vagueness and specificity, universality and intimacy, in such an array of scenarios—a vision of the cosmos (Holst's *Ode to Death*), a Brooklyn street scene of the 1930s (Weill's *Street Scene*), a show business scenario of the 1980s (*Fame*), a passionate heterosexual love scene (Delius's *Idyll*), and a passionate homosexual love scene (Michael Tilson Thomas's "We Two Boys Together Clinging")—and be appropriate in every case. The trajectory of musical styles, from Parry to Karel Husa, is exceptionally wide as well. Virtually the only type of music Whitman did not inspire was the form he loved most, grand opera.

Certainly Whitman assumed his musical connection to be self-evident. As an opera critic for the *Brooklyn Eagle* during the 1840s and 1850s and as author of the 1845 essay "Art-Singing and Heart-Singing," he had an early, intuitive appreciation of vocal music, one that, as he himself acknowledged, helped shape *Leaves of Grass*. His poems are full of musical references: from the first "Inscription" in *Leaves of Grass*, he defines his work as "varied carols" of "America Singing." "Song of Myself" unfolds as a series of instruments and voices: cellos, cornets, drums, a grand-opera chorus, a "tenor large and fresh as the creation," an orchestra "wider than Uranus." In his final poems, Whitman sees himself as the instrument for a "mystic Trumpeter" in the "symphony true" that is death. He looks back over his life as the "clangor of organ majestic" and asserts in "My Legacy" that he has "nothing to show" but a "bundle of songs." For Whitman, music was the "truest," most organic, and most inspiring art. He would no doubt have been pleased by his enormous musical legacy.

He might have been surprised, however, by how much more decisive this legacy was in the Old World than in the New. In poetry, Whitman took half a century to make his most powerful mark in the work of Allen Ginsberg and other "maskless," direct-voice poets. (Some of his earliest admirers were English writers such as Tennyson and William Rossetti.) Only in music was his influence immediate—but in Europe rather than in America. Stanford's popular Whitman setting *Elegaic Ode*, composed in 1884 during Whitman's lifetime, probably reached a wider audience than the poems themselves. In American music, Whitman has been fitfully recognized by a small, devoted following, but only recently has he been embraced with the passion typical of Europeans. Early minor settings by Ives and Converse pale beside the dramatic outpourings from Europe near the turn of the century. Since midcentury, Whitman has moved Elinor Remick Warren, Lee Hoiby, William Schuman, John Adams, Ned Rorem, Vincent Persichetti, and other Americans to write attractive, sometimes beautiful music. (Bernstein's "To What He Said," from his underrated *Songfest*, is a particularly poignant example.)

Across the Atlantic, Whitman inspired composers at the beginning of the century to move in innovative directions. They took the exploratory rhetoric in his poems literally as an aesthetic directive. Vaughan Williams, the quintessential British Whitman enthusiast, called his debut work *Toward the Unknown Region*, after a line from Whitman, and modeled important aspects of his musical style on Whitman's aesthetic philosophy; his friend and colleague Gustav Holst was also overwhelmed by Whitman early on, as was Delius, whose early immersion in the Good Gray Poet resulted in a Whitmanian serenity that remained a part of him throughout his life. The Whitman settings of the German expatriates Paul Hindemith and Kurt Weill altered these composers' sensibilities only near the end of their careers; but alter them they did, toward a new lyricism and universality.

Whitman's profound and immediate influence on British music constitutes a remarkable literary-musical phenomenon that resembles Poe's impact on the French. The novelist and critic Anthony Burgess, one of the few to explore Whitman's appeal to Holst, Parry, and other composers, claims that Whitman's lack of art makes him more suitable for artistic embellishment: "Because Whitman, like the Bible, seemed to stand on the margin of art, composers saw that they could add some art to him." As we shall see, this was not the view of Delius or Vaughan Williams, who viewed Whitman as representing a new kind of art, one they hoped would become a revolutionary model—the opposite of something on the margin. But Burgess does pinpoint Whitman's vision of democracy as being crucial in attracting a certain kind of British composer: "He was democratic, even sweaty, and the right musical librettist for a musical renaissance that turned against the Mendelssohnian salons and went to the sempiternal soil." To take this idea a step further, Whitman was ideal for British composers who wanted to be sweaty and forward-looking but were not prepared to embrace the outright assaults on musical propriety exemplified by neoprimitivism or atonal expressionism. Burgess also shrewdly points out the great advantage to British musicians of Whitman's prosody; his free verse was "a corrective to the four-square folkiness that bedeviled so many rural rhapsodies and even *The Planets.*" Actually, only Delius entirely escaped this foursquareness (the curse of British music); the others, when under Whitman's spell, at least resisted it. Another advantage was that Whitman's "rhythms were declamatory, not—like Eliot and Pound (who eventually made a pact with Whitman, having 'detested him long enough')—muffled, arhetorical, conversational."[6] Yet when we look carefully at Whitman's musical legacy, we see that most settings are of middle and late poems—the least declamatory and rhetorical in the Whitman canon. The combination of freedom of line and conciseness of diction—a kind of joyous austerity unique to the final poems—held the greatest musical promise.

On a fundamental level, what Whitman represented to the British seemed to be nothing quite so subtle, but simply liberation from inhibition and convention. British composers were similar to British writers, who were entranced with the wildness and originality of nineteenth-century American literature. D. H. Lawrence's *Studies in Classic American Literature* (1924) set the trend, along with Yeats's championing of Poe's poetry and a British enthusiasm for Melville, all long before

Max Beerbohm's caricature of Walt Whitman, whose musical influence was especially strong in England. (From *The Poet's Corner*, 1904)

Americans offered a comparable endorsement. Lawrence, who called Whitman "the greatest American" and "the greatest modern poet," complained as late as 1926 that "Americans are not worthy of Whitman. They take him like a cocktail, for fun. Miracle that they have not annihilated every word of him."[7]

Annihilation was certainly attempted: Ezra Pound called Whitman a ninth-rate poet; Henry James, T. S. Eliot, and other guardians of traditional hierarchical values in art blasted him for vulgarity, repetitiveness, and generally bad technique. To them, Whitman represented the fatal imposition of democracy and democratic values onto artistic standards; these Anglophilic American expatriates feared the fatal leveling effects of democracy even more than the British.

This second wave of criticism came after half a century of anti-Whitman censure by Sidney Lanier, John Greenleaf Whittier, and other American poets who accused Whitman of sexual immorality and blasphemy and who called for Whitman book burnings. For British liberals and freethinkers, especially those in the generation following Whitman, these outraged denunciations by what they regarded as American puritans acted as a powerful aphrodisiac. Whitman's celebration of free speech, free love, and free exchange among normally hostile nations was seen as a blow against Victorian prudery, jingoism, and repressiveness, a forerunner of the revolutionary ideals of Lawrence, Bertrand Russell, and other British writers.

The embrace of Whitman was part of a general softening of official British attitudes toward America in the 1890s, in stark contrast to the belligerent anti-Americanism of the preceding hundred years. Oddly, this trend was strongest among Conservative politicians, who suddenly saw America, recently empowered by stunning industrial success, as a useful ally, just as the British Left, for the same reason, suddenly viewed America as an evil exploiter rather than a worker's paradise. The Tories exultantly celebrated "our American cousins" and "Anglo-Saxon Brotherhood." Never mind that only a few years earlier Matthew Arnold, among many others, was still denouncing America for its vulgarity, triviality, and denigration of beauty.

This trend, by no means confined to Britain, was part of an endless cycle in which European left- and right-wingers repeatedly switched sides in cycles of American adoration and denunciation. But for musicians who worshipped Whitman as the embodiment of radical American ideals, the pattern became permanent. More than a fad or a subject of youthful infatuation, Whitman became a benign obsession, a continuing source of optimism and renewal bordering on a kind of primitive religion. John Updike's shrewd characterization of Whitman as America's "happy pagan" captures what was permanent about Whitman's appeal to European intellectuals, especially composers.[8]

The most original art to emerge from the Whitman renaissance in England was the music of Frederick Delius. In spite of Delius's alleged arrogance, severity, and aloofness — distinctly un-Whitmanlike qualities — his pantheism and militant rejection of conventional Christianity echoed Whitman's. More than that, his musical style blended with Whitman's prosody in ways that seem uncannily organic, as if Delius's sound and Whitman's poems were made for each other.

As noted in Chapter 1, Delius's artistic personality was forged in the New World, where his dramatic early encounter with African-American spirituals made a deep and lasting impression. The other New World influence in his career was Whitman, the catalyst for Delius's memories of America after he returned to Europe. Whitman became, thanks to Jelka Rosen, a doorway to the New World, opening memories of the Eden that had first stirred his imagination and art. As was the case with his discovery of black music, the process was sudden and dramatic. When Rosen introduced him in 1903 to *Leaves of Grass*, Delius disappeared into his room with the collection and quickly began to compose *Sea Drift*, the work many believe to be his masterpiece.

Delius's discovery of his own voice was intimately connected with this discovery of Whitman, although no one knows precisely the intellectual process that took place. "How he found himself so suddenly," said his amanuensis Eric Fenby, "is a mystery. That it was the effect of some strange inner happening or revelation seems the only reasonable explanation.... But I do remember his saying during a conversation about Walt Whitman: 'It was a long, long time before I understood exactly what I wanted to say, and then it came to me all at once.' "[9] However this epiphany manifested itself, it is clear that for Delius the New World and Whitman's rendering of it increasingly became one, so much so that all his Americana after *Sea Drift* continued to be Whitman settings.

Indeed, Delius viewed his entire life and career in Whitmanian terms. "Look at Walt Whitman," he told Fenby near the end of his life. "Whitman spent his whole life writing *Leaves of Grass*. It is his individual contribution to art. Nobody else could have written it. So with my own work."[10] Delius viewed his iconoclastic career—his rebellion against his businessman father, his revolutionary discovery and incorporation of black American harmonies, his rejection of Christianity and British nationalism—as a Whitmanian affirmation of the indomitable self. The intuitive strength of his connection to Whitman is demonstrated by his appending of Whitman-like lines in 1899 to the score of the early tone poem *Paris*, even though he was not introduced to Whitman until four years later. As the statement to Fenby indicates, he viewed his works as one vast, unified composition comparable to *Leaves of Grass*, an epic entirely individual and unmistakable. Above all, he was inspired by Whitman's rocklike courage: Whitman had spent his whole life forging his art, even when he was sick and paralyzed; the dying and paralyzed Delius did the same in the *Songs of Farewell* during the period when he made this remarkable statement to Fenby.

The first Whitman poem Delius chose to set was "Out of the

Cradle Endlessly Rocking," which became the basis of *Sea Drift*, after Whitman's title for the set of poems that "Out of the Cradle" opens. (The same year, in a striking coincidence, Vaughan Williams began work on his *Sea* Symphony, another major setting of poems in *Sea Drift*.) Whitman's poem is an evocation of the Long Island shore, which Delius, according to Thomas Beecham, had visited in the late 1880s, following his stints in Florida and Danville, Virginia. The powerful memory of this single visit, with Whitman as catalyst, became the basis of *Sea Drift* and the *Songs of Farewell*, some of the most sublime seascapes in music.

But Delius did not intend *Sea Drift* to be merely an evocative local setting any more than Whitman did. Whitman's vision of the Montauk, Long Island, shore is clearly meant to take on universal, indeed cosmic, significance, and Delius's imagination worked much the same way, the New World always being a metaphor for larger revelations. The initiation of a boy into the mysteries of life and death through observation of birds on a seascape, the subject of "Out of the Cradle," provided an ideal subject matter for Delius, who wrote *Sea Drift* as a glowing reminiscence of his early formative experience, much as Whitman wrote "Out of the Cradle" as a memorial to his own youth.

From the first notes of *Sea Drift*, languid descending woodwinds depicting the lapping of waves, we are in a world of rapturous melancholy. Unlike Vaughan Williams and other later Whitman composers who emphasized the boldness of Whitman, Delius was interested in his voluptuousness. There are no "barbaric yawps" here; even the "coarse surging of the sea" sounds like low tide.

There is nothing conservative or Victorian about Delius's treatment. Along with *Appalachia*, Delius's other masterpiece of Americana, *Sea Drift* inaugurates the harmonic experiments and sumptuous indeterminacies that were to define his musical style for the remainder of his career. The wavelike woodwind regressions caress a constantly shifting shore; the ostensible brass cadence immediately preceding the chorus's entrance is denied its resting place, as if the crest of one wave is merely the prelude to another; the indeterminate harmonies throughout, dense with accidentals that keep the music from "progressing," keep the listener suspended in a state of euphoric ambiguity, a musical emotion peculiar to this composer and this poet. In its denial of closure, the music seems modern, yet it eschews the harshness normally associated with modernism. Whitman is not usually associated with sultry, laid-back sounds, but Delius's musical rereading asks us to take a second look. Part of the trick here is that Delius chose his text shrewdly, lighting upon a particular type of Whitman poem (others include "There Was a Child Went Forth" and "Of the Terrible Doubt of Appearances") in which the percussive vigor of Whitman's *Song of Myself* rhetoric is replaced by tender resignation and benign doubt. The point of this Whitman poem, like all Whitman poems, is to celebrate the life cycle. But the celebration here is poignant rather than rowdy. Delius used only the middle section of "Out of the Cradle," a self-contained narrative depicting love, separation, and loss through a "curious" boy's observation of two mating seabirds. He sees them constantly together until one day the

> she-bird crouched not on the nest,
> Nor returned that afternoon, nor the next
> Nor ever returned again.

The poem is about the inevitable loss of love and life, the central tragedy of existence; yet, typically, Whitman's despair is strangely contiguous with a state of ecstasy. Although the lovers are separated forever by death, a climactic repetition of "loved!" rings out from the surviving lover, "in the air, in the woods, over fields," even as he realizes the two will be "together no more." The life cycle continues, a "song of joy." From *Sea Drift* on, the transience of life would be Delius's major theme, and the Whitman equanimity would remain as well. The music in *Sea Drift*, as its title implies, floats continually onward, despite the drooping line and harmony in passages such as the "lone singer" calling in vain for his lover, "pour[ing] forth the meanings" of lost love. In passages such as the remarkable chorus "O rising stars!" the dense, jazzlike harmony achieves a remarkable static serenity suggesting repeating cycles; the indifference of nature, traditionally treated in poetry as harsh and disturbing, is here merely indifferent.

The music thus creates anew the experience of reading a Whitman poem. Like the poetry, the music does not seem to be going anywhere; Whitman's notorious lists and namings—here a piling up of seascape images—resembles Delius's accretion of unresolved cadences. Yet when we reach the end, with the passionate juxtaposition of "loved!" and "no more" that constitutes the poem's great paradox, we realize we have been on a considerable journey. These repetitions, first soaring, then aching with loss, convey a feeling for the infinite only suggested in Delius's earlier music. Everything in *Sea Drift* sounds the same even as it reveals endless variety, a quality exactly in touch with the world of Whitman.

Just how Delius arrived at this state of hypnotic equanimity is a mystery he himself did not understand. The music sounds spontaneous, almost improvised, beyond conventional analysis. As Delius explained it, he found himself under the spell of Whitman's poem, the text of which influenced his musical discourse in ways not always within his control. "The shape" of *Sea Drift*, he told Eric Fenby, "was taken out of my hands so to speak as I worked and was bred easily and effortlessly of the sequence of my particular musical ideas and of the particular poetical ideas of Whitman that appealed to me." The unpredictability of *Sea Drift* reflects both the poem and the organic method of composition advocated by the poet. "Good work," Delius told Fenby, "always shaped itself according to the laws of its own inner being."[11]

The persona in "Out of the Cradle" speaks of "peering, absorbing, translating," of learning "to sing, now translating the notes." And this is what Delius did, absorbing Whitman's vision, then translating his poetic notes into musical ones. Eschewing "tone painting," with its implied gloss of surface imagery, Delius went for a direct translation of Whitman's thoughts and feelings, a transference of meaning from one language to another. That Delius found this process effortless is a comment on how close he felt to Whitman, closer certainly than to other composers of his day, for whom he had lofty contempt.

According to Delius's contemporaries, other composers meant little to him, certainly less than literary figures. He admired Whitman, Twain, and Nietzsche above all, each for his iconoclastic individualism. (It did not seem to bother him that the peculiarly communal individualism of Whitman was sharply at odds with Nietzsche's and, for that matter, Twain's.) Like Debussy, whose music he regarded as "palely lascivious," Delius was a literary composer who refused to imitate or even take seriously other musicians of his day, preferring the influence of literary images and atmospheres to the emulation of musical formulas.[12] As we saw in Chapter 3, Debussy also used the translation metaphor to explain his relationship to his literary model, Edgar Allan Poe, but his attempts to set Poe were slower and more strenuous, fitting Poe's own aesthetic of meticulous calculation. Conversely, Delius's musical reading of Whitman, like the poems, was fluid and spontaneous. In both cases, musical sound embodied literary philosophy in a strikingly close manner.

Delius returned to Whitman near the end of his life in the *Idyll*, a piece for baritone, soprano, and orchestra, and in the *Songs of Farewell*, for chorus and orchestra. Composed between 1930 and 1932, by which time he was blind and paralyzed by syphilis, these remarkable swan songs owe their existence to Eric Fenby, who wrote them down from Delius's dictations—another example of the ease with which, in the Delian universe, verbal communication became musical sound. In both works, Delius's choice of Whitman texts was profoundly personal. In the *Idyll*, a long-ago love affair with an unnamed woman—now widely believed to be a secret black lover from Delius's Florida days— is reinvoked through some of Whitman's most intimate love poetry, with Whitman's lovers represented by soprano and bass;[13] in the *Songs of Farewell* Delius returns to the misty seascapes of *Sea Drift*, with a distant chorus drifting over a large orchestra like lazy shafts of sunlight.

The libretto of the *Idyll*—more a short opera than a cycle—is based on what Delius scholars euphemistically refer to as "Whitman miscellany" compiled by Delius's friend and admirer Robert Nichols. Unfortunately, it is full of cuts that compromise the rhythm of Whitman's line and sometimes distort his meaning. In the original opening line—"Once I passed through a populous city imprinting my brain for future use with its shows, architecture, customs, tradition"—the phrase "for future use" disappears, along with "architecture, customs, tradition," thereby removing both the central conceit of an imaginary city for poetic "use" and Whitman's characteristic enumerations. The rest, consisting of snippets from *The Sleepers, Children of Adam*, and other collections, has similar distortions, especially the cutting of "truant" from "My truant lover has come" and line eight from "Once I Passed" (the "woman who passionately clung to me"), a prudish and silly bit of censorship.

But Delius's music, like all successful musical settings, ultimately takes flight from words. The text is a point of departure for sensual excursions in sound. From the rapt pedal point in the introduction (first used in the 1899 tone poem *Paris*) through a journey into the "sphere of lovers" to the final passionate cry that "all is over and long gone, but love is not over," the *Idyll* is as close as we get in music to an ecstatic reminiscence of sexual love. Whitman states in "A Clear Midnight," which appears in the middle of the *Idyll*, that poetry itself is a "flight into the wordless," suggesting, along with Poe and Walter Pater, that poetry strives for the condition of music, a world beyond words.

Only two voices, clear and direct, sound out in this intimate work. In the *Songs of Farewell*, however, the vocal part calls for a large, distant chorus, chanting in densely chromatic harmonies that are delicately woven into the orchestral texture. The text is blurred, sometimes indecipherable, which increases the work's mysterious power. These *Songs* are even more a flight into the wordless than the *Idyll*, with its appeal to human love. Here Delius depicts the nonhuman, first Whitman's sky and sea, then the mountains, prairie, and "winding creeks and rivers." There is another remove as well: in the poems, written near the end of his life, Whitman renders these splendors not as he immediately experiences them, as in *Song of Myself*, but as he ecstatically remembers them, as "silent backward tracings." These poems are more concise and inward than the more celebrated early work, making them ideal for Delius's musical style. Delius's circumstances were movingly similar to Whitman's: like his poetic mentor, he was physically paralyzed, waiting for death.

Like Delius's music, the poems used in this cycle (from *Sands at Seventy* and *Songs of Parting*) are compact, unsentimental, yet densely sweet, like the apple in Whitman's "Halcyon Days" that "at last hangs really finished and indolent-ripe on the tree." They speak of final things, but in a clear, serene voice. Deftly selected and copied out by Jelka Rosen (who followed up on Delius's idea from a decade earlier), these haunting miniatures were given musical manifestation by a composer who had totally entered their world.

The poems depict the soul's leave-taking as it prepares to "hoist instantly the anchor" and "depart upon the endless cruise." The mystical rapture of the chorus, which concludes *pianissimo possibile* at the end of the cycle, is a glimmer of infinity. Unlike the laden-down sounds of black singers on the river from Delius's youth, these singers sound unfettered, disembodied, untied to anything mortal. The orchestra too, with its distant brass and liquid strings, is pure, elemental color: sea, sky, glinting sunlight. The structure, a musical equivalent of Whitman's free verse, avoids predictable sectionings and symmetries; it is constantly fresh, constantly reinventing itself, like Whitman's vision of "the eternal, exhaustless freshness of each early morning."

The opening song, "How Sweet the Silent Backward Tracings," sets the tone of reminiscence, its suspended seventh chords basking in the "yellow, golden, transparent haze of the warm afternoon sun"; in pungent contrast, "Passage to You!" "Joy, Shipmate, Joy!" and "Now Finale to the Shore" thrust vigorously outward, taking off toward the horizon as the poet shouts, "Away O soul! hoist instantly the anchor!"

Standing aloof in its elemental power is the masterpiece of the cycle, "From Montauk Point." Here the stricken composer, like the poet, looks down on sky and sea from a perspective of infinity; the eight-part chorus floats in over mystical horn and wind motifs with the un-forgettable opening line, "I stand on some mighty eagle's beak," then soars toward "the wild unrest, the snowy, curling caps—the rebound urge and urge of waves," and finally vanishes, "seeking the shores for-ever." After the chorus has gone, scraps of orchestral motifs, rather than returning as simple recapitulation, climb upward toward the limitless and vanish as well. This song, so inexpressibly tender, is the ultimate manifestation of Delius's lifelong belief that each individual must face death alone, as fearlessly as possible.

Delius's friends and colleagues (the ones who were not driven away by his alleged orneriness and arrogance) were awed by the *Songs of Farewell*, not only by the quality of the work but by its very existence. Fenby, who transcribed the text, called it "a monument of what can be done when, the body broken, there still remains in a man the will to create."[14] According to the composer and critic Peter Warlock, to give "such a title to a last work is a courageous but not a difficult action; to write music that is worthy of the title's full meaning is a task for genius."[15]

As Delius was putting the finishing touches on *Sea Drift*, another British composer, Ralph Vaughan Williams, was beginning his own Whitman sea piece, the *Sea* Symphony, his Symphony no. 1. Vaughan Williams was introduced to Whitman at Cambridge by Bertrand Russell, a fellow student, in 1892, the year of Whitman's death. As was the case with Delius, Whitman proved a lifelong influence on Vaughan Wil-liams, artistically and spiritually. An agnostic freethinker with a deeply mystical sensibility, Vaughan Williams eagerly latched on to Whitman's pantheism and egalitarianism; during the first decade of the new cen-tury, he carried a pocket edition of *Leaves of Grass* with him, and throughout his life he continued to saturate himself with the Poet of Democracy.

For Vaughan Williams, Whitman's sea was a metaphor not for transience or life cycles but for voyages of the imagination. Whitman's call to sail toward the "limitless" and "steer for the deep waters only" was, from the beginning, the composer's guidepost in his own journey as an artist; he quoted this injunction repeatedly, both in his Whitman settings and in contexts that had nothing explicitly to do with Whitman. In the most dramatic instance, it is invoked by the chorus at the end of the *Sea* Symphony in a long fade-out coda, establishing a motto for the remaining eight symphonies. Even the *London* Symphony, Vaughan Williams's most programmatically British work, concludes with the symphony's invisible narrator heading down the Thames toward the open sea.

Vaughan Williams's attitude toward Whitman is reflected instantly in the opening of the *Sea* Symphony, "A Song for All Seas, All Ships," in which a whole world opens up with the chorus's words "Behold, the sea itself." Lacerating brass fanfares and surging strings evoke a sea strikingly different from the tranquil paradise in Delius's early *Sea Drift*; here the waves are "fitful, like a surge," their "limitless, heaving breast" conveyed by harmonies that move irresistibly forward rather than curling back on themselves as Delius's do. The boldness of this opening gesture, and the transparency of the orchestration, announce that we are sailing in clear waters, not the hazy dreamworld of Delius.

More than any other setting, this symphony captures the sheer hugeness of Whitman. Vaughan Williams would later render Whitman's tenderness and intimacy; here, Whitman's epic transcendentalism fires his imagination. Its vigor and directness make it seem very much a young person's music, the eager gestures of someone at the beginning of a career. Actually, Vaughan Williams was in his thirties, as was Whitman in *Song of Myself*; the deliberate illusion of youthfulness coincides with a sophistication in the handling of large structures, an artistic firmness that becomes apparent only after repeated listening.

Critics, however, have often listened with one ear. British commentators in particular have been condescending toward this magnificent symphony, which is typically described as immature and full of gaucheries, saved only by its individual intensity and sheer earnestness. This style of criticism is strikingly similar to what Whitman sustained until very recently, even by friendly voices. It is the inverse of the Poe-Ravel criticism analyzed earlier, which views both poet and composer as technically brilliant but decadent and shallow.

In fact, the *Sea* Symphony has a freshness, quirkiness, and unpredictability that make it a more exciting piece than Vaughan Williams's parochially English works, so often praised for their maturity and solid British traditions. His distinctive voice is already present, yet the largeness of vision gives it an unusually bold range. Early as it is, the piece is subtly enriched with English church modalities and the mysticism they impart; but these are rescued from folksy provincialism by being part of the broader scheme contributed by Whitman's poetry. To be sure, this is Whitman with a trace of an English accent, but Vaughan Williams uses the text in a way that is surprisingly apt and moving, one that offers the kind of cross-cultural mélange Whitman himself advocated. Aside from the open sound so often associated with America, the piece has American touches in its harmony; the flattened seventh chords at "chanting our chant" and "farther sail" in the finale, for example, resemble the kind of blues progression later to be taken up by Gershwin.

Vaughan Williams chose his text by deftly stitching together sections from individual lyrics as well as from *Passage to India* and *Songs of the Exposition,* making additional cuts and shifts within those fragments. In doing so, he re-created his own Whitman text to suit musical needs that were inspired by Whitman in the first place. Music and poetry interpenetrate and determine each other, as they do in any piece that is more than a decorative setting. Sound and verse form an inseparable unity, whether in the wavelike undulations of orchestra and voices in "A Song for All Seas, All Ships," the spectral contrast of low strings and pianissimo cymbals in "On the Beach at Night, Alone," the diminished chords and "liquid, uneven" rhythms of the Scherzo, or the sudden irresistible lunging of chorus and full orchestra in the finale at "sail forth."

Like the poetry, the music has a little of everything. It is part symphony, part oratorio, part opera, and part fantasia (a favorite Vaughan Williams form). The slow movement and Scherzo have traditional ABA formats, but the huge outer movements (despite the hidden sonata form in the first) seem to invent their forms as they proceed, echoing the organic principle of Whitman's free verse. The hymnlike finale, aptly subtitled "The Explorers," is almost a symphony in itself, though one

without closure. Refusing to end, it fades "farther" and still "farther"
out to a sea whose depths are subliminally suggested by whispers in the
lower strings.

This New World Symphony, coming a decade after the more famous one by Dvořák, is less concerned with the native culture of that
world than with its larger implications for Europeans, its call by Whitman for peoples on both continents to be internationalists and transcendentalists. Here the New World is defined as an Oversoul
incorporating all worlds: the political world in the first movement, its
procession of ships forming a kind of floating United Nations, each
comfortable with its own national identity but all united by the sea, all
carrying the "pennant universal, subtly waving"; the night world of nature in the second movement, its precession of stars passing over the
ocean in a "vast similitude" that "interlocks all"; the physical, as opposed
to emblematic, world of the sea in the Scherzo, with its "motley procession" of waves; the mystical world of space and time in the vast finale,
whose "restless explorations" gradually drift into infinity.

The *Sea* Symphony was a pivotal work, one that enabled Vaughan
Williams to find his voice; he worked on it for seven years, beginning
in 1903, and conducted the premiere himself in 1910. During the same
period he composed another Whitman setting, *Toward the Unknown
Region*, again a kind of free-form oratorio (although a much briefer one)
bearing a title suggesting experimentation and exploration. The actual
title of the text, "Darest Thou Now, O Soul," from "Whispers of Heavenly Death," was rejected in favor of the phrase concluding the poem's
second line, which Vaughan Williams made into a more enticing, less
archaic title.

Again, the ruggedness of Whitman is emphasized in this work,
more so, indeed, than in the *Sea* Symphony. He had not yet undertaken
his studies in orchestration with Ravel, which came just before the final
version of the *Sea* Symphony, and commentators are fond of citing the
Brahmsian sound of this early work. But the bold brass fanfares that
gradually carry the piece aloft do not sound like Brahms, any more than
do the searching harmonies that precede them. Vaughan Williams experiments with a new sound here, exhibiting the kind of adventurous-
ness that came to characterize all his Whitman settings.

From the beginning of his career, Vaughan Williams was a deeply
philosophical composer, and the content of Whitman's verse meant as

much to him as its musical possibilities. This particular poem embodies what Vaughan Williams's wife, Ursula, called his "cheerful agnosticism," something he "drifted into" from an initial position of straightforward atheism:[16]

> I know it not, O Soul,
> Nor dost thou, all is a blank before us,
> All waits undreamed of in that region, that inaccessible land.

The blankness here is not negative or fearful, as in Poe (Usher's bleakly abstract paintings) or Melville (the atheistic voids in the Whiteness of the Whale). Whitman worked through the anxiety of mortality in such earlier poems as "Of the Terrible Doubt of Appearances," where love and comradeship—the warm human center of the Whitman cosmos, located in the here and now—are enough to satisfy the man or woman facing mortality, even without answers to questions of "identity beyond the grave." By the time he wrote "Sands at Seventy," Whitman had arrived at a philosophy in which blankness had become a state of equanimity, a release from anxiety, even more than the Zen-like indifference of the earlier poem. This insistence on facing death with courage while existing in the present moment had great appeal to British composers, notably Delius, Vaughan Williams, and Gustav Holst. The state of not knowing what lies beyond is not only accepted but embraced. In this work, a happy blankness is immediately apparent in the excited diminished chords and rising suspensions moving in constant crescendo toward the unknown region. Brass fanfares "float[ing] in time and space" take the listener into a mysterious, chromatic world with no "bounds bounding us."

Vaughan Williams's composition teachers, Charles Wood, Parry, and Charles Villiers Stanford, were all influenced by Whitman and all attempted Whitman settings of their own, but they were bound by musical Victorianisms that Vaughan Williams, always an intuitive rather than theoretical artist, seemed to transcend spontaneously. Stanford's "To the Soul," completed a year after *Toward the Unknown Region*, sets the same poem, but in a more conservative style: thick, churchy chords support a hymnlike tune that rises to a conventionally inspirational climax. The most atemporal of Vaughan Williams's works, *Toward the Unknown Region*, is bound neither by his later reliance on English folk and church music nor by Stanford's post-Victorian rhetoric; it floats in a rarefied symphonic discourse that follows the freedom of Whitman's lines. Conventional analysis of Whitman's musicality—to the extent that he is regarded as musical at all—dwells on his operatic devices, but there is little trace of aria-recitative or other nineteenth-century operatic structures in Vaughan Williams's mystical treatment. The music picks up on the poem's fluidity and goes with it. Like the poem, it does offer tentative closure, an exultant major chord in the brass expressing joy in the face of "inaccessible" ambiguity.

Toward the Unknown Region premiered at the Leeds festival in 1907, three years before the *Sea* Symphony, where it instantly earned Vaughan Williams a reputation as the foremost young British composer of the time. But his Whitman odyssey had just begun. The next year he wrote another Whitman setting but never published it (although the music appears in the central section of the visionary cantata *Sancta Civitas*). Three years later he composed the magisterial "Dirge for Two Veterans" but decided that the song was insufficient alone and needed a broader context. This somber piece, an eerie forecast of Vaughan Williams's experience in World War I, remained in limbo for some twenty-five years.

Meantime, in 1925 he embarked on another Whitman work, simply called *Three Poems by Walt Whitman*, or even more starkly (in a manuscript copy), *Three Songs on a Ground*. The straightforwardness of both titles reflects the music, which uses a deliberately primitive ground bass throughout. In contrast to the fluid experimentation of the earlier Whitman settings, these songs with piano accompaniment are compact and firm, always sure of their destination. Vaughan Williams had found his voice by this time, so for the most part we get an Anglicized Whitman rather than the expansive, free-floating Americanness of the cantata and symphony. Vaughan Williams's use of English church modes makes "A Clear Midnight," for example, sound like an Anglican hymn, a sharp contrast to the amorous version in Delius's *Idyll,* not to mention the spooky nontonal setting by the American radical Carl Ruggles. One song that does approach a stereotypically American sound is "Joy, Shipmate, Joy!" with its spare, open piano chords—again, a vigorous contrast to the sumptuousness of Delius's setting. The masterpiece of the set is the opening "Nocturne," a setting of "Whispers of Heavenly Death." Here the spirit of experimentation so central to Whitman breathes through every note. The poem depicts an anonymous soul "passing over" to the

"impenetrable" frontier, a vision suggested by stars appearing and disappearing in "great cloud masses" of a night sky. Vaughan Williams
conjures Whitman's night world with slow showers of piano notes. At
first these are solidified by modal harmonies, encodings of the Anglican
tradition Vaughan Williams apparently needed as an aesthetic backdrop
even though he rejected Christian theology. These descend in endless
drooping regressions, but at the end the piano climbs into "the frontiers
to eyes impenetrable," leaving the tenor soloist, with his mere words,
behind.

Like Poe, Whitman believed that music was the way into untranslatable transcendence. In the "Nocturne," we once again find that the
most haunting and original moment in a piece of vocal music is non-
verbal. Words can take us only so far toward the "unknown region"; at
some point, pure music takes over, even though words are required to
spark the inspiration. (In the second line, Whitman calls "Whispers of
Heavenly Death" a "sibilant chorale": a chorale does have words,
though the strong melody can easily survive without them.) After words
have ceased in the "Nocturne," the piano reaches into icy, celestial
dissonance and vanishes. The music floats out into the night like Whitman's "saddened far-off" stars. The other songs from this cycle, invigorating as they are, impose a neo-Anglican musical style on the text,
reducing its potency; but in the "Nocturne," poetry and music saturate
each other, as the composer allows the poet's vision to stretch and
broaden his harmonic language.

This union of language and music takes on a different mix in the
1936 antiwar cantata *Dona Nobis Pacem,* Vaughan Williams's final
Whitman setting. Only part of the text is from Whitman, however; the
rest incorporates fragments from the Old Testament and a speech on
the angel of death given by John Bright during the Crimean War of
1855. Whitman is therefore integrated into the kind of traditional mosaic
Vaughan Williams used in overtly Anglican pieces.

Dona Nobis Pacem is a passionate, sometimes despairing plea for
peace by a composer who had witnessed the ravages of one world war
and was horrified by the prospect of another. Both in its antiwar stance
and in its modernist juxtaposition of English war poetry with older religious texts, this cantata anticipates Benjamin Britten's epic *War Requiem.* But whereas Britten uses the apocalyptic antiwar poetry of Wilfred

Owen, Vaughan Williams treats selections from Whitman's *Drum Taps*, a device that gives his piece a more oblique political slant.

Whitman's Civil War poems, far from being ideological, are sublimely objective, recording the ravages of war in unflinching, painterly detail. The poems evoke awe, not anger, at the war machine. Whitman, of course, was an intense supporter of President Lincoln and the Union cause, and although he deplored the human cost of the war—which resulted in the deaths of more young Americans than all the rest of the country's wars combined—he supported its aims.

Vaughan Williams's music therefore reflects sorrow more than anger, the distinctive Whitmanian equanimity rather than protest, even though the work has an antiwar structure and sensibility. The brutality of war is immediately invoked in "Beat! Beat! Drums!" where the percussive harshness of Whitman's repeating consonants is echoed in the eerie bitonalities of Vaughan Williams's 1930s modernist style. After the violence dies down, the poem "Reconciliation" floats in with its folksong modality and beautiful violin solo, reconciling the "deeds of carnage" and "soil'd world" of war with a healing universe—the "sisters of Death and Night"—which ultimately wash war away. The central insight toward which antiwar poetry invariably moves—the recognition of the humanity of the enemy—is the capstone of this poem as well: "For my enemy is dead, a man divine as myself is dead." Typically, however, Whitman takes the abstraction and makes it physical, startling us with the final image of the wound dresser kissing "the white face in the coffin." The music too is unusually sensuous for a war piece—indeed, it is more ravishing than many of Vaughan Williams's love songs.

An earlier Vaughan Williams is recalled in "Dirge for Two Veterans," composed in 1908 but not used until its incorporation in this work. The solemnity of this piece recalls the march in the slow movement of the *Sea* Symphony. Here again, the grimness of war, as exemplified in the lines

> Two veterans son and father dropt together
> And the double grave awaits them

is mitigated by the benevolent indifference of nature and the loving compassion of the poet. The melding of music and poetry is complete, for Whitman invokes music as the final healing force with the "strong dead-march" of bugles and drums, which Vaughan Williams works up into a stirring climax.

Whitman often uses "mystic trumpets" and bugles to herald untranslatable truths. Vaughan Williams's fanfares offer their own compelling translation, as does the cantata as a whole. The voice of this work is at once thoroughly British — the song of the only self Vaughan Williams could possibly know — and true to Whitman's vision. If the old English modes in *Dona Nobis Pacem* give the effect of an Anglicized Whitman, it is also true that the poetry shapes the sweeping, visionary quality of the music. The ethereality of English church music and the earthiness of Whitman's verse exist in haunting counterpoint.

In *Dona Nobis Pacem*, Vaughan Williams reached the end of his Whitman exploration. That the results of this journey on Whitman's "open road" were so fresh and original should not be surprising: Whitman's New World was philosophically and temperamentally closer to Vaughan Williams than the high-church Anglicanism that formed his public profile. His deeper interest in the folk motifs of laboring people was thoroughly Whitmanian. Even after *Dona Nobis Pacem*, Whitman remained an enduring tonic. As we shall see, Whitman moved Vaughan Williams toward an increasingly democratic vision of art, with folk music at its center. In his eighty-fourth year, a few days before his death, Vaughan Williams said of Whitman, "I never got over him, I am glad to say."[17]

A remarkably similar case of British infatuation with Whitman is that of Gustav Holst. Although Holst's Whitman-inspired works are not quite as extensive as Vaughan Williams's, they similarly result from a deep philosophical resonance created by Whitman's poetry and represent an important series of breakthroughs in his evolution. Indeed, to a significant extent, Holst, like Delius and Vaughan Williams, found his voice and vision through reading Whitman.

Holst was first exposed to Whitman as a student in 1892–93, reading him, like Vaughan Williams, as a New World prophet of tolerance and internationalism as well as a new breed of mystic whose transcendentalism offered an antidote to encrusted Victorianism. Whitman had a special meaning, in that the equanimity and meditative calm in his poetry reinforced Holst's burgeoning interest in Hindu and other Eastern modes of thought. In 1899 he wrote a "Whitman Overture" to a new century. Holst's wife, Imogen, remarked that this early piece (which, unfortunately, was not published) was "an attempt to convey what Whitman's poetry had meant to him" as a young man.[18]

Holst's first published Whitman setting was "The Mystic Trumpeter," a setting for soprano and orchestra from 1904. He could not have chosen a more apt poem for this important early piece. "The Mystic Trumpeter" is Whitman's major poem about music; here he makes clear that the poet himself, as Emerson proclaimed, is the sounder of divine truths, not just the passive recipient, and that music — "The cornet echoing, pealing" — offers the best means of translating them. We have seen the translation metaphor before, in Debussy's reference to his Poe settings: here too, music is viewed as the realization of the poet's ultimate intentions, those he can launch but not complete with mere words. It is the trumpeter who sounds the "higher strain," the "culminating song." The nourishing process is therefore mutually beneficial: the poet needs the composer to complete his New World song, just as the composer needs the poet for his musical inspiration.[19]

The stylistic freedom in this early work was a culmination for Holst as well. According to Imogen Holst, "The Mystic Trumpeter" was a concentration of "all his genuine thought and energy.... It was the most important work he had yet written, and it was his nearest approach to an expression of what he wanted to say."[20]

The "Molto sostenuto" motif haunted him "throughout the whole of his life," erupting ten years later in a far more volatile form — the terrifying fanfares of "Mars," from The Planets, Holst's most popular work. At the end, Whitman's "atmosphere of joy" is captured in a quadruple pianissimo, a telling contrast to the fortissimo ending of the more Victorian version by Holst's colleague, Hamilton Harty.[21] After the "alarums of war" have faded, the piece suggests the ecstatic tranquility of "Venus" in Holst's treatment of the poet's withdrawal from "the fretting world." To be sure, Holst was attracted to the nonconformist rhetoric of Song of Myself, but like Delius he moved increasingly toward the tranquil side of Whitman. Whitman's "barbaric yawp" — the caricature of Whitman perpetrated by so many Americanists — was not for Holst or his British colleagues. Again, it is the late poetry such as "The Mystic Trumpeter" that attracted European composers.

In the middle of his career, Holst's Whitmania intersected with that of his friend and colleague Ralph Vaughan Williams. The two composers hit upon the happy idea of attempting two settings of the same Whitman text, in this case "Darest Thou Now, O Soul," then comparing them in an amiable competition. In the end, both agreed that Vaughan Williams's setting—which became *Toward the Unknown Region*—was superior, and Holst apparently scrapped his. A similar competition occurred in 1914, when both composers set "A Dirge for Two Veterans." Again, the Vaughan Williams version seemed to be the winner, becoming the majestic final poem in *Dona Nobis Pacem*.

Nevertheless, "A Dirge" represented another important moment for Holst. According to his wife, Whitman's "sad procession" never "ceased to move through his mind until the very end of his life." The "passionate intensity" and "relentless rhythm" of this work cut "through the last shreds of worn-out idiom."[22] Published in June 1914, "Dirge" was an ominous forecast of World War I as well as another premonition of the fierce ostinato of "Mars."

Holst's final Whitman setting was his greatest, the 1919 *Ode to Death* for chorus and orchestra. The text is the last section of "When Lilacs Last in the Dooryard Bloom'd," another instance of late Whitman providing potent musical material. Written just after World War I, as a memorial for his fallen friends, the *Ode* anticipates Hindemith's use of the same poem twenty-seven years later in a memorial to his own friends lost in World War II. (William Stone's characterization of Whitman as the most "timeless" poet for composers again seems right on the mark.) Partly because of its unfortunate title, *Ode to Death* remains a rarity and was not even published in full score until 1974.

Holst invests Whitman's vision of "lovely and soothing death" with luminous open chords that suggest a sense of infinite space—more vast, indeed, than anything in *The Planets*. The middle section, "approach strong deliveress," offers another sad procession in regular march rhythm, but it is brief. Holst is interested here in indeterminacy, a feeling of the infinite, not in predictability and closure. At the end, delicate celesta and harp colors shine like stars over Whitman's "prairies wide."

Holst follows a strategy similar to that of Vaughan Williams in *Toward the Unknown Region*, depicting the mystery of death in a "fathomless universe" through highly ambiguous harmonic suspensions—some of the most free-floating harmonies he ever attempted. This rare, astonishing work again demonstrates the strangely revolutionary power of Whitman's verse on a normally conservative British composer. Another example is Frank Bridge, whose Whitman song "The Last Invocation" is a piece of harmonic wizardry. Composed the same year as Holst's *Ode* (the centenary of Whitman's birth and a fertile year for settings of his music), this work also depicts the soul letting go at death, a process that Bridge, like Whitman, manages to make sad yet exalted. A misty crescendo-diminuendo glides "noiselessly forth" toward eternity; an exquisitely ambiguous piano chord at the climactic line "Let me be wafted" raises goose bumps.

In addition to his inspirational appeal as an American, Whitman was also a powerful force for composers seeking to *become* Americans, most notably the German expatriates Kurt Weill and Paul Hindemith. These artists were deeply affected by American musical culture, although Weill made far more consistent and successful use of it; as their affection for Whitman attests, they were inspired by literature as well.

For Weill and Hindemith, Whitman was an expression of American patriotism and a means of forging a new American identity. The paradoxes in Whitman's reputation made him a perfect passport; in mid-twentieth-century America (and perhaps more so in Europe) he was still regarded as a bohemian artist, one who was American precisely in his otherness and eccentricity. As such he was an ideal American icon for expatriates like Hindemith and Weill, whom the Nazis had denounced as practitioners of "Entartete Musik," a decadent modernism spawned in impure, egalitarian places like America.

Both of these political orphans—especially Weill, who was Jewish—were eager to renounce the political crimes of their homeland and embrace America. Whitman's poetry provided them a perfect musical subject in that it explicitly rejected racism and nativism and openly welcomed immigrants from all nations. And Whitman had one other advantage: the all-encompassing humanity of his Civil War poems could, without too much stretching, be yoked to the American war effort. Earlier European composers had shown that these poems made excellent vehicles for ruminating on the nightmare of a first world war and warning of a second; now they were dusted off again, this time as patriotic vehicles.

Weill, in his quest to remake himself into an American composer, found Whitman a perfect match. He could retain a vestige of his avant-garde past because Whitman was a radical poet, yet in the actual music he could lavish Whitman's words with a newly forged American style based on American literature, folk songs, and pop idioms such as Broadway. Because jazz was already part of Weill's music, his Americanization was well under way. The sardonic jazz idiom of *Threepenny Opera* and the bittersweet vision of the American South and West in *Mahagonny* were part of his musical identity. Now Whitman was to provide a softening of that profile.

Weill collected his Whitman settings, composed between 1941 and 1947, into a *Walt Whitman Cycle* for voice and piano. Two of the poems he chose had previously been set by British composers, but Weill's are strikingly different. In "Beat! Beat! Drums," Weill's piano thumps out a percussive but upbeat march accompaniment for a singer who bellows out warlike sounds that mimic a commanding officer shouting orders. This is a patriotic Whitman, a far cry from Vaughan Williams's darker reading (or Coleridge-Taylor's post-Victorian rendering) in which anguished bitonalities warn against the horrors of another war. Now the war has arrived, and Weill is clearly heartened by its prosecution.

In "Dirge for Two Veterans," regarded by Weillians as the most American song in the cycle, the treatment is again more upbeat than that of Vaughan Williams (or, for that matter, of Holst), featuring the kind of open fifths associated with Copland during the 1940s and a striding vocal line that gradually incorporates "Taps" before melting into a soaring cadence on "my heart gives you love." This is the kind of unabashed sentimentality combined with rigorous structural sophistication that made Weill a major Broadway composer. If this "Dirge" seems like a vulgarization of Whitman's text, one should remember that Whitman himself purported to write for the masses, not for intellectuals, and a popular audience was certainly what Weill was after. Vaughan Williams's "Dirge" may be more artful, but Weill's apparent artlessness has its own seductions.

The two other songs in the cycle, "Come Up from the Fields, Father" and "O Captain! My Captain!" have a similar melodic simplicity and clarity; they too represent a popularized Whitman suitable for Broadway. (Another striking example is "Look Down Fair Moon," from 1940, a nocturnal vision of death on the battlefield improbably yet powerfully set in an American pop idiom by the Cairo-born composer Charles Naginski.) For Weill, Whitman was not a visionary alternative to post-Victorian stuffiness and parochialism, as he was to so many British composers. Rather, he was an anchor for Weill's determination to live in the present as a practical American artist, grounding him in a new democratic directness.

Weill's most beautiful Whitman setting occurs not in a separate piece but in the first act of his Broadway opera, *Street Scene*, in which lines from "When Lilacs Last in the Dooryard Bloom'd" are interpolated into a duet between the would-be lovers, Sam and Rose. Wrenched from its Civil War context, the poem works seamlessly in this mid-twentieth-century urban setting, demonstrating both the universality of Whitman and the ingenuity of Weill and his librettist, Langston Hughes. The sprig of lilac Sam offers Rose from a park in Brooklyn is a way of transcending the grayness of the streets, the subtle near-poverty of the American middle class so presciently depicted in the opera. The lilac observed by Rose and Sam in the park each day is an emblem of love ("Remember that I care") and the promise of a better life, a flower picked "in our dreams," where "nothing can take it away." Sam's recitation of "When Lilacs Last in the Dooryard Bloom'd" as a love poem is at first a somewhat eccentric romantic gesture: a paean of love to President Lincoln, it is also a funeral dirge, the appropriateness of which is sadly apparent by the violent end of the opera. Its inclusion works here because of Whitman's powerful, palpable desire to speak to the common man and woman; he would undoubtedly have been pleased by its use in an opera about ordinary American working people. The long, arcing melody, reaching a passionate climax in Sam's "Remember that I care," constitutes some of Weill's most ravishing music.[23]

Like Mark Twain, whose *Huckleberry Finn* Weill was setting to music at the time of his sudden death, Whitman was a vernacular artist who helped Weill turn his back both on his own earlier work and on the entire European modernist movement that he found isolating and financially untenable. There is considerable irony in all this. Whitman — whose bisexual celebration of "sexes and lusts" was second in controversy only to his alleged blasphemy — is not the first poet one thinks of as a passport to patriotism and wholesomeness. Nevertheless, the Whitman phenomenon is precisely about his appeal to remarkably diverse audiences, from Carl Sandburg middlebrows to Allen Ginsberg's beat generation. (Weill was shrewd enough to choose Whitman's safer, more accessible poems such as "O Captain! My Captain!" avoiding riskier material such as "Reconciliation," the sensually charged centerpiece of Vaughan Williams's *Dona Nobis Pacem*.) Whitman did, after all, aim for the "Divine Average," even though his actual work may seem better suited for pagans and pantheists. And he did adore bel canto Italian opera, the most overtly popular, deliberately vulgar form of serious music. For better or worse, Whitman got the democratic averaging he was always after in the songs of Kurt Weill.

Whitman also provided Paul Hindemith a vehicle for the expression of a new American identity and a concomitant patriotism. Hindemith's *When Lilacs Last in the Dooryard Bloom'd*, commissioned in 1946 by Robert Shaw and his remarkable Robert Shaw Chorale, at a time when Hindemith was searching for ways to express gratitude for his newly adopted country, is his most thoroughly American work. Indeed, scholars such as David Neumeyer, reflecting a tendency to downplay Hindemith's Americanness, regard the *Lilacs* Requiem as Hindemith's "only profoundly American work."[24] Lukas Foss, who was Hindemith's student at Yale in 1939–40, feels that the Requiem is "not quite as convincing" as Hindemith's jazz pastiches or the Americana of other Europeans. Hindemith was not the kind of artist, said Foss, to easily "put on an American hat."[25]

Subtitled "Requiem for Those We Love," this solemn work certainly meant a great deal to Hindemith. The occasion of Shaw's commission was the death of Franklin Roosevelt, whose New Deal represented an egalitarian vision close to Whitman's. According to Robert Shaw, Hindemith was "extraordinarily moved by this piece." The vision of community in the Civil War poems, in which Whitman proclaims the "breadth of this land" for all and recognizes that we are, finally, each other's keepers, was fundamental to Hindemith. Much of the piece is choral, for "brotherhood is the natural ambiance of choral art."[26]

Shaw, like so many other musicians, regarded Whitman as an irresistible subject for music: "His passionate declamation seems to cry out for musical elaboration—an invitation to add the unspeakable to the already spoken." For Hindemith, "When Lilacs Last in the Dooryard Bloom'd" was felicitous on several levels: compatible with his own values and those of the Roosevelt era, Whitman's poem was a threnody for another visionary American president, Abraham Lincoln, who had fallen eighty years before Roosevelt, almost to the day. In Hindemith's setting, the poem also became a Requiem for Americans killed in World War

The opening of Paul Hindemith's *When Lilacs Last in the Dooryard Bloom'd*, one of the most epic Whitman settings. Whitman was Hindemith's passport to American identity. (Yale Music Library)

II. Finally, on a profoundly personal level, it became a metaphor for Hindemith's loss of his own friends, many of whom by 1945 were gone or dead. In the words of Shaw, who lost his wife days after this interview, the Requiem is the testament of "a lonely, broken heart." Yet it is by no means sentimental or crowd pleasing. "No one *heard* this work at first," recalls Shaw. "It is too gray-brown, like the bird in the poem, too thoughtful. Hindemith wrote it for Lincoln, for his Yale students, and for those who perished in the Holocaust." It is "not public mourning," and despite its deeply patriotic gesture, it is "not a goddamn political speech."[27]

In the mind of Hindemith, who had been condemned by Goebbels's propaganda machine for associating with Jews and for creating "degenerate and decadent" art, Lincoln, Roosevelt, and Whitman were all heroic healers and unifiers. Furthermore, Whitman's poem manifests the kind of transcendental unity—a mystical triumph over ugliness and evil—that Hindemith constantly strove to translate into his later music, especially the works he wrote in the 1940s in America such as *Die Harmonie der Welt*. Like Holst and Vaughan Williams in their Whitman Civil War settings, Hindemith saw music as a mystical healing force.

Shaw answers the cliché that Hindemith was "all craft and no heart" by pointing out that for this composer, craft *was* heart: "For Hindemith, structure and symmetry were mystical and communicative; they were transfusions of truth, the juice of a piece. The spirit is in the letter: getting a chord in tune means the truth is at stake."[28] Given Hindemith's fondness for symmetry and structural complexity, it is not surprising that he was drawn to "When Lilacs Last in the Dooryard Bloom'd," which boasts an emphasis on craft, a repeating trinity of symbols, a formal voice (unusual for Whitman), and an intricate structure.

The Requiem was not the first time Hindemith had worked with "When Lilacs Last in the Dooryard Bloom'd." He is another striking example of a European composer who was influenced by American culture from the beginning of his career. Twenty-seven years before the *Lilacs* Requiem, during his first experiments with jazz, Hindemith had composed three Whitman settings, including "Sing On There, in the Swamp," the beautiful mezzo solo that became no. 5 in the Requiem. Shaw initially took this single song to Hindemith, who had reworked it in 1943, with the proposal that it be used as a memorial to Roosevelt. Hindemith's admiration for both the president and the poet was so great, however, that he responded, "No, we should do the whole thing." A two-minute song became an hour-long New World Requiem, an American epic set to European forms, including a sinfonia, a chorale, marches with trios, double fugues, arias, choruses, motets, fanfares, and much else.[29] (Hindemith presented the original manuscript of the song to the judge who presided at his U.S. naturalization ceremony on January 11, 1946, six days before beginning work on the Requiem.)

The first thing one notices about the Requiem is its astonishing formal scope and variety, as if the relief of being in the New World, free from Nazi censorship, paradoxically enabled Hindemith to bring to bear an array of Old World techniques—the European academicism of which he is so often accused—in a fresh context. The marches, fugues, and relentlessly classical symmetries that bring Whitman's passionate verse to life have a vitality here that is sometimes lacking in his purely instrumental works.

Nonetheless, Hindemith's European formalism ultimately proved to be an insuperable problem in his efforts to become, like Weill, an American artist. Foss was correct on this point: Hindemith had been more convincingly American when he was living in Europe and dabbling in jazz. After he gave up his Yale post and moved to Zurich in 1953, he remarked sadly, "Nobody ever bothered to call me an American musician. I always remained for them a foreigner."[30] As Shaw pointed out, few really heard *When Lilacs Last in the Dooryard Bloom'd* during its early exposure; only in the 1990s, when major performers besides Shaw finally began performing and recording the Requiem, did it begin to enjoy a genuine revival.

Unlike Weill, Hindemith chose not to simplify Whitman with an American pop vernacular; instead he set one of Whitman's most lengthy and uncompromising poems—all of it, without cuts—in his own most dense and uncompromising musical language. The result is a work that is not as immediately inviting as settings by other European composers but one that impresses with its purity and granitelike integrity. One of the grayest and least prettified of Whitman settings, it comes closest to embodying Whitman's determination to deglamorize poetry, to celebrate the grittiness of ordinary life.

Hindemith was an astute, utterly unsentimental reader of "When Lilacs Last in the Dooryard Bloom'd"; in his setting, the poem emerges as a drama of personal and cultural recovery from trauma and death. Light shines into Hindemith's thick, dark textures only gradually, after it is fully earned. The music moves from the grim orchestral prelude—a terrifying depiction of despair in Hindemith's most stark expressionist style—through stages of mourning captured in delicate arias, recitatives, and choruses, toward a quiet acceptance of death.

The final stage of equanimity is depicted in a rapt chorale, "Come, Lovely and Soothing Death," the austerity of which contrasts strikingly with the voluptuousness of Holst's setting. Hindemith's love of medieval and Renaissance plainsong is glowingly apparent in the a cappella sections, while the strict passacaglia woven by the orchestra exemplifies his continued attachment to neobaroque structures. The purity of Whitman's late verse is curiously compatible with these Old World techniques, making this one of the most subtle unions of Old and New World art.

But subtlety is by no means the whole story in this Requiem. Embedded in the poem is a majestic celebration of the American landscape, the "miracle spreading," an occasion for one of Hindemith's most complex double fugues. (According to Shaw, Hindemith, an astonishingly fast worker, wrote this fugue on a train.) The complexity of Hindemith's polyphony again seems an appropriate musical form for Whitman's vast panorama of people and places, the "varied and ample land" of America. Each fugal voice becomes the embodiment of a different place:

> the South and North in the light,
> Ohio's shores and flashing Missouri.

And all voices interact with a simultaneity not possible on the printed page. Here is an instance where music, because of its ability to combine a multitude of voices instantly, in a vast sense of space, genuinely enhances a poetic text by going beyond the boundaries of literature.

Again, late Whitman works best for musical settings, at least in the work of European composers, who carry the weight of symphonic traditions they either invigorate (as in the case of Hindemith) or renounce (as in the case of Delius). The prosody of "When Lilacs Last in Dooryard Bloom'd" has a freedom that makes it suitable for musical manipulation, yet the relatively formal structures—the recurring symbols, the allegorical journey of Lincoln's coffin, the dignified march cadences and funeral dirges—fit the formality of Hindemith's musical style. Most important, the passionate calm at the center of Whitman's poem is an ideal sounding board for Hindemith's mature aesthetic. Glenn Gould, one of Hindemith's most astute advocates, once characterized Hindemith's style, "when properly adduced," as the "true amalgam of ecstasy and reason: repose."[31] Hindemithian repose found its happiest counterpart in Whitman's poetry.

A year after Hindemith composed his Requiem, Hans Werner Henze wrote another important setting of late Whitman, the delicate and sensuous *Whispers from Heavenly Death*. Several other Austro-German composers contributed settings as well, many long forgotten. Like Hindemith, German and Viennese Whitmanians tended to be enemies of the Third Reich, including Friedrich Wildgans, who wrote his *Mystic Trumpeter* the same year as the Lilacs *Requiem*; Franz Schreker, who enhanced his fatal "decadence" credentials with the Whitman settings *Vom Ewigen Leben* and *Zwei Lyrische Gesänge*; and Karl Amadeus Hartmann, who composed a Whitman-inspired First Symphony shortly before disappearing from German musical life during the Nazi regime.

For the émigré Robert Starer, who fled the Nazis in 1938 after they marched under his window in Vienna, Whitman's verse became a vehicle for profound retrospection. Between 1983 and 1997, Starer wrote three Whitman settings, including his own version of *The Mystic Trumpeter*. "I came to Whitman late in life," Starer told me in a 1997 interview, "but I adore him." Like Parry near the end of the nineteenth century, Starer admired Whitman's focus on real human problems. He wrote *To Think of Time*, a song cycle for soprano and string quartet, in 1985, when he had turned sixty and was searching for a poet who faced mortality honestly. He was struck by how Whitman "shares real things," how he "deals with death in a true way—and poetically at the same time."

Starer infused *To Think of Time* with the cool lyricism characteristic of his late work. The stillness in "After the Dazzle of Day" evokes the night and stars "after the dazzle of day is gone," when, at life's end, we hear the silence of "the symphony true." In the title poem, gently dissonant strings suggest the possibility of "nothing," repeated four times in the final stanza. They suggest it more lugubriously in "Yet, Yet Ye Downcast Hours," as the soprano insists that "Matter is conqueror." Yet the soul moves through the void undaunted; at the end of "Darest Thou Now, O Soul," singer and strings shimmer upward into darkness. Ninety years before Starer's setting, Vaughan Williams used bracing fanfares for the same poem, and Stanford used staunchly Victorian cadences. Starer is more in tune with Whitman's final austerity, but he delivers what he regards as the poet's "wonderful vital quality" as well.

Whether in the elegant lines of Starer, the polyphony of Hindemith, or the supple melody and accompaniment of Weill, it is this fundamental optimism—along with a peculiarly American ampleness and multiplicity—that European composers took from Whitman and transcribed into music. Vaughan Williams put the matter most explicitly when he praised Whitman for his rejection of narrowness, his repudiation of anything remotely highbrow or undemocratic. In his provocative essay "Bach the Bourgeois," he placed Whitman in the same category as Bach—as a supreme middlebrow artist. Bach is a great artist "because his music appeals to everyone—not only the aesthete, the musicologist or the propagandist, but above all to Whitman's 'Divine Average'—that great middle class from whom nearly all that is worth while in religion, painting, poetry and music has sprung."[33]

To Vaughan Williams and others of this persuasion—certainly Kurt Weill, although he never said so quite as bluntly—Whitman's Divine Average provided a New World model of total inclusion, a sharp challenge to the hierarchical conception of art propounded by Whitman-haters such as T. S. Eliot and Ezra Pound. In this Whitmanian view, all divisions between classical and popular, highbrow and lowbrow, are false and pernicious, especially in music. Vaughan Williams wrote that Whitman represented a democratic art "in which all can take part. . . . Is this popularization of art merely a Whitmanesque fantasy? At present it is only a dream, but it is a realizable dream."[34]

In Vaughan Williams's lifetime, this dream remained mainly that; indeed, the gap between classical music and everything else grew ever wider. As we saw in the early part of this chapter, Anthony Burgess and others placed Whitman and his aesthetic on the margins of art rather than in the center, where Vaughan Williams and other celebrators of the Divine Average locate it. But as the twentieth century drew to a close, old dichotomies began collapsing, as postmodern fluidity rendered the landscape increasingly complex and chaotic. Antihierarchical notions of total inclusion reemerged in the multiculturalism of the 1990s—though with an emphasis on ethnic separatism that neither Vaughan Williams nor Whitman would have sanctioned; just as confusingly, conservatives joined liberals in regularly denouncing elitism, embracing serious music based on, of all things, pop idioms. So much for the conservative defense of high culture! Traditional chant suddenly became marketed as "New Age." In this blurred scenario, one thing is clear: Whitman musical settings are becoming more visible in the culture. Although the astonishing extent of Whitman's impact on music is acknowledged only infrequently, we are no longer in the state of ignorance that existed, say, in 1934, ironically the year of Holst's death, when the *British Musician* complained that no composer had attempted to set "The Mystic Trumpeter." Whitman settings are finding new audiences in pop songs ("I Sing the Body Electric") and neo-Romantic works by Craig Urquhart, John Adams, Ned Rorem, and other Americans.[35]

As we have seen, Europeans led the way, both in epics by Vaughan Williams and in minor settings such as Kurt Weill's *Walt Whitman Cycle*, the forerunner of what we might call Broadway Whitman, a genre between pop and highbrow that attempts a Whitmanian disruption of hierarchies. To paraphrase George Orwell, who once described himself as "upper lower middle-class," settings in the Weill tradition are upper lower middlebrow—a negation of distinctions that many American composers now seek as a matter of course. The downside of this endeavor, especially for composers who lack Weill's melodic sophistication, is a tendency toward blandness.[36]

The egalitarian Whitman of Weill, Vaughan Williams, Holst, and even Hindemith (whose musical pragmatism is a kind of democratic utilitarianism) represents the dominant branch of Whitman musical setting. But there is another, rarer type as well. The greatest Whitman settings, surely those by Delius, move in a more mysterious, frankly elitist direction. Delius represents the nonconformist, radical Whitman, the one who broke all the rules, who steered away from the Average, whether Divine or otherwise. The scathing contempt Delius and Vaughan Williams had for each other's music—Delius thought his colleague's music was provincial and dull, Vaughan Williams accused Delius of writing "restaurant music"—reflected a philosophical as well as aesthetic divide. Delius's Whitman has nothing to do with community or democracy, values utterly foreign to his sensibility.

Yet the tension between Delius, the arrogant, rabid individualist, and Whitman, the "apostle of friendship" (as another Englishman, George Saintsbury, called him), produced greater, not lesser, art. Christopher Ricks's contention that the best criticism of art is other art finds eloquent confirmation in Delius's "criticism" of Whitman. Delius's interaction with Whitman is a kind of concerto, in which two forces oppose as well as compliment each other.

Whitman, who worshipped the all-conquering "I," but uttered "the word Democratic, the word En-Masse," embodied the same split, a dilemma common to New World artists: a passionate democrat, he was also a daring experimenter, a tough paradox given that mass democratic audiences are far more comfortable with the safe and predictable than with the radical and experimental. It was the rarefied, ephemeral side of Whitman—the side often ignored—that interested Delius. In keeping with his Nietzschean, antidemocratic proclivities, Delius embraced Whitman's experimental structures and neopagan content, producing the most original and mysterious of all Whitman settings. *Sea Drift* and the *Songs of Farewell* seem to come out of nowhere, erupt into being, then vanish like forces of nature. Like the poems (and compared to the settings of Stanford, Hindemith, Vaughan Williams, and most others who use sectional structures), they are completely organic, with a new form for each subject, bearing little resemblance to traditional patterns. Visionary in the truest sense, they are what Whitman called his poems: "New World Songs."

CHAPTER FIVE

Beyond the Frontier: New World Landscape

*I did not think of Amériques as purely geographic, but as symbolic of discoveries—
new worlds on earth, in the sky, or in the minds of men.*
—Edgard Varèse

THE idea of open sound defining American music is one of those persistent clichés that is annoying because it is so true. From Puritan hymns to Copland's cowboy scenarios, American composers do indeed tend toward sonorities associated, in the popular imagination, with the vastness of the prairie and the lonely integrity of the pioneer spirit.

Some of the earliest American landscapes in symphonic music come from New World Europeans, who were as guilty as anyone of inaugurating this myth. Europeans broadened the horizons of American landscape considerably, but they began for the most part where Americans did. Indeed, it was Dvořák's *New World* Symphony that largely established the metaphor of openness in American symphonic culture, both in the actual music and in the criticism describing it. The assessment of Victor Herbert, Dvořák's contemporary, is typical: "If I wanted to point out something vitally and poetically American in music, I should point to that movement in Dvořák's beautiful symphony, 'From the New World,' wherein he depicts in passages of extraordinary poetry and sustained beauty the musical feelings aroused in him by the idea of the vast expanse of star-lit, wind-swept prairie."[1]

Concomitant with expansiveness in this mode of criticism are other American traits such as directness, clarity, and spontaneity; commentators either reveal or impose these qualities (depending on one's point of view), both as antidotes to turgid European academicisms and as responses to the unadorned beauties of the American landscape. James Creelman wrote in 1894 that Dvořák's symphony was composed "spontaneously" and was "marvelously free from affectation"; Henry Krehbiel was convinced that the symphony was profoundly different from Dvořák's European efforts, by virtue of being "more spontaneous" and "less labored"; James Huneker, echoing the spontaneous description, also used landscape analogies, calling the symphony "clear, airy, healthy."[2] Coleridge-Taylor, inspired by Dvořák's example, praised the master's " 'open-air' sound."[3]

For better or worse, the *New World* Symphony engendered a series of tropes that came to characterize criticism of American music for more than a century. This work, however, was by no means Dvořák's only evocation of the American vista: as we have noted, the E-flat Quintet is what Dvořák called a musical picture of Spillville and its Czech community, as is the more famous *American* String Quartet; the Violin-Piano Sonatina, small and charming though it is, was associated in the composer's mind with Minnehaha Falls; and in general, the extreme spacing between high and low tones in works from Dvořák's American period suggests, as Michael Beckerman points out, the spaciousness of the American landscape.[4]

By the time Dvořák returned to Bohemia, European admirers like Herbert had gleaned from his work a ready-made package of images and analogies suitable for marketers of cowboy chic, a fad intensified by the emergence of Westerns in the new medium of cinema. Buffalo Bill's Wild West Show, for example, was one of numerous cowboy-and-Indian marketing gimmicks that have persisted in tourist enterprises such as Cherokee, North Carolina.

Puccini, of all people, picked up on the trend in 1907, when he launched the first—and surely the best—Wild West musical drama. The potential tackiness of the project worried him from the beginning: "The idea of the 'West' appeals to me," he wrote his producer, Tito Ricordi, but the actual Westerns he had experienced on stage offered only "bad taste and 'vieux jeu.' " Nevertheless, in his restless search for new, tougher subject matter and sounds, he settled on David Belasco's play

The Girl of the Golden West. Belasco, a master of Americana, had himself labored to circumvent the genre's bad taste, and the collaboration was surprisingly smooth. The legendary Metropolitan Opera premiere of *The Girl of the Golden West,* conducted by Toscanini and starring Caruso and Emmy Destinn, was a smash, despite the grumblings of critics. In happy dismay, Puccini wrote his wife that his New World Opera was apparently a huge success (and a gratifying antidote to the disastrous La Scala premiere of *Madame Butterfly*): "The performance was superb and the singing marvelous. Belasco himself took care of that. . . . Caruso was splendid both as singer and actor. The audience, rather reserved first, soon got carried away. . . . There were more than fifty curtain calls. . . . They call me the Belasco of opera. . . . They all publish my ugly face." After the performance, according to this breathless letter, Puccini was taken to the Met's foyer and introduced to "all the millionaires: the Astors, Goulds, etc."[5] He had definitely made the American scene.

Like other Europeans, Puccini did surprisingly fresh things with American material. Avoiding the horse-clomping and cowboy-song pastiches of later composers such as Ferde Grofé, Puccini invented an imaginary, exotic American West out of whole-tone scales and other Puccini-cum-Debussy devices — *Pelléas* on horseback spiked with pentatonic Orientalisms from the world of *Madame Butterfly.* Puccini further refined this advanced idiom with surpassingly delicate orchestration. (Ravel exhorted his orchestration students to study the score.) At the same time, he bowed to America's macho cowboy idiom by using a male chorus in unison, minimizing his usual lyrical effusiveness, and emphasizing masculine bass sonorities.

Somehow bad taste is never an issue in *The Girl of the Golden West.* The work has a powerful unity of atmosphere and a lonely grandeur, as in the haunting four-note motif that announces the arrival of the men chasing Johnson, Puccini's outlaw hero. Although the relative lack of big arias and florid set pieces has made it less popular than Puccini's other standard-repertory operas, he achieved a fascinating union of his notorious stylistic neuroticisms and a new poetic freedom. Having suffered a six-year block, Puccini needed a fresh jolt of inspiration, and the New World provided it.

Puccini's heroine, Minnie, a forerunner of numerous gunslinging cowgirls in American culture, is rough and resilient, beautiful yet una-

Final scene from the Metropolitan Opera premiere of Puccini's *The Girl of the Golden West*, 1907. Puccini's American West was both tough and exotic. (Metropolitan Opera Archives)

dorned, the ultimate embodiment of her landscape. Her log cabin, swept by wind and bitten by frost, nonetheless exists in a world of unspoiled beauty; her vision of the Sierra, described in the libretto, is of another planet, "far from earth," where "you suddenly feel like knocking on the gate of Heaven to be let in." Puccini's music captures the threat of the Sierra as well as its benevolence. His moody use of whole-tone harmony evokes a Wild West that can seem claustrophobic as well as open, barren and endless in its isolation.

A world bereft of history and Old World tradition, Puccini-Belasco suggest, is both intoxicating and dangerous, a place where mythmaking is still possible. As W. H. Auden noted in an essay on his libretto to Benjamin Britten's *Paul Bunyan*, the highly original choral opera that was maligned in the 1940s, revised in the 1970s, and revived in the 1990s, "America is unique in being the only country to create myths after the

A scene from Benjamin Britten's Broadway opera *Paul Bunyan*. Britten's pioneers and prairies preceded those in Aaron Copland's *Rodeo* or Rodgers and Hammerstein's *Oklahoma!* (©Glimmerglass Opera. Photo: George Mott)

occurrence of the industrial revolution. Because it was an undeveloped continent with an open frontier and a savage climate, conditions favorable to myth-making existed. . . . In the New World the struggle between [civilization] and Nature was again severe enough to obliterate individual differences in the face of a collective danger."[6] Certainly this sense of danger is present in *Paul Bunyan's* forest prologue and chorus for trees, where Britten's spare harmonies depict a pristine New World landscape before it is tamed by America's mythical lumberjack. As Dvořák and Puccini demonstrate, Europeans were often captured by New World mythology before Americans. Britten's potent images of pioneers and prairies came before *Appalachian Spring* or even *Billy the Kid*, just as the rollicking cowboy song in act 1 ("Slim's Song") came before *Rodeo* or *Oklahoma!*

A less familiar example of the early lure of the frontier in European music occurs in Ernest Bloch's *America*, a New World Symphony conceived in 1916, as the Swiss-born expatriate was sailing to New York, but not composed until ten years later. "I had to absorb America," the composer said, "and then the music came." The piece is based on a hymn-like theme simply called "Primeval Nature," a bleak melody built on sustained minor chords, introduced by open fifths whispered by strings. Bloch thought of this motif as identifiably American, even without the barrage of Civil War tunes, Sorrow Songs, ragtime fragments, and other Americana that clutter the work's initial pristineness. This New World evocation of "Primeval Nature" was meant, said Bloch, to unite all the symphony's diverse ideas in one melody, just as America itself represented the "unity of all people." Echoing the outer-space imagery used by many New World Europeans, Bloch recalled that when he arrived in America it was "like another planet." His musical *America* is most compelling when focusing on that sublime remoteness rather than taming it with folksy quotations. Yet folk songs spurred his imagination, providing him with images of "the pioneers and those who made this great country."[7]

European evocations of American landscape are by no means limited to the frontier and its requisite imagery of pioneers and cowboys. Indeed, they tend toward two other extremes: the city and the jungle. Frederick Delius depicted both, and others as well: his *Idyll* takes us to a dreamlike "populous city"; *Sea Drift* and *Songs of Farewell* travel to America's East Coast. Far removed from pioneer images, these pieces evoke something far stranger: the mysticism of late Whitman.

Delius's love affair with American landscape goes back to the beginning of his career. His opus 1, *Florida*, is the first of numerous recountings of his "romantic surroundings" in Solano Grove. Critics are usually condescending in their mention of the piece, referring to it as pleasant but not terribly interesting. Words like *pretty* and *insipid* are used to describe it, even by Delians. But when it is well performed (sadly, it is rarely performed at all), *Florida* is a rapturous account of Delius's encounter with preindustrial, pre-mall Florida.

Does it have Delius's authentic voice? It certainly conveys the distinctive Delian tranquillity, as in the cello-harp sequence from "By the River." The work also has a unique vigor, its "Daybreak" bursting with birdcalls and sunlight that later flood "On Hearing the First Cuckoo in Spring" and numerous other works, though without the same innocence and wonder. Coming at the beginning of Delius's career, *Florida* breathes a New World freshness too close to its source to be etherealized in his later manner. Although the harmonies are not yet fully Delian, the free modality and floating seventh chords are distinctive, especially considering how early the piece is (contemporaneous with Debussy's *Prélude à l'après-midi d'un faune*). *Florida* is the childhood of Delius's art before the world-weary chromaticisms creep in. This is Florida bathed in brilliant sun and moonlight, without mists.

In fact, *Florida* was so early and Delius such an unknown that the first performance did not take place until 1888 — in a Leipzig beer hall. The audience consisted of Edvard Grieg, Delius's mentor, the young composer himself, and sixty or so musicians who agreed to run through the score for a barrel of beer. The work was not performed again until Beecham's revival of it in 1937, three years after Delius's death. Nothing illustrates the Delian paradox more than this bizarre premiere: Delius the arrogant, aristocratic esthete listening to his first masterpiece, based on slave music, being premiered in a bar.

The one segment of *Florida* to have permeated the culture is "La Calinda," which became a popular concert piece. In the mid-1890s this charming African-American dance also emerged in *Koanga*, the second of Delius's twin operas on American themes. The first, *The Magic Fountain*, uses the "Daybreak" theme of *Florida* in its evocation of the Florida coast. The sad fate of these rarely produced operas, beautiful and historically significant though they are, typifies the neglect of operatic Americana in the late nineteenth century. Until Joplin and Gershwin, only Europeans seemed interested in American opera. In his 1895 interview in *Harper's*, Dvořák issued a sharp challenge to the American opera establishment, asserting that the Metropolitan was a company that "only the upper classes can hear or understand." As part of his plea for an American voice in music, he called for operas based on American themes and sung in English.[8]

His own effort in that direction, an opera based on *Hiawatha*, was abandoned, and no American composer took him up on this challenge. But the same year Dvořák made these remarks, Delius, in total isolation, was working on an "essentially Indian" experiment, as he called it, though the harmonic language, especially the Gershwin-like final arias, are steeped in African-American harmony. Entitled *The Magic Fountain*, this breakthrough work is exactly what Dvořák called for, a thoroughly American essay on American themes and in an American setting, with original but accessible music sung in clear English. Yet this sumptuously compact opera was not performed until a BBC production in 1977.

Set in the "depth of the Everglades," *The Magic Fountain* involves the fatal love of Solano, a Spanish nobleman, for Watawa, a young Indian woman, despite Watawa's hatred of the white race for exterminating her people. Typical of his early works, it is a narrative of unconventional, doomed love set against an obsessive search by Solano for the magic fountain of youth. Delius wrote the libretto himself, along with some of his most rapturous music. The daybreak scene opening act 1, scene 2, evokes the Florida coast with haunted horn fragments from *Florida*; the opening seascape recalls *Florida* motifs as well. Indeed, the opera's opening scenes basically inhabit the *Florida* world. But the music gradually loosens up, becoming freer and more dreamlike, especially when Solano articulates Delius's subjectivist point of view in the phrase "there's truth but in dreams." The Indian war dance in act 2, scene 2, recalls the dance episode in *Florida's* "Daybreak" scene, but it culminates in a descending chromatic rush more harmonically advanced than anything in the earlier work.

The distant, floating chorus of sailors, Indians, Night Mists, and Invisible Spirits of the Fountain conveys a sense of mystery that forecasts enchanted Delian choruses in everything from *Appalachia* to *Hassan*. In the ending, Delius projects his admiration for Wagner, but with a New World twist: the doomed lovers vow to meet in "a sweet magnolia grove," Delius's vision of the new Valhalla.

The most original piece of landscape painting is the depiction of the Everglades at the end of act 2, described in Delius's poetic set directions: "Night gradually falls over the scene. Stars are seen twinkling above the tree tops; fireflies glimmer by hundreds in the heavy fragrant air, flitting to and fro" (although Delius lived too far north to technically be in the Everglades; he was actually in the wild, undeveloped Florida marshland). The music captures this quintessentially Delian landscape with flitting woodwinds and the heavy fragrant air of suspended harmonies that were not yet in the harmonic range of *Florida*, although they have a way of resolving with cadences that offer more closure and stability than later Delius. *The Magic Fountain* is a transitional work in the best sense, moving from one paradisal world toward another, with no loss of sunlight or stars.

The libretto is fascinating and revealing. Delius's sea, as seen by the restless Solano, is a Melvillian nightmare, an "endless space" imbued with a "terrible calm," a forecast of the ocean in *Sea Drift*, specifically its fearful aspect. This is a psychological sea, not a Whitmanian force of nature. In his existential despair, Solano cannot accept this serenity, to him a "dead calm," though Delius's exquisitely flowing seascape, with an English horn singing the *Florida* "Daybreak" oboe tune, tells another story. Instead of absorbing the beauty around him, the "pale and weary" Solano searches for the fountain of youth, an obsession that renders him "dead to everything else."

This is the first working out of Delius's lifelong theme: the absolute imperative to accept change and mortality through the solace and regeneration of nature. The search for endless youth is, of course, doomed, resulting in no more than a "phantom quest," as the distant sailors' voices warn. Indeed, the Magic Fountain turns out to be a deadly poison that kills both Solano and Watawa. In the final scene, a kind of Indian *Liebestod*, the lovers drink the poison, finally submitting to the "sweet magnolia grove," the paradise Delius was to resummon endlessly in later works. Delius himself became involved in Solano's quest, seeking constantly to recapture his youthful adventure in the Everglades, but he did so through art, the one place where a fountain of youth can soothe mortality.

Delius's libretto is a paean to his Everglade Eden, the most extended essay he ever wrote on New World landscape: the "gently breaking" sea at dawn and the sunset on the Florida coast; the "soft and dreamy woodland"; the "stillness of the night" in the "great swamp," with its "rank and luxurious" vegetation; the fireflies in the "heavy, fragrant air." All this is captured in just under two hours of enchanted music. With the exception of the final death scene, the best moments are orchestral, especially the preludes and postludes to each scene, exquisite Everglade tone paintings with different slants of sun and moonlight. That Delius never got to hear this opera—that no one did for over eighty years—is a sad and ironic commentary on the very fleetingness the libretto depicts. (It is especially disheartening that no one has put together a concert suite of the largely self-contained orchestral music.) Like its doomed characters, the opera sank into a great swamp.

Delius's *Koanga* (discussed in Chap. 1) is also an early evocation of American landscape, in this case the swamps of Louisiana. The opera's most original touch is a "Negro Quartet," which floats into act

2 with an a cappella evocation of "strange lights wander[ing] o'er the
dark lagoon." This disembodied sound is spiced with Delian harmonies
as mysterious as the setting. A similar chorus appears in the more familiar *Appalachia*, with similar imagery. In *Koanga*, the magnolias'
"heavy scent" and the whippoorwills' nocturnal song anticipate *Appalachia*'s "scented woods" and "radiant moon." *Koanga*'s most peculiarly
American moment—fifty years before Gershwin—is the strumming of
distant banjos, an effect that, far from gimmicky, seems merely part of
the Delian mist and flow. Only Delius could make Dixieland banjos
sound ethereal and ghostlike, part of the scenery in this voodoo Valhalla.
Contemporaneous with *Koanga* was *Over the Hills and Far Away*, a
fantasy-overture that shares the opera's haunted enchantment as well as
its variation structure. As its title implies, this tone painting communi-
cates a feeling of distance and lostness, established immediately in the
ethereal ascending motif that is the work's variation theme. But like
Delius's other early New World landscapes, it has a surprising robustness
that the fragile later pieces often lack. Like *Koanga*, *Over the Hills* builds
strong climaxes and ends in a shower of light. The closer in time Delius
was to his lost New World, the more palpable was his evocation of it.

Following his Everglade odyssey, Delius revisited America once,
in the middle of writing *Koanga*, probably in an unsuccessful attempt
to reunite with his New World lover and son. He did not return again,
but the New World was by then imprinted in his imagination and musical style. By the time he revised *Appalachia*, at the turn of the century,
he no longer needed a full libretto; the vision of the "mighty river,"
with its twin images of loss and renewal, provided the necessary spur for
his imagination. It is no accident that Delius admired Mark Twain,
whose *Huckleberry Finn* depicts another mighty river in a story of loss,
separation, and racial oppression. Indeed, Twain's prose gives the distant
music that Huck and Jim hear from dying towns as they float downriver
a Delian quality of mystery and nostalgia.

After settling in Europe, Delius considered cutting the choral parts
of *Appalachia* to make the work more practical and performable, but
Peter Warlock, the most notable Delius worshiper after Thomas Beecham, voiced an eloquent protest: "These little choral doxologies that
round off the variations are so full of mysteries and haunting suggestiveness that the work would lose much of its unique charm by their
omission. The voices enter pianissimo and the effect is almost as though

Frederick Delius's house in Solano Grove, Florida, an American paradise complete with romantic surroundings, spirituals on the river, and a secret love affair. (From the collection at the Jacksonville Historical Society Archives)

the spirits of the forces of Nature invoked by the music become suddenly articulate to acknowledge the master who called them forth."[9]

No one has so succinctly spelled out the pagan quality of Delius's New World aesthetic. These hypnotic doxologies parallel the voodoo incantations in *Koanga*, the composer becoming a magician summoning "spirits of the forces of Nature." Later, in *Song of the High Hills*, Delius invoked the poetry of Dowson to ask, "Knowest thou Pan?" But during his two years in the Florida marshlands, the question would have been irrelevant: in America, Delius was Pan.

The most daring and original landscapes in American music came from a Frenchman in New York, Edgard Varèse. Inventing a new American myth, Varèse also mythologized himself. In 1920, five years after arriving in the New World from Paris, with ninety dollars in his pocket, Varèse wrote *Amériques*, subtitled *Americas, New Worlds*. "I did not think of *Amériques* as purely geographic," he said, "but as symbolic of discoveries—new worlds on earth, in the sky, or in the minds of men."[10] This New World aesthetic, linking America with discoveries in the outer and inner universe, was one from which Varèse never departed.

Determined to reinvent himself as an American composer, Varèse forged an identity as the consummate American immigrant. He literally left behind his European identity: all his pre-*Amériques* pieces were destroyed or lost.

With its brutal sensuality and sheer noisiness, *Amériques* is distinctively American. More specifically, it is a piece about New York, its unique power and electricity. Unlike Dvořák, who sailed to New York only to write about the prairie—establishing a pattern later followed by Copland, Thomson, Foss, and other New York composers—Varèse was inspired by the city itself and was perfectly content to write music about it: "When I wrote *Amériques* I was still under the spell of my first impressions of New York—not only New York seen but New York heard. For the first time with my physical ears, I heard a sound that had kept recurring in my dreams as a boy—a high, whistling C sharp. It came to me where I worked in my Westside apartment where I could hear all the river sounds—the lonely foghorns, the shrill, peremptory whistles, the whole wonderful river symphony which moved me more than anything ever had before."[11]

This dreamlike description—a poetic antidote to Varèse's many quasi-scientific elucidations—is one of the earliest documentations of a European musician "under the spell" of New York, an intoxication later responsible for the Americana of Kurt Weill and such grandiose urban sculptures as Milhaud's *A Frenchman in New York* and Poul Ruders's *Manhattan Abstraction*. There are many pastoral river symphonies in America, of course, from Ferde Grofé's *Mississippi Suite* to Steven Albert's *River Run*, but the waters of *Amériques* are anything but placid. This is a raucous, modernist city version of a New World Symphony.

Here again is a work identifiably American, yet one only a European could have conceived—a view of America from the outside. As with so many aspects of Varèse, the Old World dimension has to do with architecture. He traces the grandeur of his music to the Romanesque cathedrals of his childhood; in *Amériques* this sense of massiveness and monumentalism is uniquely combined with the noise, vulgarity, and anxiety of American life, resulting in a soundscape that has never lost its shattering power. The "shrill, peremptory" siren in *Amériques* has continued to scream throughout the twentieth century, long after serialism and other European academicisms have fallen silent.

Attracted as a young man to Debussy's obsession with pure sound, Varèse pushed further, making "sound masses" the basis of a New World aesthetic. As its title implies, *Amériques* represents a break with what Varèse called Europeanisms. As far as he was concerned, new inspiration had to come from the New World; the Old World was dead but constantly rising zombielike from the grave. "American music must speak its own language," he insisted "and not be the result of a certain mummified European formula."[12]

Images of death and mummification associated with European musical tradition permeate Varèse's essays and letters. A living aesthetic, he was convinced, must be in touch with the noisy excitement of modern life; what was needed was not a new classicism or a New Viennese School (he believed neoclassicism and serialism to be equally reactionary) but a New World entirely—new materials as well as content. "What I am looking for," he said, "are new technical mediums that can keep up with thought."[13]

Jacques Barzun has noted that Varèse came at the point where there could be "no positive principles, only negative: 'Let us do just the opposite; let us forget what we know; let us not even suppose that we possess the simplest means of our art.' Thanks to the genius of Varèse, exploration along these lines, coupled with technologically new sources of sound, led to a genuinely new *possibility of music*; and here we are, listening to *Ionisation, Déserts*, and *Poème électronique*."[14]

Barzun told me in 1995 that Varèse admired America for its "wonderful organization of technical and industrial things, an organization dependent upon steady relationships between human beings. I wonder if he knew how much it declined after World War II."[15] Decline is certainly the last thing we hear in the early music, which vibrates with, as Varèse himself put it, "pulsation from a thousand points of vitality."[16] But the haunting desolation of late works such as *Déserts* and *Nocturnal* do hint at deterioration; the great machine that at the end of *Ionisation* chugs into infinity finally seems to be breaking down. The music itself suggests that Varèse may have suspected the decline of which Barzun speaks.

In her charming *Looking Glass Diary*, Varèse's wife, Louise, wrote that her husband used to say: "I like Americans; they are natural, like the Russians; they don't have the 'slavic charm' and are not mad, but more reliable."[17] This resembles Varèse's own insistence that to be modern is to be natural. In America, or at least in Varèse's version of it, the natural is redefined as the mechanical, as long as the machine is dynamic and in motion. To Varèse, the New World and the natural are the same thing, a relentless process of change, a seeming chaos animated by a hidden Emersonian "internal structure."

As the first musical poet of American technology, Varèse reconfigured the boundaries of the New World. To Dvořák, Delius, and Coleridge-Taylor, the New World represented a new Romanticism, a postfrontier aesthetic that kept romance and mystery alive by celebrating a state of nature that was rapidly vanishing. It became, ultimately, a new nostalgia. Varèse vehemently rejected nostalgia, opting for an equally American love of modern machines and optimism about the future.

Otherwise Varèse does, to a surprising extent, fit the pattern of his predecessors, at least theoretically. It is difficult to imagine anything more different from the grinding, crashing dissonances of *Amériques* than the mellifluous sounds of Dvořák and Delius. Yet Varèse regarded himself as a New World Romantic—though a radically new type. As he said many times, all revolutionary art is inherently Romantic, becoming classical only with the passage of time. Like the early Romantics, Varèse regarded Romanticism as a synonym for modernism.

Varèse's position on the outer edges of Romanticism explains the curious parallel between his aesthetic statements and those of Dvořák. His use of sirens in *Amériques*, for example, was not, he insisted, simply imitative of the noises of urban life, as critics asserted. Sirens and other noisemakers were meant to be poetic and metaphorical, "the interpretation of a mood.... The theme is a meditative one, the impression of a foreigner as he interrogates the tremendous possibilities of this new civilization.... The use of strong musical effects is simply my rather vivid reaction to life as I see it, but it is the portrayal of a mood in music and not a sound picture."[18]

This clarification—the same kind made by Beethoven in describing the program of his *Pastoral* Symphony—strikingly resembles Dvořák's reaction to commentators who misconstrued his use of black folk materials as real quotations rather than as poetic impressions and moods. Similarly, this music derives from the "impression of a foreigner" (almost exactly the phrase Dvořák used thirty years earlier), with all the enthusiasm, freshness, and objectivity unique to that vantage point. No one else in America wrote more vivid impressions of Sorrow Songs and the prairie than Dvořák, just as no one wrote more powerful impressions of modern American life than Varèse. The sharpness of these musical observations are those of outsiders.

That Varèse's aesthetic is poetic rather than literal or realistic, even though he specified precisely what kinds of sirens and other noisemakers he wanted, is illustrated by what happened while making a pioneer recording of the piece. In 1965 Vanguard Records transported equipment — including the massive percussion battery and the New York City Fire Department siren specified by Varèse — to Salt Lake City to make the first stereo recording of *Amériques* with the Utah Symphony, under Maurice Abravanel. This was a risky, expensive undertaking. To everyone's horror, the siren broke down in the middle of the session; there was definitely no other New York City Fire Department siren to be found in Utah. According to Seymour Solomon, Vanguard's president, an anguished producer, fearing financial disaster, jumped into the percussion section where the broken siren had been and said, "You want a siren, I'll give you a siren." He then proceeded to groan and shriek, sirenlike, where the score indicated, for the rest of the session. His efforts were so seamlessly dubbed in that no one has ever known the difference: this recording was, and remains, one of the most powerful and acclaimed accounts of the score. In addition to illustrating that Varèse's machines are not as mechanical — and his music not as inhuman — as one might think, this incident also demonstrates that a process as seemingly technical as recording is really an art, an idea Varèse surely would have applauded.[19]

In addition to his many other detonations, Varèse exploded clichés about American prairies and open spaces. No longer was the American musical frontier purely pastoral, the space of nature. Now it was urban and mechanical. By dragging music kicking and screaming into modern reality, Varèse also created new myths of his own. Wide-open space became outer space (Andrew Lloyd called Varèse "the first space age composer") or the frantic industrial space of New York. "North America impresses him with a sensation of vastness and extent," wrote Varèse's friend the writer Alejo Carpentierc; "in passing, one can cast an absent-minded glance from the window of a railroad train at the largest water-falls on earth. In the depths of canyons, there are cities creating their own storms." Carpentier goes on to point out that Varèse's aesthetic was removed from the usual staples of American culture, including jazz, a peculiar shortcoming in a 1920s avant-garde composer. To Varèse, New York was "neither jazz nor 'musical comedy,' nor even Harlem dives. He stands apart from these ephemeral characteristics of this new world, but feels himself profoundly moved by the tragic meaning which he perceives in the implacable rhythm of its labor, in the teeming activity of the docks, in the crowds at noon, in the bustle of Wall Street."[20]

This urban repertory of New World images was a new contribution to music, but its antecedents were literary. It hearkened back to Whitman in its American obsession with direct experience and its exuberant urbanness. Both Varèse and Whitman embraced the sciences, especially astronomy, and were nourished by the noise of Manhattan (what Whitman called the en-masse), yet both prized individual vision above all else. Whitman declared, "You shall no longer take things at second or third hand, nor look through the eyes of the dead, nor feed on the spectres in books"—like Varèse invoking an imagery of specters and mummies associated with deadening tradition.

But because music is essentially a direct appeal to the senses—in this case a direct assault on them—Varèse is harder to take than his literary soul mates. His music has a rawness that refuses to be refined, that is outside the boundaries of taste and artistic decorum. He utterly rejected the ideology of accessibility practiced by Dvořák, Korngold, Weill, Martinů, and other New World Europeans, just as he abhorred the orthodox, clubhouse serialism inundating academia. For him, art was not communication but confrontation, an opening of space, a New World that can exist only to the extent that it blasts away the old. By definition Varèse *cannot* be accessible. The standard pedagogical strat-egy in music appreciation—that of making modern music more com-fortable through repeated listenings—does not apply. The more we listen, the more bizarre and uncomfortable the music gets, which is precisely its appeal. *Amériques* particularly—partly because it is simply longer and therefore harder to endure—retains to this day its radical

edge, its terrifying raucousness. Its grandeur is contiguous with its ob-
noxiousness.

The most vivid portrayal of Varèse's rejection of norms, including
jazz (which in mid-century rapidly changed status, moving from "cool"
to conventional) comes from another Whitmanian voice, Henry Miller's. Like Debussy, Varèse preferred the company of writers and painters
to that of musicians, and it is fitting that writers were among the first to
understand his achievement. Miller considered Varèse the only genuinely original composer in America — and as such he was lucky to be
ignored. If his music were widely disseminated, Miller argued, "he
would be stoned. . . . Aesthetically we are probably the most conservative
people in the world." Miller characterizes Varèse's music as "not sensational, as people imagine, but awe-inspiring. . . . What new music have
we to boast of other than Boogie Woogie? What are our conductors giving
us year after year? Only fresh corpses. Over these beautifully embalmed sonatas, toccatas, symphonies and operas the public dances the jitterbug."
More than any writer, Miller, whose imagery of living corpses echoes his
subject's, is in touch with the apocalyptic quality of Varèse, the cleansing
brutality that makes him the most physically cathartic of the great composers. "After listening to [Varèse]," Miller writes, "you are silenced. . . .
Varèse wants to bring about a veritable cosmic disturbance. . . . When he
talks about his new work and what he is trying to achieve, when he men-
tions the earth and its inert, drugged inhabitants, you can see him trying to
get hold of it by the tail and swing it around his head. . . . He wants to
speed up the murdering, the buggering, the swindling, and have done
with it once and for all. Are you deaf and dumb and blind? he seems
to ask. . . . *Death is one thing and deadness another.*"[21]

The Americanness of artists like Miller comes through in their
hostility to what they view as America's deadening reality, in contrast to
its liberating mythology. Again, as Michael Wood has noted, the central
idea of America is a "picture of possibility" rather than anything historical or real. Only in art, especially music, does the myth fully come to
life. Yet aside from his acute perception of Varèse's music, Miller's diatribe says more about his own attitude toward America than Varèse's,
which was always upbeat. Varèse's statements about his art were never
the invigorating rants one finds in Miller. (Then again, what writing is?)
Rather, they tend to be quasi-scientific discussions of such things as
"musical outer space" and "external forms of crystals," a dismaying fore-

cast of 1980s New Age jargon, although Varèse's nerve-wracking tumult is worlds removed from that movement's unrelenting mellowness.

What Miller captures most brilliantly is the uniquely American impoliteness of Varèse. In its sheer fierceness, the music itself does pretty much what Miller advocates. The ear-splitting violence of *Amériques* and its descendants is cathartic in an exact sense, releasing pity, terror, and all other pent-up emotions. Varèse delivers music as electroshock treatment, a way of shaking up the "inert, drugged inhabitants" of what Miller calls the "air-conditioned nightmare." If nothing else, *Arcana*, *Ionisation*, and Varèse's other "cosmic disturbances" do wake up the slumbering, "drugged" subscribers in an American concert hall, even if (as I once experienced in a Varèse program performed by the New York Philharmonic under Boulez) they awaken only to flee the hall in a streak of blue hair. As a partisan advocate, extreme but on target, Miller served Varèse well. Many Varèse aficionados (myself included) discovered his music through reading Miller, exemplifying the life-giving crosscurrents that once flowed easily between literature and music, even in the air-conditioned nightmare.

Another prominent interdisciplinary figure who struggled to bring the Varèse revolution before the American public was Paul Rosenfeld, the controversial mid-century art and music critic who, like Miller, championed the avant-garde but belittled jazz. Rosenfeld promoted important American composers such as Ives, Sessions, Ruggles, and Copland long before their achievement was widely recognized. But for him the ultimate American revolutionary was Varèse, whose incendiary music found an ideal complement in Rosenfeld's powerfully overheated prose. Rosenfeld presents Varèse as the Old World confronting the New. On the one hand, Varèse was an "alchemist. . . . Like the medieval scientists, he is moved by the desire to unveil god-nature and its divine or diabolic springs." At the same time, "his music gives us an overwhelming feeling of life as its exists in the industrial sites, and of the perspectives of recent science." Rosenfeld understood Varèse's caveat about not being a "tone painter": "Not that his art is in any way illustrative. His medium is independent, and his expression is 'metaphysical.'" Above all, this musical metaphysician is American, a "skyscraper mystic" whose "golden screams" have the potential to change musical reality.[22]

This vision of Varèse as skyscraper mystic was not the last attempt to link the composer with contemporary American cultural landscapes.

After Miller and Rosenfeld, the major Varèse guru for the second half of the twentieth century was Frank Zappa, who sponsored a huge, noisy Varèse concert at Madison Square Garden and who regarded Varèse as the foundation behind rock and roll. Whether Varèse would have liked being regarded as a granddaddy of rock, not to mention Zappaesque post-rock fusions, he has become just that.

In the late 1980s, Zappa told the lexicographer, conductor, and raconteur Nicolas Slonimsky that his own music was based on the discontinuous architecture of Varèse. Slonimsky, who pioneered Varèse in the early twentieth century and was a consummate musical detective, analyzed Zappa's scores in his charming memoir *Perfect Pitch,* and declared the Varèse influence to be real.

Zappa initially encountered Varèse's music when he was thirteen. "I read an article in *Look* about Sam Goody's Record Store in New York. . . . It was praising the store's exceptional record manufacturing ability. One example of brilliant salesmanship described how, through some mysterious trickery, the store actually managed to sell an album called 'Ionisation'. . . . The article described the record as a weird jumble of drums and other unpleasant sounds. I dashed off to my local record store and asked for it. . . . I was so hot to get that record."[23] When Zappa finally tracked the record down, he was delighted to find that the picture of the composer on the jacket "looked like a mad scientist." The music he heard on that LP—the many loud parts of which he marked with chalk so he could listen to them repeatedly—became a lifelong obsession.

This anecdote illustrates Varèse's status as an extreme outsider in the culture: he was the ultimate hard sell, a "mad scientist," a marketing challenge for a culture that even in the 1960s valued convention over originality, conformity over self-reliance, no matter how much its mythology proclaimed otherwise. Varèse's position was much the same in high culture: many of his peers indeed regarded him as a mad scientist, to the extent he was recognized at all. Varèse embodied antiestablishment energies that only a cross-cultural revolutionary like Zappa would pick up, energies that exist on the fringe of the culture, working their way into the mainstream only in safe, marketable dilutions such as rock and roll. Varèse exists where the New World of music he helped define remains new.

Varèse's New World was not limited to the United States. In the

1933 *Ecuatorial*, the first orchestral music to incorporate an electronic keyboard, he invoked the beautiful and sinister landscape of South America. Unlike his New World predecessors, Varèse did not usually require the poetic mediation of literature and folklore. For him, architecture or cubist painting, rather than poetry, served as the proper analogy to music; the immediate landscape of a city and its machinery was usually enough to fire his imagination.

But *Ecuatorial* (like the surrealist song cycle *Offrandes*) was an exception. The text, by the Guatemalan poet Miguel Asturias, treats an ancient Mayan invocation to the Spirit of the Sky and Earth, the "All-Enveloping Force" that gives life. Varèse, whose music is nothing if not an all-enveloping force, confessed to being awestruck by the "imploring fervor" of this poem. At once mystical and starkly concrete, it was close to his own art. In wonderfully exotic terms, Asturias described the text as "an invocation of the tribes lost in the mountains after abandoning the City of Abundance." Here was a New World of austere strength, suggesting to Varèse "the regions where pre-Columbian art flourished. I wanted the music to have something of the same elemental rude intensity of these primitive works."[24]

Modernism frequently bolts the primitive to the new, but the visceral power of this conjunction is unique. Varèse's weird electronic glissandi, thunderous percussion, and what he called incantatory vocalise deliver in twenty shivery minutes the kind of primal energy sought by searchers after the American life force such as Melville's Ishmael, Twain's Huckleberry Finn, and Whitman's roving "Self." Like Delius's voodoo-obsessed *Koanga*, *Ecuatorial* is a re-creation of music as pure magic, unsullied by the European tradition its creators needed so desperately to jettison. South America was ideal for Varèse because it had even less of a canonical tradition than North America. It was a new frontier capable of inspiring a new music. In *Ecuatorial*, primitive instinct based on ancient religion — through the aid of electronic machinery — becomes the alternative to Western musical conventions. Varèse moved back to the primal beginnings of the New World even as he pushed its sonic boundaries forward with new sounds. By the time he wrote his final work, *Nocturnal*, he was able, with the help of Anaïs Nin, to create his own magical incantations, his own primitive text.

The alluring remoteness of *Ecuatorial* is a landmark in the evocation of the South American New World. But as Varèse himself commented, it is only "roughly geographical," inspired by its wondrous landscape but not limited to it. Andrew Porter, music critic for the *New Yorker* in the 1970s, told me that when asked to name an appropriate piece to be performed at a festival in the Acropolis, he could think of only one work, *Ecuatorial*; only it carried a sense of awe and infinity capable of filling this ancient, magic spot. Once again, the grandeur and sheer strangeness of Varèse insured that he would remain an isolated figure, championed by only a few.

As Varèse got older, his music turned increasingly inward, as roughly geographical New Worlds increasingly contracted into "New Worlds within the minds of men." In *Nocturnal*, Varèse's death-haunted swan song, the text by Anaïs Nin repeatedly invokes "you belong to the night" over dissonance and ghostly silence. In the 1954 *Déserts*, the geographical opposite of *Amériques*, the American "river symphony" becomes a desert, a blasted, barren landscape fulfilling Miller's vision of Varèse as apocalyptic bomb thrower. It is tempting to view *Déserts*, composed at the height of Cold War paranoia, as the aftermath of a nuclear explosion. Varèse again insisted that the title was mainly poetic and psychological, representing not only "all physical deserts . . . but also deserts of the mind of man . . . that remote *inner* space no telescope can reach, where man is alone, a world of mystery and essential loneliness."[25]

With this haunting statement we reach the end of all Varèse discoveries, the space where no telescope can reach. The hollow chimes and ominous stillness of *Déserts* suggest the frightening Melvillian possibility that the American vastness might be a huge emptiness, a profound blankness. The tumultuous excitement of a work like *Ionisation* is replaced by a mysterious attenuation that the usual Varesian explosions only briefly disturb. The interpolated sounds of electronic tape, some of the first in music, add another layer of austerity; here they have none of the loopiness that makes so much later electronic music sound like what Pierre Boulez called the "music of science fiction."

Déserts suggests a profound affinity with Debussy's Poe-inspired works. Debussy was attracted to the fundamental loneliness, the "naked flesh of emotion," he discovered in Poe's quest for the beautiful. Varèse took this search to the outer limits of mystery and remoteness.

What is true of the music is true of the man. In spite of his gregariousness, reflected in his Sullivan Street apartment, a lively hangout for writers and musicians, Varèse was an isolated figure, regarded by many as a crackpot. He died, Jacques Barzun told me, "a disappointed man after being heroic and sticking to his own line." He was shunned by his musical contemporaries even though "he wasn't difficult, egotistical, or vindictive at all. Varèse had the misfortune to come during the high noon of serialism, when anyone who didn't fiddle with a tone row was a nobody." Immediately following his death, Stravinsky and others lavished him with praise — "a shameful thing," noted Barzun, given that during his life these same luminaries "sneered, laughed at, and made fun of him, claiming his music was a dead end — as if *theirs* wasn't a dead end."[26]

Varèse's status exemplifies a doubleness in American culture that simultaneously nourishes — indeed, insists upon — the idea of originality, then shuns it when it actually occurs. As composer Eric Salzman remarked in 1970, two decades before the Varèse revival of the 1990s, Varèse was an artist who "suffered immensely from his voluntary transplantation to this country — there has never been much of a place for powerful and original musical minds in established musical life here — but to the end he considered himself an American composer; the concept of New World music had both literal and symbolic meaning for him."[27] For this New World Prophet, America was simultaneously the toughest and the only possible place to be.

By the end of the twentieth century, most of the mummified Europeans Varèse inveighed against had gone creaking back to their tombs. Serialism and its academic offshoots were indeed the real dead end. Yet the New World of Varèse, which eschewed systems and formulas, is by definition a legacy without heirs. Lacking an army of disciples like Zappa, it lives on in increasing numbers of public performances, and perhaps more significantly, in a growing body of recordings: more than any composer, Varèse benefits from digital technology, almost as if it were invented to manage his huge dynamic range. As he dreamed, new mediums are catching up with new thoughts.

Stereotypical American images of the frontier meant little to Varèse, yet he himself was a lonely pioneer. When asked by Henry Miller what he was trying to capture, he spoke of the Gobi Desert and other remote landscapes as offering a state of utter outsiderness. For other New World composers as well, loneliness and foreignness were ideal states. Delius gloried in his adventure in the Florida marshland, shut off from contaminating formulas from the Old World, content with immersing himself in the instruction offered by black hymns and wild nature; Darius Milhaud spent two years in Brazil, "that marvelous country, surrounded by the experience of the tropical forest . . . isolated from the rest of the world, for even letters from Europe took a month to reach us."[28]

This experience yielded the remarkable ballet *L'Homme et son désir,* an evocation of the Amazonian rain forests. The mystique of *L'Homme* lies not just in the music itself, intoxicating as it is, but in the circumstances of its composition. *L'Homme* was one of Milhaud's early collaborations with Paul Claudel, a team that became the equivalent of Richard Strauss and Hugo Hofmannsthal. The ballet was written for Nijinsky and the legendary Ballets Russes, who were touring Rio during the last stage of Nijinsky's career. "Working together toward the final realization of the work," said Milhaud, "afforded us some of the happiest moments of all our years of collaboration." They had "time to enjoy the gentle unfolding of the ballet as though it were a kind of beloved plaything."[29]

Even with Milhaud's enormously sophisticated polytonality, *L'Homme* does seem like a beloved plaything, its childlike primitivism invading its French elegance like a jungle taking over a Provence garden. (Milhaud once said that for him Provence reached all the way from Constantinople to Rio.) Milhaud's Amazon is basically benevolent, like Delius's Everglades, despite all manner of sinister forest creatures cavorting under a spectral moon. His musical style is right for the subject: the dense, snakelike polytonalities sliding over hypnotic drummings, rattlings, and whistlings in duple meter sound like the clammy heat and clashing colors of the rain forest. Five planes of sound, each with its own ensemble, tonality, and pulse, form a complex foliage that envelops the listener, with or without Claudel's allegorical depictions of Night, Sleep, and Desire. Milhaud's polytonal chords—"more subtly sweet, more violently potent" than normal ones, he once said—are in tune with the violence and sweetness of Amazon rain forests.[30]

L'Homme is one of several remarkable European works depicting New World jungles. Each is strikingly individual, but they share common traits. The sultry Brazilian setting and offstage chorus in *L'Homme* anticipate Constant Lambert's *The Rio Grande,* a genre-defying cantata-piano concerto that conveys a poetry and freedom unique even for Lambert. In addition to the jazz element, *Rio* has a south-of-the-border sexiness, as evoked in Sacheverell Sitwell's text:

> Of the soft Brazilian air
> By those Southern winds wafted

The mystical, faraway choruses in both of these Brazilian travelogues are presaged by those of Delius, in his depiction of the Everglades—the Spirits of the Forest—in *The Magic Fountain* and the hymns floating upriver in *Appalachia*. *Ecuatorial* is far noisier and starker than any of the above, but its elaborate percussion section resembles that of *L'Homme*. Varèse, like Milhaud, uses woodblocks and primitive whistling noises in his sounding of the elements.

In 1930, the same year Varèse unveiled the Mayan landscape of *Ecuatorial*, Milhaud presented *Christoph Colomb*, an opera redolent of the barbaric splendor of Aztec murals, its penultimate scene an incantation by Aztec gods "stirring up maelstroms" to thwart Columbus's destruction of their culture. This rarely performed masterpiece (first staged in the U.S. in 1992 by the Brooklyn College Opera Theater) presents a complex portrait of Columbus and an epic vision of the New World he discovered, a glimpse of the limitless—in the words of the libretto, "the boundary after which there are no boundaries." As with Varèse's *Amériques*, the focus is more on pure imagination than on physical landscape. Part opera, part film, part spoken word, this dizzying hybrid depicts the New world as a vast repository of poetic images.

In *Christoph Colomb* Milhaud (again collaborating with Claudel) depicts a more frightening South America than in the languid rain forest of *L'Homme et son désir*. Just before Columbus discovers America, his terrified sailors cower in the ship, unable to confront a ghostlike world of "palpitating whiteness." As with Delius and Varèse, Milhaud voyages into an alluring but terrifying New World that is Melvillian in its vision of endless blankness, what the narrator in *Moby Dick* called "heartless voids and immensities."

A similar doubleness complicates the character of Columbus himself. Both demonic and heroic, Columbus is as ambiguous as the New World he discovers, the fearless voyager into the New World but also the destroyer of the ancient culture he finds there, a brilliant visionary but also a failed bureaucrat abandoned by friends as well as foes. Describing himself as the "Ambassador of God," Columbus brings turmoil and violence, yet at the opera's conclusion, a flashback showing his great moment of discovery, the dove of peace appears as the choir sings a radiant Te Deum: the quest for the unknown, the ultimate value, redeems everything. In the original version of the opera, this hymn was buried in the middle; by breaking up the chronology of the narrative and putting the actual discovery of the New World at the conclusion, the revised version more clearly dramatizes the opera's focus on the ecstasy of discovery.

Milhaud's music is as complex as his interpretation of Columbus, combining knotty polytonality with the simplest, most austere diatonic chant. To the extent that critics have noticed this important work at all, they have ignored its fluorescence of New World musical genres. Yet Milhaud was acutely aware — as he was in *La Création du monde* — of his American sources. The diverse musical styles he works into this opera suggest the New World landscape encountered by Columbus and those who immediately followed him. Spanish modes and syncopated rhythm, mingling Moorish, Aztec, and African flavors, invoke "Nueva España," the intoxicating cacophony that erupted in the New World in Columbus's time. From the very beginning, as Milhaud's score demonstrates, New World sound was wild and syncopated. The music celebrates Columbus's legacy even as the libretto presents his dark side; the mixing of opera, drama, film, and religious ritual parallels the delightful jumble of *villancicos*, polyphonic hymns, arabo-andalou motifs, Indian chants, and African dances that miraculously came together in "Nueva España." As in *La Création du monde*, polytonal chords coalesce into provisional or temporary cadences, a metaphor for the divergent traditions that Columbus discovered clashing, gradually mixing, and finally coexisting in uneasy harmony.

Christoph Colomb is an example of Europeans treating New World subjects in new, complex ways that avoid frontier commonplaces. Olivier Messiaen's 1974 *From the Canyons to the Stars*, one of the most ambitious pieces of Americana in music, portrays a subject that has certainly seen its share of triteness. Yet once again, the outsider status of its creator helped insure that the observations would be sharp and novel. As a foreigner, Messiaen encountered America's canyons and prairies, the domain of Copland and Grofé, with new eyes and ears. Messiaen had already explored New World landscape in his *Song of Love and Death: Harawi*, a song cycle from 1945 that depicts an erotic love story set in the Peruvian mountains. The earliest part of a "Tristan Trilogy" that includes the Turangalîla Symphony (covered in Chapter 3), *Harawi* is one of Messiaen's first fully characteristic works, combining piercing dissonance and tonal lyricism, mysticism and carnal sensuality, Western modernism and non-Western primitivism, in this case Mayan symbolism, Peruvian dances, and syllable sequences from the ancient Indian Quechua language. In Messiaen's South America, shrieking bird-song alternates with mystical mountain vibrations, sultry sunlight with visions of the planets. The first of Messiaen's New World landscapes, *Harawi* helped establish sound and images that reverberated throughout his career, culminating in *From the Canyons to the Stars.*

As with Milhaud's *Christoph Colomb* and Hindemith's *Lilacs* Requiem, *From the Canyons to the Stars* was both a new direction and a work of retrospection. The New World was a catalyst that enabled Milhaud to bring together the diverse aspects of his style, including the jazzlike swing of *La Création du monde*, the hair-raising polytonality of his *Oresteia* series, and the dancelike charm of his pastoral works. Paradoxically, the poetry of Whitman unleashed in Hindemith a dizzying parade of European forms from his earlier periods. For Messiaen, too, the New World was a unifying experience. *From the Canyons to the Stars* is a synthesis of his theological, ornithological, and harmonic contemplations over a period of forty years, not only the New World of *Harawi* but many others as well. From the elaborate cacophony of birdsong in what Messiaen called this "symphony of birds" through the numerous religious allusions (Eastern and Greek as well as Catholic) to the evocation of celestial lights and colors, *Canyons* recapitulates Messiaen's career. Beginning in a cavernous desert, a fearful reminiscence of *Et expecto* and other modernist works by Messiaen, the music gradually sweetens into the diatonic splendors of the mountains and stars, recalling earlier pieces such as *The Ascension.*

Messiaen used lean, unadorned sounds to bring the American West to life. His ensemble includes a wind machine, a large percussion battery, and solos by a resonant French horn and a piano. This New World Symphony, like Dvořák's, is conceived on an epic scale. Indeed, in size *From the Canyons to the Stars* is the most epic of all New World landscapes, a twelve-movement extravaganza that depicts the canyons of Utah—Bryce, Cedar Breaks, and Zion Park. Messiaen discovered photographs of these wonders in an art book and immediately decided to fulfill a commission from Alice Tully for a piece of Americana. But first he flew to Utah to see his subject before attempting a setting. He was not disappointed. Like Dvořák, Delius, Bloch, and so many other European composers, he was overwhelmed by an "American paradise": "We were immersed in total silence—not the slightest noise, except for the bird songs. And we saw those formidable rocks tinted with all possible shades of red, orange and violet . . . the shapes of castles, towers, bridges, windows, columns!"[31] Not surprisingly, this description combines New World exuberance with Old World imagery. Superimposed onto the wilderness of Utah's canyons is a European monumentality, complete with images of castles, towers, and ruins, much as Varèse's American landscapes were sculpted in the Romanesque architecture of his earlier life. There are no cowboys, Indians, or pioneers either in Messiaen's commentary or in his colorfully stark music.

As we have seen, European composers coming to America tended to describe it in extraterrestrial terms. Getting off the boat in New York, Bloch experienced America as "another planet"; Varèse imagined the New World as "outer space." With his otherworldly predilections, Messiaen went a step further. To him, planets and outer space were more than metaphors: the canyons in Utah were "landscapes like those we'll probably see after our death, if we then have the chance to visit other planets." *From the Canyons to the Stars* explores not only "the miraculous beauties of our planet" but "the hope of still greater beauties after death," a state in which we will move "from light to light." As its title implies, the New World of *Canyons* points toward paradise: by the eighth movement, the work is in the heavens, glossing Messiaen's discovery in the Book of Job of "an extraordinary phrase in which it is said that 'the stars sing.' "[32]

It is easy to make fun of such commentary, and the convoluted specificity of Messiaen's theological and bird-watching musings has not helped his cause among intellectuals. It would be charitable simply to let the music speak for itself, but the composer makes it hard for one to assume that posture. Like Wagner, Scriabin, and others who were taken with their own mythologies and theologies, Messiaen has a way of imposing himself on his art, issuing a torrent of words with each piece and insisting that the theology and philosophizing are an intrinsic part of the music and its appreciation.

They are not, of course, and the listener has the option of ignoring them. The hallucinatory colors and near-painful ecstasy of this music cannot be bound by words, even those of their creator. Indeed, *Canyons* is wilder and harder to label than Messiaen himself may have realized, as revealed by the work's premiere in 1974. The early 1970s in American culture were largely an extension of the 1960s, and the (inadvertently) psychedelic sensibility of this piece was not lost on its New York audience, many of whom were visibly members of the counterculture. (American performers specializing in Messiaen during this period, notably the chamber group Tashi, marketed themselves with all manner of flower-child imagery and regalia.)

The lyricism and spaciousness of *Canyons* are paralleled in a number of American works by Europeans, including composers not known for these qualities. In some cases, the New World Symphonies of these composers were bold intensifications of tendencies already in play before they arrived in America. Hindemith's evocation of America's "prairies wide" in his *Lilacs* Requiem is an overt naming of a new expansiveness in other works from his American period, such as the powerful Symphony in E Flat and the exuberant *Metamorphosis on Themes by Carl Maria von Weber*. A vivid example of the American Hindemith is the oddly neglected Clarinet Concerto, written for Benny Goodman in 1947. In spite of the Goodman commission and Hindemith's keen interest in jazz, this New World Concerto offers only a tantalizing taste of that genre in the swingy, percussive Scherzo: the rest offers polyphonic lyricism in the style of the *Lilacs* Requiem, with suggestions of a brilliant, starry night in the opening and closing tutti. The grandeur of the pieces Hindemith wrote at Yale was first apparent in *Mathis der Maler*, the banning of which by the Nazis impelled him toward America. Once in the New World, he broadened this tendency.

Other Europeans followed a similar pattern. Bartók's poetic sounding of birdcalls in Asheville, North Carolina, during his struggle with leukemia—movingly captured in the Concerto for Orchestra, the Third Piano Concerto, and the Viola Concerto—are a more passionate version of a lyricism that was beginning to take flight in the Music for Strings, Percussion and Celeste and the Violin Concerto. As in the case of Hindemith, critics characterized this change in Bartók, which began just before his journey to the New World, as a stylistic "softening," a move-

Paul Hindemith and Benny Goodman rehearsing Hindemith's Clarinet Concerto, 1946. The King of Swing both inspired and performed numerous European concert works. (Yale Music Library)

ment toward a new "humanism." But both artists were humanists from the beginning. What did develop was a new soulfulness, spontaneity, and nostalgia, qualities found in numerous World Symphonies since Dvořák's.

But there is more than one kind of New World sensibility. What is unveiled by Varèse, Milhaud, and British composer Nicholas Maw in his voodoo-haunted *Ghost Dances*, from 1988, is something darker, more explosive and dangerous, the remote outer reaches of American landscape that lie beyond the frontier. It is an awesomeness more likely to be noticed by outsiders, by Europeans, than by those who live too close to the waterfall to hear it any longer. It is a vision articulated by the British travel writer Jonathan Rabin when, speaking for other Europeans, he described American landscape as "shockingly bigger, more colorful, more deadly, more exotic, than anything they'd seen at home."[33]

CHAPTER SIX

Broadway, Hollywood, and the Accidental Beauties of Silly Songs

Every day America's destroyed and recreated.
—W. H. Auden's libretto for Benjamin Britten's *Paul Bunyan*

I'm an American!
—Kurt Weill

T HUS far, this book has explored the lure of the New World as idea and ideal. Commercially, America proved felicitous as well. When Erich Korngold discovered Hollywood in the 1930s and Weill conquered Broadway in the 1940s, they reversed more than their artistic fortunes. Suddenly American greed and materialism—even the dreaded leveling effect of democracy—seemed not so bad after all. In spite of its notorious philistinism, America became the place where commerce could become art, as well as the reverse. These two artists and their émigré colleagues converted the crassly commercial genres of American culture into a new, glitzy species of musical poetry, a crossover between the elite and the democratic, the sublime and the vulgar. As W. H. Auden put it in his libretto to Britten's *Paul Bunyan*, the Broadway and Hollywood dream machines allowed Europeans a "life of choice."

Kurt Weill's *The Rise and Fall of the City of Mahagonny*, the precursor to Broadway opera, is an emblem of this phenomenon. A leftist European's nightmare of America, *Mahagonny* is also a stand-in for postwar Germany during the rise of the Third Reich, a signification not lost on the Nazis, who banned the work. On an obvious level, *Ma-*

hagonny is a symbol of unregulated avarice, an endless cycle of compulsory scamming in an empty culture where the ultimate crime is a failure to make money. This is what American capitalism does to people, the piece insists. But it says something else too, which Weill's music suggests even if Brecht's text does not: the ragtime, jazz, and Tin Pan Alley idioms that inspired so much of Weill's haunting music are the quintessential products of the very culture the piece so mercilessly lampoons. No socialist society has produced jazz, just as no capitalist society has conquered the poverty and social displacement that enabled jazz to erupt. This is the paradox that no ideology has resolved and that Weill celebrates in his brittle way, even if Brecht, in his orthodox Marxism, does not. The Europeanized jazz mined by Weill in *Mahagonny* was the product of American show business, which Weill mastered and then enriched after arriving in the New World. The facility with American popular music he gained with the composition of *Mahagonny* enabled him to prosper two decades later on Broadway, his own "city of nets." Unlike the nets of the doomed characters in *Mahagonny*, his did not turn up empty.

The story of European émigrés making it in American show business is laced with ironies. It could only have happened the way it did in Roosevelt's America, a culture that for a brief time shared the progressive values of Weill, Britten, and other émigrés who participated in New Deal programs for the arts such as the Federal Theater and Works Progress Administration. It was the anti-Roosevelt, Mahagonny version of America, the world of unregulated capitalism, that made the New Deal necessary in the first place, just as the Depression made Hollywood's golden age and its escapist fantasy world necessary. In a grimmer irony, it was the Nazis who gave a big push to this new alliance between art and commerce: in their zeal to rid Western culture of "decadent" art, the Nazis ensured its spread; in banning *Mahagonny* and its offspring, they forced some of the greatest talents of the century to emigrate to a New Mahagonny, where that art could easily flourish. Hollywood and Broadway made it possible for composers who were forced to flee political persecution with virtually nothing—no cash, no publishers, no contacts—to suddenly strike it rich.

Music, of course, is not the only art form where crass commerce spawned significant contributions. Later in the century, the same pattern became evident in other fields (for example, in the pop art of Andy Warhol and Roy Lichtenstein and in the pop minimalism of late twentieth-century novelists who chronicled life in the mall, then sold vast numbers of books there). But the phenomenon occurred first in music, most notably in the collaboration of European composers with Hollywood and Broadway producers, who sometimes actually delivered on the American dream of instant glamour and wealth.

Often the promise was fulfilled at the high price of artistic reputation. Because their commercial success in America outshone their earlier European triumphs as "serious" artists, Korngold and Weill inspired the liveliest, most outraged vituperation. The controversy they engendered was the inversion of the Dvořák case, where Americanists felt threatened by the incursions of a prominent European espousing inferior black music in American citadels of high culture; in the case of Weill and Korngold, Europeanists who had championed their Old World music were horrified that these artists had allowed their standards to be lowered by an inferior American culture. As Kim Kowalke has persuasively argued in regard to denunciations of Weill on Broadway, "Most of these appraisals barely disguised an underlying belief in the innate superiority of European culture"; objective appraisals are hard to come by, and indeed, as late as 1993 "adequate studies of the primary context in Weill's case, the American musical theater, and the secondary context, émigré composers' experiences in the United States, have yet to be written."[1]

Recent commentators have avoided the outright snobbery of earlier critics: American show business did not exactly ruin European composers, this kinder argument goes, but merely kept them from becoming what they might have been. Assessments of Weill and Korngold tend to be remarkably parallel, even in phraseology. The *New Grove* calls Weill "one of music's great might-have-beens";[2] a 1995 article in the *New York Times*—tellingly entitled "A 'Serious' Composer Lives Down Hollywood Fame"—asserts that Korngold's "few masterpieces, early and late, are flickering visions of what might have been."[3] America seems to confer upon "serious" Europeans who profit from it a curious future-conditional status, placing them in a perpetual limbo of unfulfilled promise.

That the might-have-beens might really be in the critics' heads is suggested by the quite different assessment of the educated public. Audiences do not share this tortuous ambivalence; they have always loved the American works of these composers, just as they cheered earlier Old World re-creations of New World music. The circle explored earlier in this book persists: European composers receive something vital from the New World, then re-create it, in the process conferring upon it a new viability and respectability. When Dvořák and Delius reimagined African-American Sorrow Songs, when Victor Herbert pioneered the early Broadway musical and silent-film score, they were nurtured by an American vernacular that, thanks partly to their efforts, soon became incorporated into high culture. As the historian Karen Greenberg has pointed out, "Finding their own voices in America, the émigré did much in turn for the American voice. Not afraid to consider the music of the people, they brought a new level of sophistication to what might otherwise have been considered trivial."[4] At least in this might-have-been scenario, American culture is raised rather than the European composer being lowered.

Initially, Hollywood and Broadway diverged in what they offered European sojourners. Hollywood appeared to sanction the creation of a European fin-de-siècle beachhead in America, while Broadway demanded an unmistakably American vernacular. As we shall see, the realities were more complex, and it is worth noting that even if accurate, the pattern reversed itself after mid-century: European film composers (writing for spaghetti Westerns or jazz-drenched French crime films) went increasingly American in their materials; Georges Delerue, one of the most prominent in this group, began his career composing sharply etched scores for François Truffaut and Alain Resnais but ended up in California writing in a post-Korngold Hollywood idiom for Oliver Stone and other filmmakers. Broadway, on the other hand, increasingly allowed itself to be taken over by gaudy British musicals—ersatz Saint-Saëns and Puccini—while the innovations of Gershwin and Bernstein were put on hold until the rock revival of the 1990s brought American idioms back. Transatlantic offerings from both sides became increasingly complicated and mutually nourishing.

The case of Hollywood's golden age is fascinating in its complexity and strangeness. It is a supreme example of the American immigrant experience at its most efficient and inspiring. Many of Hollywood's early composers—such as Erich Korngold, Ernst Toch, Franz Waxman, and Dimitri Tiomkin—were émigrés who had fled political oppression. America provided not only a safe haven and a fresh start but its most glamorous myth, Hollywood, a make-believe world that offered fame and wealth virtually unheard of (and still rare) in serious concert music. The music establishment, however, condemned the resulting music as shallow and degenerate—ironically, the very terms the Nazis had used to vilify Korngold and his colleagues (though in a far more deadly context).

The Korngold case is especially poignant. He is conventionally regarded as the most successful of the European émigrés who escaped the Nazis, and from a strictly commercial point of view he probably was. But precisely because he was a major composer—in the judgment of Strauss and Mahler, the greatest of his generation, and the bearer of their mantles—he was accused most intensely of being a sellout. Some of the harshest commentary came from fellow émigrés, memorably illustrated by the icy response of Otto Klemperer (who had premiered *Die tote Stadt* in Cologne) to the lament by Austrian Radio's Heinrich Kralik that Korngold had "wasted" his talent on Hollywood: Korngold had "always composed for Warner Brothers," Klemperer said, "he just didn't realize it."[5]

Korngold was incapable of neatly segmenting his career, either artistically or chronologically, into movie versus serious music, as did Miklos Rosza, Dimitri Tiomkin, and Franz Waxman (the first two writing much of their "serious" music at the beginning of their careers, the latter at the end). For Korngold, it was all or nothing: every note he produced was "serious," even the most schmaltzy. Depending on one's point of view, he was either the most naive of composers or the most daring in terms of ignoring traditional distinctions, taboos, and hierarchies.

Korngold had the temerity to think he might actually make money from his art to support his family, and that this might be a respectable thing to do. The remarkable photograph of Korngold arriving in New York in 1936 with his wife and children, all wide-eyed in the wondrous anticipation of the American immigrant experience, reveals a sense of promise the composer was determined to convert into reality. Before

Erich Wolfgang Korngold and his family arriving in New York, 1936. Korngold invented
Hollywood music and a new American romanticism. (Lebrecht Collection)

Hitler's Anschluss destroyed his world, he was the most illustrious composer in the Viennese classical tradition. Except for his life and family,
he lost everything. Then Hollywood—a myth premised upon fast, spectacular fantasy gratification—offered money and the dream of all artists:
the opportunity to write for a new, revolutionary medium.

Off the record, Korngold embraced Hollywood with reluctance; he
was certainly shrewd enough to know his artistic reputation might suffer.
Furthermore, the genres he was asked to work in—swashbucklers and
sentimental romances—clashed with his sensibility. Even his biggest hit,
The Adventures of Robin Hood, was undertaken grudgingly; first Korngold turned down the commission from Hal B. Wallis, stating in an
impassioned letter that the very notion of scoring action films was painful and pleading with Wallis not to try seducing him into changing his
mind. But when Korngold's father called with the news that everything
they owned in Vienna had been confiscated by the Nazis, Wallis was
able to tell his *Robin Hood* production team that Korngold was on board.

Officially, Korngold was enthusiastic about his Hollywood work, insisting that movies were the newest form of opera. He was not the earliest composer to make this connection: Victor Herbert, his émigré predecessor, was credited with creating "the first grand opera for film" in his music for the 1915 silent film *The Fall of a Nation*, the debut through-composed movie score. But Korngold was the first to sustain a career with film music and to establish an aesthetic for the new medium of talkies, the dialogue of which he regarded as a new kind of libretto. In print, he "never differentiated" between opera and film music; both, he insisted, were different but equally respectable varieties of "dramatically melodious" music.[6] He treated all the genres he worked in with exactly the same intensity and perfectionism.

For a while, Korngold enjoyed spectacular success. In 1935, shortly after Max Reinhardt talked him into writing the delightful Mendelssohnian pastiche for *A Midsummer Night's Dream*, Warner Brothers hired him for *Captain Blood*, the first of several Errol Flynn blockbusters, a huge hit that garnered Korngold a Warner contract just in time to escape Hitler, who had banned his opera *Die Kathryn*. Three years later, Warner produced *The Adventures of Robin Hood*, for which Korngold — despite his painful reluctance — wrote some of his most stirring Hollywood music, full of sonorous fanfares and an outpouring of lyricism that set a near-unreachable standard for future Hollywood composers. Wallis and his Warner colleagues, who knew the quality of what they were getting, gave Korngold the freedom to compose what he wanted, when he wanted.

Like other golden age movies, *The Adventures of Robin Hood* is saturated in continuous music. The musical equivalent of early Technicolor, the score is manifestly "overdone," as it must be. This *Robin Hood* feels like a nineteenth-century opera, much as Korngold fantasized, its stylized actions and dialogue matched by lush, tightly written diatonic music. Cinema critics continue to deplore this "reactionary" music composed for the revolutionary "new" art of cinema. But what was new in Depression- and war-weary America was a revolution in fantasy, an American version of opera that provided an instant and total escape into the dark.

Presiding over Hollywood's golden age, Korngold provided *Anthony Adverse*, *Of Human Bondage*, *The Prince and the Pauper*, *King's Row*, and his other projects with scores remarkable both for their quality—often considerably higher than the films they grace—and for their manner of composition. The notoriously mechanized corporate conditions under which film composers work did not exist for Korngold, who enjoyed the right to choose his own projects, compose without interference, and show the finished product to producers only during the final cut. His method, as he described it, consisted of sitting at the piano in the projection room "watching the picture unroll" while "improvising or inventing themes." His immediate inspiration came not from Old World tradition—a muse he reserved for Viennese pastiches such as the finale of the Second String Quartet—but directly from the movie at hand: "If the picture inspires me, I don't even have to measure or count the feet. If I am really inspired, I simply have luck. And my friend, the cutter, helps my luck along."[7] Korngold's method of improvisation, more akin to jazz than to opera, resulted in scores consistent in their disciplined opulence, melodic distinction, and atmospheric unity, so much so that they came to define Hollywood sound in its golden age as well as in its frequent revivals by neo-Korngoldians such as John Williams and Pino Donaggio. (Williams, who in interviews rhapsodizes about the similarity of film music to opera, recaps Korngold's words as well as notes.)

Korngold rendered obsolete the distinction between music serving an invisible support for film narrative and music capable of standing on its own. The debate over the genre's function in this regard rages to this day, enlivened by all manner of technical and ideological twists. But Korngold, whose earliest movie music came before its film criticism had been invented, was benignly ignorant of such distinctions. As far as he was concerned, film music enhanced the film while retaining an integrity of its own; one was impossible without the other. Movie music, he said, was "symphonically dramatic music which fits the picture, its action and psychology, and which, nevertheless, will be able to hold its own in the concert hall."[8] Here was another judgment that was not vindicated until the hybrid movie-concert fusions of the 1980s and 1990s.

Korngold harbored few illusions about the films themselves: when critics complained near the end of his movie career that his film music was declining, he answered that when he first arrived in Hollywood, his English was so poor that he was unable to understand what the performers were saying on screen. Now he did. In any case, the continuity between his film and symphonic music was not unlike the case of Purcell, Mozart, Haydn, and others who composed theater music, incidental pieces, and divertimento for various entertainments and who later used the same entertainment material for symphonic music. Hollywood became an admirable twentieth-century solution to the age-old dilemma of the serious composer struggling to make a living—a replacement for the aristocratic patron who had hitherto supported musical artists. If many, including Korngold himself, had doubts about Hollywood movies as sufficiently elevated vehicles, it is also true that the libretti of Mozart, Strauss, and other composers were commonly denounced as trash.

Critical commentary to the contrary, Korngold's movie work did not lower the tone of his concert pieces, although it certainly slowed their pace. Indeed, many of Korngold's best concert works were based on his movie scores, either directly or in spirit. If anything, the discipline required for writing film music sharpened Korngold's aesthetic. In inventing Hollywood sound, he increased the dramatic focus in all his music, an admirable example of American commerce helping art. The American concert works have the same dreamlike shimmer as Korngold's earlier music but also exhibit a new drive and compactness, qualities first apparent in the 1937 First String Quartet, based on African-American spirituals. This is one of Korngold's most beguiling works, and one of his tightest. Its reinvented spirituals and its Dvořákian sweetness place it directly in the New World Symphony tradition. The trend intensified a decade later in the Second Quartet: the clear diatonic lines of its folklike slow movement, resurrected from *The Sea Wolf,* are classical in their simplicity; the restless, chromatic outer movements are the closest he came to writing modern music. These pieces have a wistfulness and lonely vulnerability connected with exile, most strikingly the 1943 Symphonic Serenade, a tour de force for strings with a hymnlike Lento religioso movement carrying the same marking and mood as the slow movement of Bartók's Third Piano Concerto, a touching parallel to the newly simplified idiom of another European exile in America.

Hollywood gave Korngold a way of keeping the Romantic flame burning in his symphonic works. Even the sensuous melodic line in his Violin Concerto of 1945, an outrageously sentimental bit of hedonism from the end of Korngold's film career, has a momentum that keeps it from collapsing into bathos. Based on material from *Juarez, Anthony*

Adverse, The Prince and the Pauper, Another Dawn, and other film projects, this virtuosic concerto written for Heifetz—another émigré with a
nineteenth-century aesthetic who was drawn to Hollywood—is an exuberant summation of Korngold's Hollywood period. So is the Cello Concerto from a year later and, in its final section, the charming Theme
and Variations, written in 1953 for an American student orchestra. With
their nostalgic references to Hollywood's golden age, these pieces represent movie music in a platonic form; wrenched from their film context
and poured into variation or sonata forms, Korngold's melodies retain
their dreamlike glamour while gaining interest as they interact to create
a symphonic fabric. Freed from accompaniment status, they unroll an
imaginary film in our heads, one far more voluptuous than the kitschy
images they originally enhanced. A kind of meta-movie music, they anticipate the concert-film hybrids of George Pelecis, Michael Torke, and
other composers preoccupied with American film culture in the late
twentieth century.

Critics dismissed these works as a further comedown. Having cat-
egorized the Hollywood Korngold as a commercial panderer, they now
sneered at his post-Hollywood works as attempts to "redeem himself
artistically." (In an ugly, if less deadly, parallel, official tastemakers in
the Soviet Union were also monitoring "redemptions" by Shostakovich
and his colleagues.) Korngold found himself ostracized by virtually every
faction, from modernists, who had regarded his Romanticism as passé
to begin with, to conservatives hostile to Hollywood's commercialism.
In a double irony, this supreme Viennese reactionary, in many ways the
last composer to uphold Old World symphonic tradition, created a democratic synthesis of popular and elite culture, only to be attacked by
American upholders of new hierarchies. The title of one of Korngold's
final, most poetic film scores, "Between Two Worlds," was sadly apt.
Rather than bridge two worlds, as Gershwin had managed to do briefly,
Korngold fell headlong between them. By the late 1940s and early 1950s,
he was in the wrong place at the wrong time, just as he had been in
the perfect place at the perfect time in the late 1930s.

In post-Roosevelt America, the chasm between highbrow and popular culture began to gape once again, pushing Gershwin, Weill, Korngold, Britten, and other popularizers to the sidelines, at least in the
academy. While these Europeans looked to America for new sources of
color and vitality, many established American composers forsook the

New World and began latching onto twelve-tone music — the latest European system, the guarantor, in Schoenberg's words, of the "supremacy of German music." By the time the Milton Babbitt school officially renounced the idea of an audience altogether, it was merely making explicit what was already the practice among American academic composers. Tuneful composers like Barber, Diamond, and Korngold were out, along with audiences, but Korngold, as a film composer, was held in special disdain.

His biggest sin in the eyes of the critics was apparently being a *successful* film composer. No one deplored Stravinsky, Rachmaninoff, or even Schoenberg for their abortive attempts at writing for Hollywood. If anything, their naiveté in dealing with show business was a badge of honor. Nor did critics go after Prokofiev, Honegger, Britten, Walton, Shostakovich, Vaughan Williams, Arnold, or others who made more modest money from the Russian, French, and British cinemas. Composing for American pictures, where one could make big money fast, conferred a special disdain. (Only Copland, whose musical nationalism was all the rage, was able to write Hollywood music — some of the most beautiful in the genre — with impunity.)

Unlike the endlessly prolific Steiner-Tiomkin group, whose sellout was so total it ceased being an issue, Korngold wanted desperately to reinvoke the great-composer status of his Viennese wunderkind days. The loneliness of this struggle is reflected in the bleak clarinet-percussion opening of his only symphony, his final work, a gesture of alienation unlike anything he had written before. Begun in 1947 as a memorial to Franklin Roosevelt, this heartbreaking symphony, in the remote key of F sharp, received only a single radio broadcast in 1954 and was not performed again until 1972, when it was discovered by Rudolf Kempe in the first wave of Korngold revivals in the 1970s and 1990s. A quintessential New World Symphony, Korngold's is alternately mournful and exuberant, drenched in Old World nostalgia even as it celebrates American subjects, in this case an American president. Like Dvořák's imaginary black spirituals, Korngold's symphonic manipulation of what resembles Hollywood film music is newly composed. It anticipates film music to come, the heroic horn theme in the Scherzo an exact harbinger of John Williams's scores for Steven Spielberg thirty years later. The cyclical structure of Korngold's symphony also echoes Dvořák's, the recapitulation of earlier themes in the finale adding an epic dimension to something already larger than life. And like Dvořák, Korngold managed a slow movement (one beginning, as Dvořák's does, with quiet, suspenseful chords) that may well be the most soulful he ever wrote, rising to a series of climaxes that exceed in grandeur even his early operas. Of musical memorials to Franklin Roosevelt, only Barber's *Adagio for Strings* equals this movement in emotional power.

Unlike Dvořák's instantly popular "New World," Korngold's took some thirty years to find its audience. Korngold died a lonely orphan. He was revived near the end of the century he was allegedly out of sync with, the musical establishment having finally decided that Romanticism — even the Hollywood variety — was not so passé after all. The fruits of Korngold's pop-classical synthesis did not become clear until the 1980s and 1990s, after American imitators of European modernism had virtually serialized themselves out of existence. (Like Virgil Thomson, Korngold predicted the collapse of academic serialists — the "complexity boys," as Thomson called them — during their mid-century dominance.) Suddenly Korngold film scores began to be played as concert suites and tone poems; major orchestras such as the New York Philharmonic performed Korngold's movie music as excerpts from the films were projected in back of the orchestra — this time the images accompanying the sound rather than the reverse. These performances revealed in a vivid way what Korngold aficionados had long suspected, that the music upstaged the images it supposedly accompanied, just as Wagner's "continuous melody" often soared above its narrative. Recordings tell the same story: the 1997 Marco Polo release of the score for the long-forgotten Errol Flynn flop *Another Dawn* (which includes a rousing final fanfare that was cut from the original) features love themes of such sultry intensity, harmonic ingenuity, and sheer sexiness that standard neo-Romantic concert fare of the 1990s seems neutered by comparison. No wonder Korngold plundered this haunting score, otherwise destined for oblivion, for his Violin Concerto.

As Edward Rothstein has pointed out, by the 1990s Korngold and the aesthetic he "almost single-handedly created" were responsible for a welcome cross-pollination in concert venues: "What need do concert halls have of the gimmicks that have been proposed for revitalizing American concert life — interior decoration, elaborate light shows or color-coordinated ambiances — when the halls are becoming host to these more powerful combinations of image and sound?"[9] If we accept

Korngold's definition of narrative film as the new opera, these concert-film fusions become another realization of Dvořák's dream of a distinctly American opera. By the 1990s, "postmodernists" such as Michael Nyman and Philip Glass were busily writing music to films both new and old, played in concert halls and movie houses.

The situations of Korngold's more prolific colleagues, such as Steiner, Rozsa, and Waxman, were simpler and happier. Less encumbered by artistic ambitions, they manifested little of Korngold's painful ambivalence. A self-deprecating aesthetic, which regarded film music as largely functional and invisible, helped enormously: Waxman believed a film score should not be "full of secrets," like concert music, but instead be "simple and direct."[10] If a film like Hitchcock's *Rebecca* was premised on secrets, he could skillfully provide those as well: the music he composed for the tracking scenes in front of Rebecca's mysterious bedroom door are voluptuously haunting, establishing a Gothic Romance sound in the American cinema that no one has surpassed.

Miklos Rozsa initially complained about the stupidity of producers, one of whom demanded that the hero's theme be in a major key and the heroine's in a minor, and that the two be sounded together during their encounters; he also bemoaned the "Broadway-cum-Rachmaninoff" clichés of his colleagues. But he became increasingly pragmatic, able to modulate easily from the pseudo-Resphigi of *Ben-Hur* to what he called his "anti-Ben-Hur," the dreamlike score of Alain Resnais's *Providence*.[11] Happiest of all was the extraordinarily prolific Max Steiner, who in 1934 alone wrote music for thirty-seven RKO films. Steiner scored masterpieces such as *Casablanca*, one of the most seamless blendings of narrative and music in film history, and *The Treasure of Sierra Madre*, where the obsessiveness of the music exactly mirrors the story. Although not associated with Westerns, Steiner scored one of the best: Aside from a few obligatory "Indian music" sequences, his music for Ford's *The Searchers* has a tragic grandeur generated with remarkably simple materials; like the film itself, it is memorable and endlessly imitated.

Dimitri Tiomkin, a pianist turned movie composer, had the most authentic American pedigree of the group: before emigrating to America, he launched the European premiere of George Gershwin's Concerto in F. In *Shadow of a Doubt*, he helped Alfred Hitchcock, another permanent émigré, capture the ambiance of small-town America, establishing through his music a surface amiability and, at the same time, a sinister undercurrent that came to define a whole genre of American thriller concerned with outward normality and hidden terror; in Hitchcock's *Spellbound,* he developed the genre further, combining lyricism in the Ingrid Bergman–Gregory Peck love scenes with the kind of eerie, partially electronic special effects that later became the signature sound of *The Twilight Zone, One Step Beyond,* and countless quasi-supernatural pieces.

It was in the most quintessentially American form, the Western, that Tiomkin did his most characteristic work. In his collaborations with Frank Capra, his mentor in American popular culture, he learned to borrow American folk songs, spirituals, and cowboy tunes to create spacious, luminous scores such as *High Noon, Giant,* and *Rio Bravo.* In the Westerns particularly, Tiomkin's music is identifiably American, yet for him the New World grew so casually and organically from the Old that there was little gulf: when he accepted the Academy Award for *The High and the Mighty* in 1954, he thanked not his producers and agents but Tchaikovsky, Strauss, Brahms, and Beethoven.

American movies offered European composers a solution to the old dilemma of how an artist in a philistine culture puts food on the table. It also provided a new way of dealing with the rift between popular and elite culture. Golden age composers were eloquent on the subject. Franz Waxman, in particular, considered it "deplorable" that in America "the song writer goes one way and the serious composer goes another," whereas Haydn and Mozart sustained a "close contact" between the two.[12] Hollywood, of course, is rather philistine itself, but to anyone with an Old World perspective, this was nothing new. Composers, like other artists, have always had to contend with the vulgarity and mediocrity of benefactors. Purcell had to endure the Restoration stage, Mozart the Emperor Joseph, Beethoven a Viennese management that allowed the soloist premiering his Violin Concerto to hold the instrument upside down and perform his own showpieces between movements.

Not all émigrés were able to play the Hollywood game. The priests of high modernism had trouble from the beginning. Otto Friedrich recounts a legendary story in *City of Nets:* in 1935 the MGM producer Irving Thalberg offered a nearly broke Arnold Schoenberg twenty-five thousand dollars to score a film treatment of Pearl S. Buck's *The Good Earth.* When Schoenberg arrived in Thalberg's office (after getting lost in an MGM tour that he thought was part of the interview), he began the discussion by denouncing the vacuousness of American movies, then demanded complete control of all sound, including dialogue. When the astonished Thalberg asked what he meant by complete control, Schoenberg answered that he "would have to work with the actors," who would be required to declaim their lines on pitch in the manner of *Pierrot Lunaire*—an excerpt from which his disciple Sadka Vertiel, whom he had brought with him for the interview, proceeded to wail on the spot, as a demonstration. When the dumbfounded Thalberg replied that the director "wants to handle the actors himself," Schoenberg explained that the director could have the actors after they "had studied their lines with me." Assuming all this to be temporary dementia, Thalberg told his associates later that no one as broke as Schoenberg would decline an MGM commission. The next day, Schoenberg had his wife call Thalberg, restating the demand for complete control and doubling the fee to fifty thousand dollars. After Thalberg canceled the deal—the "Chinese technical advisor" suddenly came up with "some very lovely music"—Schoenberg expressed relief. Writing for Hollywood, he said, "would have been the end of me."[13]

Whether one views this incident as a fable about naiveté, arrogance, or integrity, Schoenberg's attitude is the diametric opposite of that of the Steiner-Rosza-Waxman school. Like Schoenberg, they came to America virtually without money, projects or contacts, but they managed to reinvent themselves and make a new life, viewing Hollywood as a new start in the New World rather than as the end. It was an opportunity they made the best of, usually without apologies. (Schoenberg's attitude toward Hollywood extended to other aspects of his life in America: his lectureship at UCLA, he said, was a waste of time comparable to Einstein's having to teach mathematics at a middle school.) Had he played his cards differently, Schoenberg might conceivably have scored films in specialized genres. His twelve-tone *Accompaniment to a Cinematographic Scene* was not actually used for a film, but when Lukas Foss and the Brooklyn Philharmonic resurrected it in the 1980s as an accompaniment for F. W. Murnau's *Nosferatu,* it proved the perfect music for that film's magnificent creepiness.

Schoenberg's Hollywood misadventure occurred the same year as the premiere of his *Suite in Olden Style for String Orchestra* in G major, his first work composed in the United States. That the Suite is a tonal piece, as were two others from his American period, the Chamber Symphony no. 2 and the Theme and Variations, raises fascinating psychological questions. Why, immediately after settling in Hollywood, did the master of twelve-tone music return to a system he had so decisively renounced? Did he, as his student Winfried Zillig claimed, have secret yearnings to be a tonal composer? Were these desires somehow released by his exile in America? As with his attitude toward movie music, Schoenberg was deeply ambivalent about tonality, as indicated by his tortuous, defensive preface to the *Suite*, in which he proclaimed he in no way meant to retreat from the direction of his previous work. Although his American neotonal pieces are less tightly wound than his European serial pieces, they are still dour, recondite, and tough-minded. They often begin in a deceptively straightforward manner, then become increasingly clotted and complex once the basic tonality has been established. Even the *Suite* has an underlying tension, as if Schoenberg could not quite allow himself the comfort of tonal resolution. A technical tonalist only, he could not go all the way. After the Theme and Variations, he was never tempted by tonality again, any more than by Hollywood.

Emigré attitudes about Hollywood were a function of the personality, status, and ideology of the composer, and therefore varied widely. The most scathingly negative take on Hollywood, American culture, and the whole idea of adjusting to the New World was articulated by Theodor Adorno, the provocative Darmstadt Marxist critic who in the 1970s and 1980s became the darling of deconstructionist and gender musicologists. (In a cleansing antidote, Otto Friedrich wrote in 1986 that Adorno and his Frankfurt School colleague Max Horkheimer "never accomplished anything very substantial," but "did their best to serve as an irritant even in southern California.")[14] Trotting out the centuries-old European fear of democracy as a malignant leveler of culture, Adorno dressed up this cliché with elaborate new rhetoric, railing against the capitalist "culture industry" and all its cancerous satellites, including jazz, Hollywood film music, and eventually rock—indeed, against virtually everything since Wagner that delivers pleasure rather than instructing us in our victimization as capitalist objects. Composers from Stravinsky to Weill were sellouts as far as Adorno was concerned. Hollywood music was particularly insidious because its artificially "warm" medium seduces us into forgetting we are being manipulated by a "cold" consumer machine. Not surprisingly, Adorno's hero was his mentor, Schoenberg, whose contempt for American culture rivaled his own.

One of the oddest cases in the Hollywood émigré saga was that of Stravinsky: on the one hand, he scorned Hollywood, walking out on Sam Goldwyn when told he would have to hire an "arranger" for his music, and calling Disney's treatment of *Le Sacre du printemps* in *Fantasia* "execrable"; yet he repeatedly tried to get back in Hollywood's graces, even agreeing to option *Renard* and *The Firebird* to the loathed Disney (who had paid Stravinsky a small fee for *Sacre* "accompanied by a gentle warning that if permission were withheld the music would be used anyway.")[15] Stravinsky's attempts at writing for the movies came to nothing, but some of the outtakes were fruitful, especially the tempestuous Symphony in Three Movements, with its traumatic 1940s atmosphere based on war films and its elegant slow movement based on the score for *Song of Bernadette.*

American intellectuals, who have trouble taking Hollywood music seriously to begin with, invented a clever mythology which says that Korngold and his colleagues hoodwinked Americans into thinking Hollywood music was an American form when in fact it is really fin-de-siècle European music in disguise; there is nothing American about Hollywood music, despite what naive Americans think. In Leon Botstein's words, "the irony was that America embraced Korngold, whose movie music helped to shape and transform what most Americans today would regard as quite American clichés of music for the movies."[16]

But perhaps the irony is too easy. Surely the perceptions of most Americans cannot be so summarily dismissed, especially those of movie fans, who tend to be preoccupied with details of genre history and who know perfectly well that golden age music was written largely by Europeans. Furthermore, who is to say that the Southernized Steiner idiom of *Gone With the Wind,* the pop style of Steiner's theme from *A Summer Place,* the jazz-piano riffs in Korngold's *Between Two Worlds,* the small-town ambiance of Tiomkin's *Shadow of a Doubt,* or the open-prairie sonorities in Tiomkin's Weosterns are not American just because they were composed by émigrés whose harmonic vocabulary was learned in Europe?

It is what artists do with influences and traditions that matters. This music is as American as Nabokov's *Lolita,* a work that captures American culture with a European's shrewdness and a keen appreciation for America's love of nostalgia, or Ang Lee's *The Ice Storm*, a film that depicts American suburbia with a foreigner's cool objectivity. A particularly voluptuous example is Steiner's *Casablanca*, where story, theme, and music become one. The "Marseillaise" appears with heroic emphasis — indeed, the dueling anthems scene is one of the most stirring musical sequences in the movies — but it is the music in Rick's Café Américain, a thoroughly American enterprise, that establishes the idiom and values of the film. America is the place the trapped inhabitants of Casablanca long to be, and Sam, Rick's piano player, takes them there, playing the American showbiz riffs that, especially when developed in Steiner's haunting score, establish the bittersweet mood and strange timelessness of the film. ("As Time Goes By," the most famous tune, was written by Herman Hupfeld for a forgotten Broadway review from 1931 called *Everybody's Welcome*.) Steiner may be as foreign as the film's setting, but as someone who made it to America, he understood the desperate nostalgia of "As Time Goes By" as only an exile can.

These composers created a new Hollywood romanticism. Some, like Tiomkin and Steiner, were influenced by American folk and pop culture; others, like Korngold, were directly moved by the medium itself, by the images that erupted on the screen as they created themes for them. The tautly constructed, deliberately simple melodies, fanfares, and occasional jazz cadences of Korngold's movie music do not really sound like Wagner or Strauss, as critics claim. Nor do they sound like early Korngold scores, famous for their funhouse of chromaticisms and suspensions. The story of the Hollywood émigrés is another case of Europeans being influenced by an American idiom and creating a new art.

Broadway offered a different set of problems and satisfactions to New World émigrés. Unlike Hollywood, its tradition demanded *overt* Americanness, both in sound and sensibility, Herbert, Gershwin, Porter, and other composers having already established a national tradition and a set of expectations. Britten and Weill, who enjoyed projecting more than one persona, saw this as an opportunity rather than a hindrance. Both artists were influenced by American culture, both gave something significant back to it, and both were moved by egalitarian ideals, often more passionately than their American colleagues.

Weill, the consummate European-American, began in the cabaret-

Dooley Wilson (seated at the piano) and Humphrey Bogart in *Casablanca*, where everyone was an exile, including the composer, Max Steiner.

cum-concert hall of Berlin, where he redefined the relationship between
popular and serious art (see Chap. 7); in New York, he adroitly switched
to "Broadway opera" and again challenged traditional categories and
hierarchies. His American odyssey started in Hollywood.[17] In 1937, Weill
teamed up with Fritz Lang, who was remaking himself as an American
director the way Weill wanted to as a composer; when their project
fizzled—as most movie ideas do, Weill soon discovered—he tried Wilhelm Dieterle, who asked Weill to write music for an anti-Nazi film
about the Spanish Civil War. Ultimately, Weill's score was rejected as
being too sophisticated, as were the Broadway musicals he later at-

tempted to translate to the screen, including *One Touch of Venus, Lady in the Dark*, and *Knickerbocker Holiday*, all of which were drastically cut. Only in *Where Do We Go from Here?*, an anti-Nazi propaganda collaboration with Ira Gershwin, did he see his music and dramatic vision survive intact. By then a Broadway success, Weill did not need Hollywood, which had become a means of securing an extra income. His judgment on the entire Hollywood enterprise, typically trenchant, came as early as 1938: "They hate any kind of enthusiasm here. It is the craziest place in the world, and I have never seen so many worried and unhappy people together."[18]

Broadway proved a far more congenial place, the continuation of a fascination with American culture stretching back to the beginning of Weill's rejection of Schoenbergian modernism and his embrace of popular songs from smoke-filled bars and street parades. His Broadway works are the culmination of an aesthetic fusion of highbrow and popular entertainment, much like that of Gershwin in *Porgy and Bess*. Weill's jazz-infused operettas such as *Mahagonny, The Seven Deadly Sins*, and *Happy End* bring to life fantastical American scenarios and genres, replete with cowboys, Chicago hoodlums, and Salvation Army colonels. They are European pieces with an American overlay, whereas the Broadway musicals are American with European sophistication. These are inversions and variations, not fundamentally different Weills. Indeed, the great achievement of Weill's European period—a new simplicity and emotional focus, from an artist nurtured in modernist complexity— is precisely the achievement of the Broadway Weill. It only sounds different because the Broadway musical demands a species of catchy tune different from cabaret.

Weill's notoriously turbulent identity as an artist was stabilized largely by his lifelong entrenchment with American culture. Like Oscar Wilde, another European who was fascinated by America, he reveled in multiple personae and artistic postures. When scholars argue over which was the more genuine of the "two Weills," they miss the point: multiplicity was Weill's identity. Like Whitman and Twain, two of his literary inspirations, he was deeply committed to the American ideal of egalitarian uprootedness and multiplicity.

Indeed, a claustrophobic aversion to a single identity, especially one superimposed by an outside tradition or authority, is projected in the themes and structures of the works themselves. Weill's "lady in the

dark" seeks psychotherapy because society will not allow her more than
one identity as a woman. Even the show itself resists traditional cate-
gorization: this multihybrid work, a Broadway musical-play about American psychiatry, with a preface written by the librettist's psychiatrist, had
its genesis in Moss Hart's psychotherapy, through which he overcame
suicidal depressions. The piece itself, quite literally a therapeutic work,
became the climax of Hart's cure and the resolution of Weill's challenge
to become a successful American artist. This odd, exhilarating combination of European opera and American musical theater was an unexpected popular hit, boasting 467 performances in 1941 and making a
triumphant American tour that finally gave Weill financial independence.[19]

Another clue to Weill's loose, complex notion of identity occurs
in the finale of *Street Scene:* Rose, whose mother has just been murdered
by her father, rebuffs her suitor's passionate claim that they "belong to
each other":

> Look at my father, my poor mother:
> if she had belonged to herself
> if he had belonged to himself,
> it never would have happened.

Weill himself refused to "belong" to any one culture or genre; like Rose,
the survivor in his greatest Broadway work, he cultivated a sense of inner
belonging, a free sensibility that allowed him to be whatever he wanted:
one season an avant-garde modernist, another a cabaret entertainer, another a celebrant of the magic of American railroads (the delightful and
utterly unclassifiable *Railroads on Parade*), another a Broadway show
composer. Like Rose, Weill strove to belong only to himself. Had he
not died at age fifty, he would surely have reinvented himself again. Far
from being a might-have-been, Weill was so many things that the only
question was, What next?

Weill's unwavering commitment to Broadway must be understood
against the backdrop of his long-held fascination with American culture
and his belief in bridging the gulf between elite and popular art, an
enterprise that had already begun with the relatively accessible innovations in *Mahagonny* and *Threepenny Opera*, both runaway sensations
that juxtapose acrid modern material with light musical forms such as
tangos and fox-trots. Weill steadfastly insisted that his American period

was a logical continuation of his earlier career, not something out of nowhere, and certainly not a new Kurt Weill. He never "acknowledged the difference between 'serious' music and 'light' music" but "only good music and bad music."[20] Critics focus on the first part of this often-quoted statement as evidence that Weill abandoned the whole idea of aesthetic criteria, but the second makes clear that good and bad were still the measuring sticks.

Like his Hollywood colleagues, Weill was determined to find a solution to the age-old dilemma of how to reconcile art with commerce, the need to remain true to one's vision while making a living. What Korngold found in Hollywood, Weill found on Broadway, a medium for an art both popular and serious, commercially viable and true to the composer's collaborative talents. Both composers advanced their respective mediums in addition to taking from them. Korngold helped define the Hollywood soundtrack; and beginning with *Knickerbocker Holiday*, Weill contributed substantially to the revitalization of the Broadway musical, following in the footsteps of Victor Herbert, who inaugurated the American operetta on which the Broadway musical was based.

Despite the contentions of critics, there is no evidence that Weill relaxed his exacting artistic standards once he came to America. He was as perfectionist and meticulous as ever, to the point of overseeing the musical quality of a show through its entire run. From the bittersweet lyricism of "It Never Was You" in *Knickerbocker Holiday* through the ironic insouciance of "I'm a Stranger Here Myself" in *One Touch of Venus* to the tragic intensity of "I Never Could Believe" in *Street Scene*, Weill's professionalism was as high in New York as in Berlin. One can, of course, argue that the Broadway musical is inherently inferior to its Berlin equivalent, but that is another issue, one Weill's critics rarely engage openly, although a distinct snobbery is implicit in many of their attacks. This prejudice by intellectuals against Weill's Broadway musicals parallels the hostility toward all of Weill by resentful avant-gardists and die-hard serialists.

Conventional critical wisdom holds that Weill's Broadway shows are inferior to his earlier European productions because, unlike them, they are nonironic: what made *Mahagonny* and its offspring art was their ironic, and therefore artful, treatments of light music. With the irony removed, as in the Broadway shows, the music becomes merely light. Weill viewed both irony and his sources very differently. He never condescended to jazz, maintaining a keen appreciation of its sophistication and ironic sting. And like Britten, Tippett, and other Europeans in America, he held the Broadway show tune, especially as practiced by Gershwin and Porter, in a similarly high regard. Anyone open to the possibilities of the Broadway musical knows that it, too, in its higher manifestations, can carry an ironic charge. The notion that only classical music can be ironic and smart—and that the ironic is automatically and always superior to the straightforward—is precisely the kind of self-marginalizing provincialism that Weill was determined to transcend.

The continuing dismissal of the Broadway Weill by contemporary academics is premised on a contempt for the genre, an assumption that it can become art only by being improved by some sort of ironic distortion. To Weill and Britten, the wit and ingenuity of American show music allowed it to be constantly reinvented in forms both bitterly ironic and passionately straight, mournful and exuberant, simple and complex. It was the same attitude Dvořák had toward spirituals and their emotional range. To Europeans sojourning in the New World, the line between art and entertainment was blurry and mysterious. It existed but was hard to pin down and was often ignored, like a pesky nuisance: Britten's cabaret songs are really cabaret; Weill's Broadway tunes in *Lady in the Dark* are really show tunes, just as the dances in Mozart's German Dances are really dances. They embrace their genres even as they transcend them.

In Berlin, Weill had taken European marches and chorales and given them an American spin. On Broadway, he again enriched what he found there, adhering to the basic format while enlarging its musical resonance. In giving the Broadway musical a new edge and sophistication, he inverted the achievement of his colleague Hindemith, who embellished European forms with American tropes, as in his *Lilacs* Requiem. Weill immediately began speaking in the voice of American idioms such as the Broadway musical, just as he began speaking English practically the day he got off the boat in 1935. Not surprisingly, this voice retained the overtones—the harmonic subtleties and formal perfection—of his German heritage. The creative interaction between the two traditions was always what engaged him. As for the widespread claim that there is no development in the Broadway scores, a criticism that goes against the evidence of ears and common sense, it can just as easily be argued that there is more development from *Knickerbocker*

Holiday to *Street Scene* than from *Mahagonny* to the later Berlin works, the smoky seductiveness of which frequently sounds the same.

Like Dvořák, Delius, and Coleridge-Taylor, Weill was profoundly influenced by American literature, past and present. In addition to Whitman, Frost, and Twain, who provided texts and inspiration for Weill's earliest and latest projects during his life in America, a number of prominent contemporary writers contributed to his art, including Maxwell Anderson (*Knickerbocker Holiday*), S. J. Perelman and Ogden Nash (*One Touch of Venus*), Moss Hart (*Lady in the Dark*), Langston Hughes and Elmer Rice (*Street Scene*), and Archibald MacLeish ("Song of the Free"). These writers shared Weill's commitment to reaching a large public: "I never could see any reason why the 'educated', not to say 'serious' composer should not be able to reach all available markets with his music," he said, and for a brief, glorious period, the culture appeared to agree.[21] The Roosevelt era was a uniquely Whitmanian, unsnobbish period in America, eloquently symbolized by Helen Hayes's spoken performance of Whitman's "Beat! Beat! Drums!" set to Weill's music as part of America's World War II mobilization, a moment when patriotism, art, and commerce came together in a rare egalitarian synthesis.

During Weill's American period, the most profound and fruitful contemporary literary influences came from Elmer Rice and Langston Hughes, a collaboration that resulted in *Street Scene*, Weill's American masterpiece and a landmark in the history of modern musical drama. The story of this Broadway opera again illustrates that Weill was touched by American culture long before he settled in the States. As early as 1930 he had seen a Berlin production of Rice's *Street Scene*—a revolutionary piece of realism depicting a single day in the lives of families struggling to survive in a New York tenement—and was so haunted by it that he began asking Rice about adapting it six years later during a rehearsal for *Johnny Johnson*. The gritty hyperrealism of Rice's play appealed to Weill's values; in the tradition of Emerson and Whitman, he envisioned a musical theater in which the ordinary person, not royalty and the aristocracy, would be the center of the action. But *Street Scene* goes a step further: the heroine—the enunciator of the play's values as well as the victim of the central tragedy—is an ordinary woman, a housewife struggling against spousal abuse and a lower-middle-class financial deprivation more subtle than outright poverty. Weill felt the play had immediate social relevance—as indeed, it still does today.

Left to right: Kurt Weill, Elmer Rice, and Langston Hughes, creators of *Street Scene*, which fulfilled Weill's dream of Broadway opera. (Weill-Lenya Research Center, Kurt Weill Foundation for Music, New York)

Weill's Broadway opera fulfilled Dvořák's vision of an American music drama. "Opera should be part of the living theatre of our time," Weill insisted, adding that "Broadway is today one of the great theater centers of the world. It has all the technical and intellectual equipment for a serious musical theatre."[22] Broadway served the technical equipment admirably; as for the intellectual, that was provided by Langston Hughes, who wrote the lyrics for *Street Scene*. This was more than just an aesthetic collaboration; Hughes, a committed activist as well as poet, wanted Weill to understand the subject of *Street Scene* — the street life of America — in a direct way, and Weill was more than willing. Shortly after Weill began work on the piece, Hughes took Lotte Lenya and him on a tour of New York tenement neighborhoods, black and white, giving Weill a firsthand glimpse of poor and working-class Americans he had only imagined from reading Rice's play. Here again was a European fulfilling Emerson's call for American art based on direct experience of ordinary life. The heartrending intensity of Weill's music was therefore inspired by two American writers and a brief saturation in the drama of New York streets. Weill discovered that *Street Scene* "lent itself to a great variety of music just as the streets of New York themselves embrace the music of many lands and many people. I had an opportunity to use different forms of musical expressions. From popular songs to operatic ensembles, music of passion and death—and, overall, the music of a hot summer evening in New York."[23] From the music of passion and death in the murder scene and its eerie aftermath to popular songs such as "Hail to the School" and the irrepressibly American "Ice Cream Sextet," *Street Scene* offers dazzling variety served up with an outsider's sense of discovery.

Much of the power in this Broadway opera must be credited to Hughes's lyrics, which interact with Weill's music in a bittersweet chemistry. The exuberance of Weill's rumbas and tangos combines with the loneliness of Hughes's vision of a collapsing American Dream. Anna Maurant's "Somehow, I Never Could Believe," the tragic center of the opera, soars on the wings of a characteristic Weill melody, one that is shapely, easy to recall, and spiced with harmonic subtlety. Hughes's lyrics explore the melancholy plight of the American housewife:

> I don't know—looks like something awful happens
> in the kitchen where women wash their dishes.
> Days turn to months, months turn to years
> the greasy soap suds drown out wishes.

In this aria, the blues number, "Lonely House," and the choral ensemble "I Loved Her Too," in which Anna's husband confronts the horror of his crime, Hughes gives the work a tragic grandeur that confers poetry on Rice's stark realism. In this new kind of American opera, the greasy soapsuds that wash away Anna's dreams become startlingly real as well as metaphoric. The requisite Broadway sentimentality is there, to be sure, but darkened by Weill's collapsing chromaticism and harsh ostinatos. The substitution of spoken dialogue for recitative makes the work feel as much like tragedy as opera.

Hughes was a master of African-American polemic, but here his blackness becomes a mode of empathy for all people beaten down by drudgery. The free-spirited relationship between Hughes, Rice, and Weill was a model of the democratic moment in mid-century America that Weill embodied and nourished. "It didn't seem strange or unusual to either Kurt Weill or Elmer Rice," wrote Hughes, "that I, a black American, should write the lyrics for *Street Scene*. Both of them wanted a lyricist who understood the problems of small people. Blacks certainly do. . . . By writing a 'Broadway opera' like *Street Scene* in a national idiom that could be understood by the American people, Weill reached this American people and stirred it to compassion, concern, and self-awareness."[24]

More than anything, Weill longed to be accepted as an American artist serving a broad American culture, and statements like this from artists of Hughes's stature must have partially sweetened the sour denunciations he sustained from critics who felt he had betrayed his Berlin legacy. With considerable justification, Weill maintained that far from being a bland comedown from his Brecht days, *Street Scene* was the climax of his efforts to develop populist opera. To him, it was "the fulfillment of an old dream, the dream of serious, dramatic musical for the Broadway stage."[25] Despite fashionably cynical claims of a Weill sellout, *Street Scene* fulfilled the promise of popular opera pioneered in theory by Dvořák and in actuality by Gershwin, anticipating in turn the urban grittiness and street slang of Bernstein's *West Side Story*.

A poignant hint of how Weill's Broadway dream might have continued to unfold is found in the five numbers of the *Huckleberry Finn* show he was working on with Maxwell Anderson between January and April 1950, just prior to his death. The valedictory quality cited by David Drew and others in "River Chanty," the most haunting of these songs, comes through not only in echoes from earlier works but in the meandering flow of melody depicting the "whispering Mississippi," the godlike force that brings and takes away life, gradually pulling the piece into ambiguous infinity. Weill's love of American literature is summarized by the singer repeatedly chanting "Mark Twain," like a mantra. Twain's greatest creation obviously had a special meaning for Weill: like Huck, Weill was a survivor; he was also a perpetual exile, partly because of history and partly out of choice. Even in Berlin he estranged himself from the high-modernist establishment. His own journey down the river was hazardous and unpredictable, but like Huck, he preferred to be on the raft rather than be defined by society or fashion.

Another important Broadway opera from the Weill period was Benjamin Britten's *Paul Bunyan*. The young Britten launched this brilliant hybrid just before meeting Weill in Connecticut in 1940, while Weill was working on a (never-completed) Broadway opera based on another American frontier hero, Davy Crockett. The idea for *Paul Bunyan* came from the visionary publisher Hans W. Heinsheimer, who had a feel for American culture and had helped Weill forge his Berlin conceptions of America. In *Paul Bunyan*, a European again treated an American myth from an outsider's perspective, creating something fresh and constantly surprising. Originally conceived as a "choral operetta," it was one of several remarkable collaborations between Britten and Auden. Both had come to the New World as young men; Auden's stay turned out to be permanent, whereas Britten's was a fruitful sojourn that engendered some of his most vibrant early work, including *Bunyan*, the saucy blues and cabaret pieces that grew out of it, the wrenching war piece *Sinfonia da Requiem*, and the charming *Diversions for Left Hand and Orchestra*. Like Weill, Britten regarded music as communication; his goal was to reach an audience, and he had little patience with an increasingly academic avant-garde. Unlike Weill, he did not pass through a high-modern phase. He had populist aspirations from the beginning, which fit comfortably with the New Deal communitarianism he found when he came to America in the 1930s.

Paul Bunyan was a pure manifestation of that philosophy, a work conceived for the collective forces of a semi-amateur chorus and orchestra. As early as 1939, Britten wrote his English publisher, "Auden and I are set now to write a school operetta. . . . This has the extra stimulus of a possible Broadway performance by the well-known Broadway Caravan. . . . The probable subject is that of Paul Bunyan, the American frontier hero, who has, believe me, the most extraordinary adventures." To Hermann Scherchen's son, Britten wrote that the new Auden collaboration "is full of nice tunes and blues and things."[26]

Paul Bunyan never made it to Broadway; indeed, it disappeared for thirty years after its unsuccessful 1941 premiere at Columbia University's Brander Matthews Hall, a prestigious but hardly glamorous venue. Britten undertook a revision in 1974, near the end of his life adding such gorgeously atmospheric touches as the Prelude and the nocturnal frog croakings during Bunyan's lullaby—evidence of an Old World master revisiting the New World of his youth. According to Donald Mitchell, during a tape of the 1976 radio broadcast Britten was moved to tears "by the operetta he had created with his old friend all those years ago on Long Island"; he "simply hadn't remembered that it was such a strong piece."[27]

Even after 1974, the opera took years to get into the culture. (The obituary on Britten in the *New York Times* merely noted that the work was "poorly received and was subsequently not listed by the composer among his published works.")[28] In the early 1970s, serialism was exercising its final stranglehold on musical culture, and Britten's stock was still down. The piece languished until the mid-1990s, when finally, like so much New World music by Old World artists, it established itself as a prophetic masterpiece. As Donald Mitchell noted in 1988, the cowboy songs in *Paul Bunyan* anticipate *Oklahoma!* and its progeny; we might add that the type of blues number Britten hit upon — somewhere between parody and straight blues — became a Broadway staple.

The collapse of a Broadway production, the dream of Britten and Auden, was a great disappointment, but in the long run perhaps better for the piece. Their intention to write a Broadway opera determined the work's structure, generosity of tunes, and nonoperatic informality; the failure of the piece to actually make it to Broadway, where it might have been tamed by production demands, kept its bizarre originality intact. *Street Scene* feels like a Broadway production, albeit on an operatic level; *Paul Bunyan* feels genuinely unclassifiable, suitable for a Broadway of the imagination. No wonder initial reviewers were puzzled by the show; the juxtaposition of serious philosophical reflection with irreverent hillbilly tunes, a common procedure in the postmodern era, did not fit the norm of either opera or Broadway.

The political philosophy of the work was prophetic and complex. The ambiguous heroism of Bunyan — the American pioneer who clears a continent for civilization while submitting the environment to "irrational destruction" — defines environmental and philosophical debates that have engulfed the culture ever since. Although they were committed progressives, Britten and Auden avoided facile leftism, projecting a cautiously exuberant vision of America. Bunyan's achievement is heroic and necessary for an adult "life of choice," despite the new commercialism and "excess of military qualities" it brings with it. What is affirmed in the final scene is neither the ravages of capitalism denounced by the Left nor the "progress" in land development championed by the

Right, but an endless cycle of creation and destruction where anything is possible because nothing is permanent: "Every day," Auden's extraordinary libretto tells us, "America's destroyed and recreated."

Ultimately, *Paul Bunyan* is about choice, about the New World as a land where, despite cultural banalities and economic injustices, choices are possible, where the constant freedom to choose and create compensates for the terror of having so few traditions and so little history. The spirit of Bunyan lives irresistibly on, always impelled by the call of "other deserts" and "other forests" to conquer. Bunyan's "aggressive will," a more "complex spirit" than political clichés suggest, is in itself neither benign nor evil. Postindustrial America "is what you choose to make it." "As the frontier closes," Paul says at the end, "the life of choice begins."

This is an opera about America as a place where commercialism can suddenly, mysteriously become art. The celebratory Christmas party in the finale summarizes the ambiguous lure of show business. A telegram from Hollywood announces that the conquering of the wilderness has become an idea for an "all-star lumber picture" requiring the technical expertise of Johnny Inkslinger, Bunyan's bookkeeper, the intellectual of the crew. Having conquered the wilderness, Johnny gets the ultimate "lucky break." The American Dream of discovery and conquest has gone the next step in the postindustrial world, toward the Hollywood Dream of instant money. The "culture industry" denounced by Adorno and other European intellectuals chugs along after all the others are spent, endlessly crass yet full of possibility. For those who choose to come aboard, new creative avenues are constantly erected and collapsed, "destroyed and recreated." Tacky as it often is, show business allows artists and intellectuals to "get sufficient to eat," as Johnny puts it in the opera's longest song. It can even be an occasion for art.

America, Bunyan says, is a land where "the Actual and the Possible are mysteriously exchanged." It is a show business world that for all its vulgarity yields one of life's most mysterious surprises, the "accidental beauties of silly songs."

CHAPTER SEVEN

New World Rhythm
The Spread of Jazz

You Americans take jazz too lightly.
— Maurice Ravel

I don't even like [jazz] and I certainly don't want to hear about its influence on
contemporary music. It amuses me while I listen to records of it while taking my
bath, but it is frankly distasteful to me in the concert hall.
— Francis Poulenc

I N 1995, Bill Clinton, America's sax-playing president, declared that jazz was "America's classical music." Whatever consternation this remark caused among America's "real" classical composers, as well as those invested in the myth of jazz as eternally avant-garde, it was an idea taken for granted by European composers for nearly a century. Europeans ignorant of or indifferent to America's "serious" composers were entranced from the beginning by jazzmen from Jelly Roll Morton to Duke Ellington, whom they indeed regarded as America's classical composers. As Carol Oja has noted, "Any gangplank interview with European luminaries visiting the United States during the 1920s, whether with Stravinsky, or Ravel, revealed, sometimes painfully, that American jazz, not concert music, was what impressed them."[1] One of the first things Paul Hindemith did in America was to hear Ellington, about whom he wrote enthusiastically to his wife; one of the keenest pleasures for Rachmaninoff when he came to New York was to head uptown to Harlem to hear Fats Waller.

Instrumental ensembles like the instantly legendary Paul Whiteman Band and vocal groups such as the Blackbirds gave jazz-hungry

Europeans a tangible source of inspiration, much as the Fisk Jubilee Singers had a generation earlier; this was America's canonical music, and Europeans didn't particularly care whether it was "real" jazz, no matter how often music critics proclaimed in a superior tone that it was not.

Indeed, some of the most life-changing forms were jazz-related spin-offs such as swing. The British novelist Paul West credits his decision to move to the United States to his youthful obsession with swing, which as a boy in England he regarded as even more sexually charged and enticing than jazz. West writes in a 1996 memoir that his greatest escape growing up in the 1940s during the blitz was swing that he picked up on BBC radio. This music filled him with lurid fantasies—"chortling saxes of sundry registers, drummers insane with drugs, crooners almost overcome with erotic or climactic excess"—beckoning him irresistibly "to the source of bliss, to the country that spawned such magic . . . where life writ itself large and swing filled the streets. Has a would-be immigrant ever felt so aesthetic a pull?"[2]

The answer among musicians, from Milhaud to Foss, is a resounding yes. As West's voluptuous paean indicates, it was initially the notorious sexual energy, the rejection of tradition and formality, that gave jazz, swing, blues, and related genres their subversive cachet—though mainly in the view of white admirers. Constant Lambert impishly claimed that "while all the Europeans flung aside their carefully won training to indulge in an orgy of pseudo-Charlestons, the negro himself was moved to tears, not by his own work but by the classic elegance of *Lac des Cygnes*."[3] But the more European composers imbibed jazz, the more they realized it bequeathed not so much a new primitivism as a new sophistication—a new rhythmic and emotional complexity that went far beyond stereotypical American funkiness. Ultimately, as Kurt Weill, Michael Tippett, and many other composers discovered, it delivered a self-abandon and transcendence, a temporary but powerful release from chronic anxiety in a war-ravaged century.

The power of jazz among Europeans is dramatically illustrated by the libretto of Ernst Krenek's 1925 *Jonny spielt auf*, the first "jazz opera": Jonny, a black jazz musician visiting Europe, makes away with a concert violinist's instrument, which he transforms into a fiddle in his jazz band, seducing the townsfolk into a wild street dance celebrating the triumph of the New World over the Old. The intoxication of jazz, the "new

Josephine Baker at the Folies Bergère, 1920s. American dance music provided a powerful release from anxiety in a troubled Europe. (Beinecke Rare Book and Manuscript Library, Yale University)

unknown world of freedom," conquers all. "The idea of this cosmic music maker had been with me as far back as I can remember," the composer said, calling his jazz hero a "Pied Piper who strikes up the note of the times for mankind."[4]

Krenek was one of the first to articulate the idea of jazz as an emblem not only of the New World but of contemporary reality itself— as not just the music of black America but as the "note of the times." To make sure his audience got the point, Krenek resorted to the ultimate deus ex machina, having his classical violinist run over by a train. While early twentieth-century Americanists worried about Europe's influence on American musical identity, Europeans were clear that America had already triumphed.

Jazz-inspired European composers experienced distinctive, highly personal jazz epiphanies consistent with their musical vision: for Delius, who started it all, the revelation occurred in the Florida swamp, utterly removed from society; for the more gregarious Ravel and Milhaud, it happened in Harlem; for Krenek, at a Duke Ellington New Year's Eve concert in Frankfurt; for Michael Tippett, the moment was a "sudden realization" from a radio broadcast; for Stravinsky, it was the page of a jazz score brought to Switzerland by Ernest Ansermet. Jazz was like a conversion experience right out of the gospel songs from which much jazz derives. Indeed, the big moment for Tippett was the gospel line "the trumpet sounds from within-a my soul."[5] Some of the least likely candidates experienced the conversion surprisingly early: when Weill, long before his own jazz epiphany, went to a Hindemith concert, he discovered that his older colleague had already "danced too far into the land of fox-trot."[6]

As enraptured outsiders, Old World artists dabbled in New World sounds with a unique audaciousness and a certain innocence — and in the case of composers such as Schulhoff and Stravinsky, a benign ignorance of jazz clichés. Beginning with Debussy and Ravel, the French were especially hot for ragtime and jazz, which they considered a natural language. The original proprietors of New Orleans, the French always had a penchant for hot rhythms and cool sensuality. Like the French hipsters in Jack Kerouac's *On the Road*, they liked to talk "in jazz American." By the 1920s, the Russians, English, Dutch, Germans, and East Europeans were speaking jazz American, too.

There were, of course, powerful tastemakers who regarded the incursion of jazz into high culture with horror. Among composers and writers, the antijazz crowd included everyone from Adorno, Mencken, Henry Miller, and Paul Rosenfeld to Poulenc and Messiaen. To them, the new jazz grammar, whether true jazz or Gershwin crossover, was a potentially fatal blow to taste and decorum — or simply a bore. Some of the most eloquent antijazz polemicists were Americanists, who were terrified that jazz would come to define American music. "American music is not jazz. Jazz is not music," insisted Paul Rosenfeld. Long before jazz culture became notoriously associated with the drug use of its participants, Rosenfeld linked jazz to drugs metaphorically: exploiting "an extraordinarily drug-like use of the materials of sound," jazz was a "cynical" form. Pretending to be avant-garde, it perpetrated endless "duplication, conformation to pre-established pattern"; despite its noisiness and "superficial irregularity," it was conservative and "inert . . . the folly of the living dead."[7] The funniest antijazz American was H. L.

Mencken, for whom jazz was not the voluptuous occasion of sin denounced from fundamentalist pulpits but the opposite: "Jazz, in point of fact, is not voluptuous at all. Its monotonous rhythms and puerile tunes make it a sedative rather than a stimulant. . . . There are plenty of Methodist hymns that are ten times as aphrodisiacal, and the fact is proved by the scandals that follow every camp meeting."[8]

So shrill were these denunciations that they became a colorful alternate ideology, a kind of antijazz reminiscent of anti-Wagnerism a half-century earlier. But like its predecessor, this powerful reaction—as rhetorically brilliant as anti-Wagnerism and often wittier—only demonstrated the potency of its nemesis. Jazz, like Wagnerism, ultimately triumphed in a way that surpassed the worst fears of its enemies, becoming not only America's classical music but arguably the most potent musical force in the Western world. If there was a strong racist element in the war against jazz, as there was in the hostile reception to black hymns in Dvořák's music, it was clear the racists—in art if not in life—had lost again.

Intellectuals hostile to jazz were especially concerned about its deleterious effect on concert music, and Rosenfeld & Co. reserved some of their harshest dismissals for Gershwin. But they were not the only ones skeptical about jazz uniting with art music. Not surprisingly, much of the jazz community was wary of jazz-classical fusions. Because many regard improvisation as the essence of jazz, "symphonic jazz" seems an oxymoron, and the term eventually fell into such disrepute that more fashionable labels such as "Third Steam" became mid-century substitutes.

But the gap between art music and jazz is not as insurmountable as it appears. Indeed, composers from Ravel to Steve Martland have behaved as if it did not exist at all. The truth is that classical composers such as Bach, Mozart, and Paganini were obsessive improvisers who left numerous details of rhythm, harmony, and even melody to the performer; recent jazz-tinged scores by John Cage, Malcolm Arnold, Meyer Kupferman, Richard Rodney Bennett, and other modern composers leave space for improvisation as well. Conversely, jazz composers such as Joplin, Ellington, and Armstrong wrote meticulously detailed scores.

Some of the first African-American music from which jazz is derived was scored in concert form by the New Orleans Creole composer

Louis Moreau Gottschalk, a revolutionary artist who to this day remains an outsider in the culture he helped create. In the 1840s, long before anyone had conceived of jazz, Gottschalk was jotting down slave drummings and dances he heard as a boy in Congo Square, where the French allowed, indeed encouraged, slaves to practice their music. As a virtuoso pianist, Gottschalk traveled to Latin and South America, where he absorbed *tresillo* and other Caribbean rhythms; when mixed with the African syncopations recalled from his childhood and banged out on European timpani and Afro-Cuban drums, these Gottschalk experiments became an important basis of the mélange later called New Orleans jazz. With his daring exploration of the African *cinquillo* and other syncopated rhythms, Gottschalk forged a synthesis of African and island sounds that eventually caused music around the world to swing.

To Europeans, Gottschalk was the inaugurator of an intoxicating New World sensibility. A spectacular pianist, Gottschalk performed in the capitals of Europe, creating a sensation with Berlioz, Chopin, Bizet, and their literary counterparts. When Gottschalk played his "Le Bananier," "Bamboula," "Pasquinade" (an astonishing forecast of ragtime), "La Savane," and other proto-jazz dances in Paris, he hypnotized everyone who heard him, and the impression he made was by no means ephemeral. Bizet was so entranced with "Le Bananier" that he performed it throughout his life; Offenbach created a version for cello and piano, the most notable of many European transcriptions. In Russia, where the piece also achieved instant cult status, Aleksandr Borodin wrote out a copy by hand; in Italy, Filippo Filippi, the prominent music critic, covered the 1872 premiere of Verdi's *Aïda* by comparing it to the music of Gottschalk.[9]

Gottschalk made Europeans realize that a multicultural, distinctly American sound did exist, one rude yet sophisticated. The reactions of literary figures who heard Gottschalk were particularly revealing, establishing a pattern that has characterized Old World feelings about New World music to the present day. These writers usually began with paeans to Gottschalk's technical brilliance, but they were more deeply impressed by his primitive power as magus and mesmerizer, as an initiator into New World mysteries. Théophile Gautier wrote that Gottschalk's "songs of the New World have an originality that is full of melancholy, energy, and suaveness and which carry you deep into fantasy and dreams." Victor Hugo called Gottschalk "a thinker who nourishes sweet dreams, a poet . . . who can enrapture." Berlioz, as always the most astute critic of his era, discovered an odd and compelling duplicity in Gottschalk peculiar to the New World: here was an artist of "sovereign powers," of "perfect grace" and sophistication, who "knows precisely how far a fantasy can be carried." Yet he also embodied a "childish naiveté," a "charming simplicity" that seemed to "emanate from a second personality."[10]

The quintessential image of the New World as envisioned by the Old, Gottschalk personified something far more intricate than the Noble Savage. In Berlioz's analysis, he was a supremely sophisticated showman, someone who knew how to work a crowd but was nonetheless childlike and simple; the latter quality was not so much put on—although calculation and "deftness" were fundamental—as a manifestation of a "second personality," a mysterious alter ego. New World "spontaneity" and sincerity, the great draw for Europeans, were therefore in tension with an equally authentic, equally American genius for commerce and calculation. Gottschalk's vision of America was an exotic "fantasy" presented by an artist who knew "precisely how far a fantasy can be carried," but it was real because Gottschalk and his music made it live. This American doubleness, the cool and sophisticated mixed with the primitive and the childlike, was fascinating to Europeans because it was enmeshed in their own identity. In some sense, Gottschalk was their alter ego, the secret sharer who sailed to the New World and assumed a mysterious new identity, one rooted in European worldliness but wilder and freer. For Gottschalk was French as well as American, suave as well as brash. The duality he so colorfully represents characterizes a great deal of American art, from Melville and Hawthorne to Michael White and Art Neville.

As a propagandist for the New World in the Old, Gottschalk was lucky in both his lineage and occupation. A Creole who happened to be a great pianist, he was not only the inaugurator of New World music in the nineteenth century but its executant and physical embodiment. Personifying what he composed and performed, he brought to Europe what Dvořák and Delius later crossed the Atlantic to absorb. His ethnic credentials were perfect: as a New Orleans Creole, he was sufficiently exotic to be a New World prophet; as a white Creole (yes, there was such a thing, politically correct definitions notwithstanding), he was able to champion black music in a racist society and be feted everywhere he went. According to Jack Belsom, archivist for the New Orleans Opera, Gottschalk's baptismal register indicates he was born in an all-white hospital and was not a Creole of color.[11]

The paradoxical qualities attributed to Gottschalk's music—the "savage" sophistication, the "energy" yoked to "melancholy"—anticipate the complex musical emotion in New World Symphonies by Dvořák and Delius. But these composers were more interested in the harmonic freedom of black spirituals than in rhythmic innovations; the more potent Gottschalk influence came with composers interested in jazz, who picked up on his syncopated dance forms.

As composer and prophet, Gottschalk was more a force in Europe than in America. After his death, he practically vanished from American culture (and to this day remains obscure); a few pieces such as A *Night in the Tropics* (though only the rhumba finale, which is wrenched out of context) are occasionally resurrected for pops concerts and by pianists specializing in American music. This sad neglect, so typical of Americans in regard to their most important artists, continues even in New Orleans, where it is difficult to find a Gottschalk recording and where promoters of New Orleans music display an appalling ignorance of their city's first important composer.

In Europe, the energies Gottschalk set loose were stalled after his death but not killed. Half a century later, Coleridge-Taylor, Debussy, Ravel, and other Europeans revived the rhythmic swing that Gottschalk had brought to the Old World from New Orleans, Cuba, and South America when they began experimenting with rags, rhumbas, fox-trots, tangos, bamboulas, and anything else that could energize the square rhythms of the post-Wagnerian establishment. These were largely parallel developments rather than direct influences, but in the cases of Debussy and Ravel, the Gottschalk connection was direct. Jacques Durand, Debussy's publisher and lifelong correspondent, was a Gottschalk devotee, as was Ernest Guiraud, Debussy's teacher in the conservatory (and composer of the *Carmen* recitatives) and a native of New Orleans, for whom Gottschalk had served as mentor. According to Barbara Fischer-Williams, Giraud shared not only music with Debussy but "billiards, cigarettes, and nocturnal rambles."[12] Debussy knew Gottschalk's legacy, even though scholars generally assume that his interest in ragtime idioms was derived from minstrel shows and circus bands. "Those acquainted with the piano preludes, with 'Golliwog's Cakewalk,' " wrote Richard Langham-Smith, "will realize that before the jazz band had made its mark on classical composers . . . Debussy himself absorbed a good deal from its precursors."[13] Among those precursors was Gottschalk.

Debussy's motivation for experimenting with these new sounds was similar to those who followed immediately after him. Determined to overthrow both the "false profundity" of neo-Wagnerism and the "hysterical mysticism" of "Gounod & Co.," Debussy seized upon black and Caribbean music in much the way he championed Javanese gamelan sounds and Eastern chant as a means of revitalizing a Western tradition he found depressingly stagnant. To someone who preferred the "percussive charm" of Eastern music to the "pompous outbursts" of his European contemporaries, the invigorating syncopations of "Golliwog's Cakewalk" and the barbershop harmonies of "General Lavine, Eccentric" were a natural step.[14]

The other composer who admired Gottschalk's legacy was Ravel. Quipping in a 1928 interview during his U.S. tour that "you Americans take jazz too lightly," Ravel argued that jazz had a sufficiently long history and tradition to be almost classical: "I could sit down and play you some French music written about 1849 that you would take for jazz, so characteristic is it, so syncopated. . . . What is more, it is considered as classical music."[15] This classical jazz was Gottschalk's.

From Satie to Hindemith, Europeans were falling under the spell of jazz, and Ravel regarded their infatuation as the beginning of a serious love affair. Although these composers shared a need to enliven a dying tradition, they had dramatically different styles and agendas. The result was a dizzying variety of jazz experiments, many of them vital and still popular despite persistent claims by critics that they were limited and ephemeral. By the late 1920s, when Ravel gave this interview, at least three tendencies were evident, including jazz as a satirical or comic gesture (as in Walton's *Façade* and Martinů's *Kitchen Revue*), jazz as a means of extending modernism, often with aggressive dissonance (the excursions of Stravinsky and Hindemith), and jazz as a serious source of inspiration, without irony or condescension—an invocation of what Constant Lambert called the "spirit of jazz" (Ravel's Concertos, Milhaud's *La Création du monde*).

Ravel's judgment on the sweep and impact of jazz was prescient.

From what he had observed during his travels in the United States, American intellectuals believed that jazz was "cheap, vulgar, [and] momentary"; nonetheless he was convinced it would become "the national music of the United States"—the same prediction Dvořák had made about black spirituals. Ravel was one of the first to recognize the universality of jazz as a composition vehicle. Old World composers using New World jazz materials bore "the national characteristics of their respective composers, despite the unique nationality of their initial material, the American 'blues.' Think of the striking and essential differences to be noted in the 'jazz' and 'rags' of Milhaud, Stravinsky, Casella, Hindemith. . . . The individualities of these composers are stronger than the materials appropriated. They mold popular forms to meet the requirements of their individual art." Jazz was thus American precisely in its freedom and flexibility, its multicultural ability to be molded by myriad individualities. On the same remarkable tour—during which Ravel visited Harlem, conducted the Boston Symphony, and premiered his bluesy Violin-Piano Sonata with Joseph Szigeti—he told Olin Downes, "I think you know that I greatly admire and value—more, I think, than many American composers—American jazz." Again, Ravel was rapturous about jazz and bewildered at the ambivalence and hostility it inspired in so many American intellectuals. In Ravel's view, Americans were grossly Eurocentric: "You have too little realization of yourselves," he said, with uncharacteristic bluntness: "You still look too far away over the water."[16]

Ravel himself had been looking over the water—to the American side. "My recent music is filled with the influence of jazz," he told a French reviewer.[17] This influence was most overtly reflected in the Blues movement of his Violin-Piano Sonata and in the blues and fox-trot numbers of *L'Enfant et les sortilèges*. The sonata is not parody or pastiche in the Satie-Poulenc mode but a serious attempt to project a blues mood onto a chamber work. The result is the most beautiful and original movement in a piece crowded with beauties. Both instruments emulate blues-band sounds, the piano through the repetition of strutting staccato chords and flattened-seventh progressions, the violin through banjolike strummings and blue notes. But beyond its special effects, this piece has a deeply felt blues sensibility, linking sophistication with childish naiveté—the Gottschalk combination. Ravel is the ideal concert jazz composer because he loved the idiom; he did not need to exploit it to show

how hip or modern he could be. Conductor Hugh Wolff, a Gershwin specialist, once told me a story that illustrates Ravel's droll attitude toward his symphonic jazz status: when Gershwin asked Ravel to give him piano lessons, Ravel responded that given how much money Gershwin made, it was he who should be taking lessons from Gershwin. Would you rather be a first-rate Gershwin, he asked, or a second-rate Ravel?

Ravel had no illusion about his vantage point as an outsider: "I have used jazz idioms in my last violin and piano sonata, but from what point of view? That, of course, of a Frenchman. Fascinated as I am by this idiom, I cannot possibly feel as if I were an American. It is to me a picturesque adventure."[18] Ravel projects a European fantasy of jazz — not the real thing but one that is surprisingly potent, as fantasies often are.

An equally picturesque adventure was the magical children's opera *L'Enfant*. Ravel declared that the piece was written in the "spirit of American musical comedy," but it was begun so early (1918) that it seems more like a precursor than an homage.[19] (Indeed, Stephen Sondheim has said that Ravel was one of his most important inspirations.) A sense of adventure and fun characterizes Ravel's jazz-influenced works, though they were worked out with painstaking care — it took Ravel four years to write the Violin-Piano Sonata — rather than with the spontaneity associated with jazz. (We already have seen Ravel's Poe-derived theory of the importance of calculation in the creation of spontaneity.)

Ravel's most popular jazz-tinged American work is outwardly Spanish: *Boléro*, a tour de force that Ravel regarded as trivia, orchestration without music, but that had a spellbinding effect on the culture. A forerunner of American minimalism (compared to which it is far wittier), this sexy, obsessively repetitive piece of musical sorcery was the perfect signature for the jazz era. Like so many jazz-inspired hybrids, *Boléro* was instantly popular with audiences and has been ever since. Charged by the electricity of American cities as well as by jazz, filled with blue notes and fandangos, exquisitely refined yet deliberately trashy, it is a crossover piece in the truest sense, an irresistible lure for those normally indifferent to classical music. Although written by the most aloof and mandarin of composers, it remains one of the most durable bridges in twentieth-century music between elite and mass culture.

The culmination of Ravel's infatuation with jazz was the two piano

concertos, both products of the late 1920s and Ravel's immersion in the
Harlem Renaissance. Taken together, they represent two spirits of jazz,
one amiable and benign, the other mysterious and demonic: one is
champagne, the other a New Orleans Hurricane. In the G Major Concerto, bluesy trumpets, squealing clarinets, and bouncy piano syncopations combine with Basque dances and Mozartian lyricism in a tapestry
both delicate and hallucinatory. The diabolical energy and orgiastic climaxes of the Concerto for the Left Hand Alone suggest a darker side of
jazz, just as *La Valse* evokes a nightmarish vision of the Viennese waltz.

The note of malevolence just under the surface of jazzy insouciance in the Left Hand Concerto, a note also struck in the jazz experiments of Hindemith and Milhaud, suggests a sense of danger, of living
on the edge, that is fundamental to jazz (and certainly to the chaotic
lives of its executants). Europeans divined this feeling early on: Berlioz
wrote that the Gottschalk sound "cradles our own disturbing and insa-
tiable desire for the unknown."[20] This dark excitement persists; it was
summarized in 1996 by British novelist Geoff Dyer's assertion that "there
is something inherently dangerous about the form."[21] (In America, composer Donald Martino, fearing for his professional reputation, invented
a pseudonym, Jimmie Vincent, for his jazz work in the 1950s, a dop-
pelgänger critics called Martino's Mr. Hyde when he finally unveiled
the secret in 1997.) This danger, of course, is part of the lure of jazz, of
its booziness and sexiness, of the daring and risk involved in the act of
improvisation. The sultry malevolence of Ravel's Left Hand Concerto
suggests reasons for both the conservative resistance to jazz and the
avant-garde attraction to it during a century of world wars and wrenching
social change. Jazz provided a source of energy and exuberance but also
an underlying sense of the sinister, a feeling of laid-back decadence and
impending collapse. As Ernst Krenek noted, it was a fundamental reflection of modern reality: exhilarating but troubling.

Jazz is not the only American influence here. As we have seen,
the Left Hand Concerto and its darker companions reflect Ravel's other
addiction to Poe. Indeed, he sometimes discussed the twin New World
magnets of jazz and Poe in the same interview. Dissimilar as these may
seem, Ravel regarded them as parallel, for both offered a bridge between
emotion and intellect. "Poe proved that art must strike a balance between these two extremes," he told the *New York Times*, "for the first
leads only to formlessness and the second to the dry and abstract."[22] Jazz,

too, with its uninhibited emotion and cool sophistication, connected the heart with the brain, just as it connected popular entertainment with art.

Not all French composers admired jazz as much as Ravel. Francis Poulenc, a Satie disciple who attended the premiere of *Parade*, manifested a witty ambivalence that soured into hostility—surprising for someone so fond of French dance-hall music. He sat in at the piano during Saturday jazz soirees at the Gaya, a bar frequented by Cocteau and Satie, both promoters of "Les Six" (Poulenc, Milhaud, Auric, Honegger, Germaine Tailleferre, and Louis Durey), and he briefly embraced their surrealist *réalisme*. It is hard to imagine a fuller immersion in the Paris jazz scene than the one Poulenc experienced. The bar constantly swung to the beat of "St. Louis Blues" and other jazz tunes, so much so that the more conservative customers bitterly complained. Manager Louis Moyses told Cocteau he was thinking of firing house pianist Jean Wiener; Cocteau, who in 1918 had described the arrival of jazz as a sonic cataclysm, advised him to keep the pianist and get rid of the customers. Fortunately, a younger crowd gradually took over the place, and in 1922 Moyses opened another boîte called Le Boeuf sur le Toit, named after a piece by Milhaud, to accommodate his expanding avant-garde clientele. Le Boeuf became the nerve center of the Paris jazz movement, promoting not only Les Six but Gershwin, Fletcher Henderson, Vincent Youmans, and Jerome Kern, with a house orchestra conducted by black saxophonist Vance Lowry. Milhaud eagerly joined the jazz revolution, and his colleague Poulenc could easily have done the same. But he disdained the idea of jazz in symphonic music: "It amuses me when I listen to records of it while I am taking my bath," he said, "but it is frankly distasteful to me in the concert hall."[23] Nevertheless, an impish Rag-Mazurka appears in Poulenc's *Les Biches*, and a bluesy poignance creeps into the slow sections of the Sextuor and other early pieces.

The French composer most hostile to jazz was Olivier Messiaen, who sustained his irritation to the end, characterizing jazz in a 1986 interview as a "robber" whose " 'innovations' are, in reality, borrowings from earlier symphonic music." It is not surprising that the intensely religious, pastoral Messiaen would despise such a resolutely secular, urban form. He deplored the influence of jazz on his contemporaries, especially Ravel: "I've always thought that the poetic and refined figure of Maurice Ravel was spoiled in his last years by this jazz influence,

which really had nothing to do with his personal inclinations."[24] Here
again is a central irony of the century: American musical intellectuals
have worried persistently about the overpowering influence of Europe,
when the real threat, as Messiaen's complaint tartly attests, was from the
opposite direction. It was Americans who spoiled and corrupted Europeans.

It was precisely the irreverent, decadent aspects of jazz that had so
much initial appeal. Some of the earliest incursions of jazz into symphonic music were satirical, the parody preceding its object. Again, a
Frenchman was at center stage. Satie's surrealistic *Parade*, with its type-
writer, whistle, and music-hall jazz, lampooned the banality of modern
culture—including jazz itself. *Parade* came about when Sergey Diaghilev, needing something delicious and shocking to program with his Ballets Russes, assembled Cocteau, Satie, and Picasso, the three most
brilliant new stars in the Parisian avant-garde. (Satie was in this trinity
largely because of Cocteau's intense promotion.) Diaghilev asked Cocteau to astound him, and Cocteau responded with the circus parade
scenarios for a "ballet réaliste," with costumes and cubist sets by Picasso
and music by Satie. The production also boasted Léonide Massine, Diaghilev's famed choreographer. Apollinaire, who wrote the program
notes, gushed that *Parade* represented a new alliance in the arts, a new
surrealism, and a new spirit in modern culture. It made an early splash,
its scandalous 1917 premiere nearly landing the composer in jail (he was
given an eight-day suspended sentence for libeling a critic—a wonderful
coup for Satie) and providing a colorful aesthetic document for the
beginnings of surrealism, cubism, dadaism, and much else. Entertaining
as it is, *Parade* is important mainly as an efficient broom that swept away
Wagnerism, serialism, and impressionism. The ruthless evanescence of
all trends and isms was well in place by the early twentieth century, and
Parade proved as fragile as what it debunked, its performances far less
frequent today than the occasions of its ridicule. Its avant-garde pedigree—Cocteau-Picasso-Diaghilev-Massine—is as hip as they come, but
like so much vanguard art from the period, the music is a series of
technically demanding in-jokes. *Parade*'s music-hall jazz element is as
deliberately banal, fragmentary, and self-deprecating as everything else
in the piece. The dark side of *Parade*, its vision of a bleakly mechanistic
society, was a modern malaise for which jazz eventually became an

antidote, but with the exception of Wilfred Mellers and a few other perceptive commentators, this disturbing layer is often overlooked because of the work's elegantly rowdy facade.

At the other end of the spectrum—though its creator is often identified with Satie and Les Six—is Darius Milhaud's 1923 *La Création du monde*, a serious, sustained evocation of the spirit of jazz based on an African creation myth as well as on Milhaud's careful study of jazz bands during his journeys to Harlem a decade before he settled in the United States. Bluesy saxophone solos over dense polytonal harmonies create a surreal spookiness later juxtaposed with explosive jazz polyphony; the result is original, colorful, slightly wacky, and curiously moving. Unlike Gershwin's *Rhapsody in Blue*, which *La Création* precedes by three months to one year (depending on which musical historian one wishes to believe), Milhaud's work incorporates jazz into a modernist context, with plenty of spicy dissonance and cross-rhythms. More than any piece from the period, it pays tribute to the sophistication of primitive materials, as modern painting had been doing for more than a generation.

Because of his experience in Brazil (see Chap. 5), Milhaud understood his subject from a broad multicultural perspective. South American motifs enliven *La Création*, as they do jazz itself. Milhaud's harmonic signature, what he called "subtly sweet, violently potent" polytonality, seems perfectly at home: as Ravel would say, the composer's "individuality" projected itself in the way he chose to "appropriate" jazz. Milhaud's emphasis, unlike Gershwin's, is on the density of New Orleans polyphony, which he makes even more potent by allowing independent melodic lines to maintain their own keys. In the Prelude and Romance, subtly sweet dissonance travels up the listener's spine. Although Milhaud had already previewed this jazzy polytonality in the alternately delicate and violent *Rag-Caprices* of 1922, *La Création* is usually regarded as his jazz debut.

Unlike the sweet-sour pastiches of Satie and early Hindemith, Milhaud's blues are served straight up. Like Delius nearly thirty years earlier, he experienced black music as a powerful personal epiphany, though in a setting far different from the St. Johns River. Instead Milhaud was riveted by secular black music in Harlem bars and theaters during a month-long visit to the United States in 1922. Two years earlier, he had heard Billy Arnold's dance band in London. "The effect on me was so great," he later recalled, "that I could not tear myself away."[25] Writing his "Negro ballet" for the Ballet Suédois at last gave him "the opportunity I had been waiting for to use those elements of jazz to which I had devoted so much study. I adopted the same orchestra as used in Harlem, seventeen solo instruments, and I made wholesale use of the jazz style to convey a purely classical feeling."[26]

In striking parallel to Ravel, Milhaud therefore experienced jazz as classical in feeling; he saw the elegance of the form as something to be taken seriously, not as the butt of a joke or the piece of a collage. But he also liked its funkiness and anarchic volatility. In the uninhibited raunchiness of its fugue, La Création eschews the elegant formality of the Ravel style of blues. And despite its busy counterpoint, the piece is far removed from the mechanical concerto-grosso world of neoclassicism. This is a piece that staked out new ground.

For a long time the seriousness of Milhaud's gesture was misunderstood. If critics now take jazz too solemnly, they once, as Ravel complained, took it "too lightly." As Milhaud later commented, "The critics decreed that my music was frivolous and more suitable for a restaurant or dance hall than for the concert. Ten years later, the selfsame critics were discussing the philosophy of jazz and learnedly demonstrating that La Création was the best of my works."[27] Indeed, the critics did an extraordinary flip-flop. By the 1930s, La Création was held up by the anti-Gershwin faction in America—including Paul Rosenfeld, the most eloquent of the antijazz ideologues—as a superior, "deeper" example of concert jazz than Gershwin's Rhapsody. Fifty years after Dvořák, it was still true that only a European could get away with taking black music seriously.

In the 1990s, scholars did another flip. Carol Oja initiated a new controversy, accusing earlier critics of having seriously erred in their assertion that La Création preceded Gershwin's Rhapsody in Blue by a year, when in fact it had been written only a few months earlier, and of hyping Milhaud's importance at the expense of Gershwin, whom, in the late twentieth century, critics had anointed the Great American Composer. One might ask what difference it makes: if Milhaud's piece preceded Gershwin's by only a day, it still came first. Both these reactions are variations on a chronic nervousness that Americans exhibit concerning their musical identity. They both miss the point, one that should be comforting: it was American popular culture that had the epoch-changing power and impact. The real source of this extraordinary energy was neither Milhaud nor Gershwin, but black America. It all started in Harlem clubs, no matter who expropriated it first.

Milhaud's statements on the "power of jazz" parallel Lambert's paean to the "spirit of jazz"; both harken back to DuBois and Dvořák on the legacy of black spirituals. In his prose *Etudes*, Milhaud wrote that "primitive African heritage remains deeply anchored in the souls of American Negroes." From this heritage comes the "formidable sense of rhythm" in jazz, as does a "profoundly moving gift for melody that only people who have long been oppressed know how to utter."[28] Again, the similarity to earlier statements by Dvořák and DuBois is striking, especially Milhaud's view that the oppression suffered by blacks translated into a specific type of melody: "All have the same tenderness, sadness, profession of faith." But there is an important difference: as a Jew, Milhaud was closer in his vision of jazz to the manifestoes of Gershwin, Weill, and Zemlinsky. For Jewish composers, who understood racial discrimination firsthand, jazz took on a deeply personal meaning.

Jazz has always been an emblem for struggles against oppression, whether it be the result of political systems or social rigidity. In America, of course, where jazz and blues artists confronted discrimination from the beginning, race was the issue. In Europe, however, jazz became a broadly based political weapon against totalitarianism, of both the right- and left-wing varieties.

In the 1920s the Soviet Union experienced its own jazz era. Soviet composers, who soon followed the French as some of the most colorful innovators of the form, quickly incurred the hostility of the authorities, who regarded jazz as the epitome of Western decadence—which, of course, it is. The most entertaining practitioner of Soviet symphonic jazz was Dmitri Shostakovich. Like Britten, Martinů, and Krenek, he wrote some of his earliest works in the genre. During his student years, Shostakovich became entranced by jazz bands forming and touring within the Soviet Union. His first big hit, "Tahiti Trot," written in forty minutes in a 1928 competition, was the witty harbinger of two *Jazz Suites* from the early 1930s. In these rambunctious works, Dixieland trombone slides, banjo strummings, and Hawaiian guitar blue notes sound like genuine dance-hall entertainment rather than a modernist pastiche, revealing a rare side of this normally gloomy composer. (Critics who denounced Milhaud's jazz experiments as being more appropriate for a dance club than a concert hall might more profitably have attacked Shostakovich, for these suites really would be comfortable there.)

Aesthetically, these pieces are charming trifles, but they were important developments in the growing universality of jazz: Shostakovich so deftly combined jazz riffs with Russian and Eastern European folk motifs that the mix seems natural, even inevitable. Jazz was clearly a form of therapy for Shostakovich, as it would be for Hindemith, Britten, Bartók, and other Europeans, serving as an early release from the traumas of war and oppression.

These sparkling works partook more of dance-hall music than of real jazz, but even that incurred the denunciation of Soviet tastemakers obsessed with bourgeois decadence, that curiously inviting label applied to jazz by authoritarians of both the Left and the Right. The anarchic egalitarianism and unapologetic hedonism of jazz were a threat to all totalitarians; symphonic jazz, however, was regarded as particularly cancerous, for it brought the disease directly into the citadels of high culture. Contemporary critics may not view concert jazz as being terribly important, but Nazis and Stalinists certainly did, enough so to merit systematic repression. Again, the authenticity of the jazz was beside the point. Indeed, the kind of no-rules dance-hall jazz that purists later denigrated as ersatz was perhaps the most subversive of all, because it implied that anyone could be decadent at will, without authenticating pedigrees. Indeed, that is what decadence is all about. By the last quarter of the century, jazz criticism began to fragment into exclusionary absolutisms—an ironic development, to say the least—but in the "Tahiti Trot" days, jazz had an exhilarating anything-goes aura that was dangerous to tyrants of all stripes. In Shostakovich's case, jazz was one of the earliest casualties of Stalinist repression; the racy trumpet riffs in the First Piano Concerto were some of the last vestiges of the free-spirited "Odessa jazz" of his student days.

In the case of Alexander Tcherepnin, a fascination with the idiom was an early forecast of his decision to emigrate to the United States. Tcherepnin's dissonant, tightly written Second String Quartet, which appeared even before Shostakovich's jazz pieces, is an early example of modernist jazz, its dark polyphony brightened by a "walking bass" cello pizzicato in the finale and a syncopated 5/8 rhythm in the otherwise mysterious opening. Like many Old World excursions into the New, it incorporates home-based European folk elements, in this case a Russian hopak.

The Tcherepnin quartet and Shostakovich jazz suites come from the same culture and period but are radically different, the former an austere modernist experiment with jazz used for smoky atmosphere and complex rhythm, the latter a playful set of crossover entertainment pieces. Even in the jazz-starved Soviet Union, different styles of concert jazz quickly flourished.

The most prominent symphonic jazz by a Russian, if the least charming, came from Stravinsky. In contrast to Milhaud, whose interest in jazz continued after he settled in America but who wrote only a single masterpiece in the genre, Stravinsky began experimenting with jazz early and dabbled in it off and on for nearly thirty years, from the 1918 "Ragtime" and *Histoire du soldat* to the 1945 *Ebony Concerto*, written for Woody Herman's band—a long jazz period by any measure.

The music community has always been ambivalent about jazz-Stravinsky, reflecting a larger ambivalence about symphonic jazz in general. Even though *Histoire* is regarded, rightly, as an important masterpiece, historians play down Stravinsky's absorption in jazz on the grounds that his interest was artificial—he studied jazz scores only in Switzerland in 1918, when he wrote *Histoire*—and intermittent. His initial exposure was limited to jazz scores by the conductor Ernest Ansermet. But one can just as easily argue that Stravinsky's lack of exposure to jazz made his first essays in the genre more impressive as imaginative flights into the unknown. Missing out on the Paris jazz-bar scene, Stravinsky avoided the clichés that were to bedevil so many others. As Varèse pointed out when he wrote *Amériques* (the same year Stravinsky composed *Histoire*), the New World was a construct "in the minds of men," a subjective as well as physical landscape.

The Stravinsky case is full of odd juxtapositions and paradoxes. Having never heard the music, he borrowed "the rhythmic style of jazz not as played but as written. I could imagine jazz sound, however, or so I like to think." Stravinsky's jazz was therefore extraordinarily literal—right from the score—yet highly speculative: he wrote what he would "like to think" jazz sounded like. Not surprisingly, *Histoire* does not sound much like jazz at all. It projects, as Stravinsky hoped, "a wholly new sound."[29]

Stravinsky came to jazz early and in isolation; the result is the uniquely tart and invigorating sound world of *Histoire*. It is often pointed out that personnel limitations were behind the resemblance of the *Histoire* ensemble to a New Orleans jazz band. Whatever the reason, that ensemble is both evocative and prescient: the way Stravinsky uses a slithery fiddle resembles both klezmer music and what was to become New Orleans zydeco. At the end, the drum set takes off on its own with a syncopated abandon that Stravinsky would never quite duplicate, although his "Piano-Rag" of a year later also has a meter-defying freedom.

Having exhausted Russian neoprimitivism as a vehicle for rhythmic innovation, Stravinsky hit upon jazz as a new mode of liberation, one that was even fresher than *Le Sacre du printemps* because it swept away his European-Russian Romantic heritage altogether. "Jazz meant a wholly new sound in my music," he reminisced in 1962, "and *Histoire* marks my final break with the Russian orchestral school in which I had been fostered."[30] Stravinsky's statement fits the pattern we see throughout this book of Old World composers using New World culture as a way of jettisoning aesthetic baggage they find oppressive. His easy blending of jazz not only with related dances such as the tango but with traditional European forms such as chorales and marches was an early, trend-setting indication of the flexibility of jazz, as Kurt Weill, strongly influenced by *Histoire*, would soon discover.

Jazz was useful to Stravinsky as the newest weapon in modernism's war on fusty post-Victorianisms and Romanticisms. It replaced Wagnerism with a whole new "music of the future," complete with disciples and enemies. As usual, Stravinsky, the consummate musical politician, was clever enough to get much of the credit as a trendsetter; indeed, he was well ahead of the Gershwin crowd, even if Debussy and Satie preceded him.

But what next? By the early 1920s, Stravinsky had pretty much wrung what he could from the genre. Typically (as with *Le Sacre du printemps*), he had seized upon an aesthetic that put him in the vanguard, then quickly exhausted it, leaving him with no alternative but to start something else. By the end of the decade, Stravinsky was ambivalent about jazz, at least rhetorically. In an interview from 1930, he said that jazz "remained an art only so long as it does not lose its origins," a statement similar to those of Lambert and Milhaud. But he went further, stating, "I like jazz when it is the simple expression of la musique nègre, I like it a great deal less in its Anglo-Saxon transcriptions."

Furthermore, "jazz is not an art created for eternity, but a mode, and as such, destined to disappear." Most curious of all was Stravinsky's insistence, at least here, that jazz is "a response to a taste for the ersatz." It was not anything new, but simply a means of bringing rhythm, "neglected for so long," back into the foreground of Western music.[31]

This statement is odd given Stravinsky's own use of jazz, which is certainly an Anglo-Saxon variant, indeed, more removed from la musique nègre than the experiments of Milhaud and Gershwin, who made a point of visiting locations such as Harlem and Charleston. This is Stravinsky in his own mode, that of relentless debunker of Romanticisms. His labeling of jazz as ersatz (aside from the undeniable fact that much of it was) reminds one of Ravel's remark about its artificiality and sophistication. The vision of jazz projected by these cosmopolitan Europeans was as far from Noble Savage clichés as could be imagined. Stravinsky was being true to his own reality: *Histoire*, "Ragtime," and the "Piano-Rag" sound like Stravinsky, not jazz. Indeed, he used jazz as a mode, a way of extending his interest in new harmonies and cross-rhythms.

Jazz had become a bandwagon, something always abhorrent to Stravinsky—unless, of course, he was driving it. All the gushing by his colleagues about how wonderful and liberating jazz was did not fit Stravinsky's style. But instead of rejecting this mode as he had Russian Romanticism and primitivism, Stravinsky collapsed it into another trend, neoclassicism. A signifier of clarity, objectivity, formal rigor, and other clean and sober subversions of Romanticism, this newest variant of modernism became the excuse for a great deal of emotionally pinched music—excluding Stravinsky's own *Pulcinella*, one of the earliest, most charming works in the genre and one of the few with a genuinely classical sensibility.

Stravinsky's notion of ersatz jazz fit the fake classicism of the 1920s and 1930s. Many works of this period contained snatches of symphonic jazz—blue notes, brass slides, and New Orleans polyphony—but were trapped in sonata and other eighteenth-century forms. The sound was often neither classical nor jazzy but nonetheless yielded notable moments, especially the slow movement of Stravinsky's Concerto for Piano and Winds, which has the lyricism (unusual for Stravinsky during this period) of a New Orleans funeral march. Similarly, the *Ebony Concerto*, written in 1945 for Woody Herman's band—the work in which neoclassicism and jazz come together most explicitly—plays with concerto-grosso pastiche but gets deep emotional resonance at the end from a hypnotically repeated blues chord that seems to float into space as it elongates.

The merging of jazz and neoclassicism by Stravinsky, Hindemith, and other Old World composers demonstrates a European view of the idiom far removed from stereotypical notions of jazz as all funk and spontaneity: here jazz is not only classical but neoclassical, an aesthetic emphasizing classicism in the most formal sense. Some of the most elegant works in this mode came from the Dutch, including Henriëtta Bosmans, Willem Pijper, and Leo Smit, who initiated a rich jazz tradition in the Netherlands combining the austerity of Stravinsky with the disciplined hedonism of Ravel. Paul Hindemith, the most academically respectable of the Entartete composers, called neoclassical jazz the "new objectivity." In this weird twist, jazz, ostensibly a release from emotional inhibition, becomes not only classical but emotionally objective. The paradox is not altogether surprising given that jazz is cool as well as hot, but Hindemith put yet another spin on the idea. His Ragtimes, Bostons, and Shimmies, which go back to the beginning of his career, are connected to the aesthetic of Bach. Hindemith introduced his 1921 "Ragtime (Well Tempered)" with the question, "Do you think that Bach is turning in his grave? . . . If Bach were alive today, perhaps he would invent the shimmy or at least take it over into respectable music."[32] Using a Bach fugue as the basis of an experiment in ragtime riffs, this goofy tangle of polyphony, like Hindemith's Bachian jazz noodlings in his *Kammermusik* series, is a raucous joke, but with an undercurrent of danger. Similarly, the fox-trot trumpet blaring out over whirring dissonance in the 1927 Kammermusik no. 1 has a sinister jauntiness that came to define the Weimar Republic's jazz age. This is music poised on the edge of the Nazi abyss.

Hindemith finally went too far when he began irreverently throwing patriotic German marching tunes from Nazi rallies into the Kammermusik stew. Using jazz motifs was bad enough as far as the Nazis were concerned, but mingling them with songs of the Fatherland was over the line, especially since Hindemith continued to perform with Jewish musicians. Hindemith was not especially political—his attitude toward fascism was mainly one of lofty contempt—but his music had an antiauthoritarian subtext. The opera *Mathis der Maler* was an explicit, eloquent acknowledgment of what was implicit in Hindemith's defiant use of rags, shimmies, and parodies of Nazi marches.

By the 1930s, Hindemith's use of jazz was more straightforward. The five-note Harlem Renaissance motif that enlivens the Concert Music for Brass and Strings—the same one used by Milhaud in *La Création du monde*—builds to a thrilling climax worlds removed from the sassy academicisms of the *Kammermusik* period. Hindemith's music became less edgy and more lyrical after he immigrated to the New World, a tendency forecast in the Concert Music, which was written as a showpiece for Serge Koussevitzky and the Boston Symphony. As with Martinů, Hindemith's use of large-scale symphonic structures, ironically, became more European than when he lived in Europe, but unlike his Czech colleague, his interest in jazz persisted. The all-percussion cadenza in the surprise coda of the Scherzo in the *Symphonic Metamorphosis of Themes by Carl Maria von Weber* is Hindemith's most charming jazz sequence, demonstrating that jazz syncopation can amiably coexist with earlier Western dance music. This, more than Hindemith's early rags, is surely what Bach would have endorsed. The freedom and playfulness of the *Metamorphosis* communicate the feel of a dance band; indeed, the composer intended that his players stand up during the performance to blare out the big tunes and blow the audience away—something hard to imagine in most of today's stuffy concert halls.

A composer much harder to classify than Hindemith—indeed, the wild card in the whole Entartete jazz phenomenon—was Czech composer and pianist Erwin Schulhoff, whose music died suddenly after its composer did, in 1942, at the hands of the Nazis, and was not resurrected until the 1990s. Schulhoff's pedigree as an East European New World Symphonist was impeccable: his earliest advocate in Prague was Dvořák himself. He therefore encompasses the European New World Symphony tradition, beginning with its inaugurator and extending through the Entartete period. In a tragically ironic way, he also moves beyond it: his way of dealing with the Nazi threat was to become a communist (he even wrote a cantata called *The Communist Manifesto*) and to embrace socialist realism, thereby implicitly sanctioning the Nazi condemnation of his earlier jazz decadence, since the Soviets had the same antijazz sentiments as the Nazis. But his attempt to emigrate to the

Soviet Union was doomed: as a Jew and a communist, he was detained by the Nazis and thrown into a Bavarian concentration camp, where he died in 1942.

Like the jazz he so avidly embraced, his legacy is large and strangely unformed, as if improvised. From overtly jazzy pieces with titles like "Hot Music" and "Jazz Etudes" to jazz-filled quartets, symphonies, and concertos, this music is still being resuscitated and reevaluated, but some matters are already clear. One is that Schulhoff was extraordinarily early and consistent in his advocacy of jazz, both as a composer and lecturer. From 1921 on, numerous Schulhoff pieces are colored by jazz, either in overall conception or in movements with titles like "Boston," "Shimmy," or simply "Jazz." What little commentary exists on this fascinating composer insists that the Schulhoff sound is derived from the Paul Whiteman Band and its spin-offs. (Schulhoff never traveled to Harlem to hear the real thing.) But this strangely original music does not sound at all like Whiteman. Full of colorful bitonalities and chromaticisms, it is basically tonal and accessible, combining a formal, almost minimalist rigor with a willingness to embrace the steamiest, most banal aspects of American popular dance music. Its jazz-tinted waltzes and sarcastic marches punctuated by xylophone riffs sometimes resemble early Hindemith; the Double Concerto for Flute and Piano, for example, marches in with Hindemithean mock sternness, but by the wistful Blues sequence in the finale, it is in another, more rapturous world. Schulhoff often juggles more than one musical persona in a single work: the remarkable 1923 Piano Concerto begins with a dark, erotic fantasia for solo piano that sounds like a combination of late Scriabin and early Bartók, then explodes into a funky "Allegro alla Jazz" that rebukes what has gone before. The clashing moods are never resolved, but this tension adds to the work's mysterious kinkiness and sense of danger, a prophetic style that would come increasingly to define the art music of the fragile Weimar Republic. By the late 1920s, Weill was creating a jazz-infused sense of the sinister with a more unified aesthetic; that Schulhoff was unable to do so does not diminish his power, which is based on a constant capacity to surprise.

Schulhoff's career consisted of embarking on a number of roads—romantic nostalgia, neoclassicism, expressionism, asceticism—then either abandoning or bolting them together. He was postmodern long before that silly term was coined. Until his final, tragically aborted journey down the Soviet path, jazz was virtually his only constant. It pops up even in the severely ascetic Concerto for String Quartet, in a "Tempo di Slow fox." Schulhoff was one of the first European composers to consistently use jazz, normally associated with chaotic, improvised energy, as an anchor, a new kind of classicism, a means of unifying a restless aesthetic that might otherwise be adrift. The closest he came to a consistent point of view was in his short, sharply focused jazz piano pieces such as the "Jazz Etudes," "Esquisses de Jazz," and "Rag Music." These have a bittersweet bluesiness that makes them the Weimar versions of Gershwin's short piano pieces, but Schulhoff's contribution to the genre has a spicier harmonic underpinning. (One of his 1926 pieces is called "Blues for Paul Whiteman," a touching homage but certainly spookier than anything Whiteman could have conceived.) When he played these pieces himself, they took on an extraordinary freedom and swingy virtuosity, which the listener can sample now that Schulhoff's 1928 recordings for Berlin Polydor have been reissued on compact disc.

Whatever the ultimate verdict on Schulhoff, he was certainly a daring innovator: the Step movement from the deliciously sensual "Moonstruck," for example, is scored for percussion only. Derived from a 1921 chamber suite and therefore preceding Varèse's *Ionisation*, this experiment in pure rhythm—wittily subtitled "without music"—appears to be the first of its type in Western music. Although only four minutes long, it has a satisfying jazz shape, rising and gradually falling with alternately brash and delicate cymbal-snare drum syncopations. By the time he arrived at his sad capitulation to Soviet realism, Schulhoff had a great deal to renounce.

As we have seen, the clearest and cleverest summary of the story of jazz in Europe was Krenek's libretto to *Jonny spielt auf*. When Krenek's New World Pied Piper, a jazz musician visiting Europe, "strikes up the band" with an instrument he has taken from a European virtuoso, he infuses the populace with his sound so that at the end everyone is dancing in the street. The rather unpleasant symbolism of Jonny actually stealing Danielle's violin and hiding it in a banjo case indicates that Krenek was not altogether sanguine about the invasion of the Old World by the New, but the exhilaration of the final octet and dance sequence finally sweep away all ambivalence. In reality, of course, the two traditions stole from each other: jazz players used European instruments, Europeans joined black America's life-giving dance. "He must wander among us as one of us," was Krenek's judgment about Jonny. Europe needed Jonny as much as he needed it.[33]

The intoxicating upbeatness of the jazz numbers (a mood rather unusual for Krenek) begins with the banjo, piano, and brass in Jonny's band but ultimately infects the entire ensemble; to racial mixing is added a cultural melding of styles and genres, high culture with low, the tone of the latter winning the day. Even the gloomy, self-tortured Max, the noble, neurotic stand-in for the Old World composer, adopts a New World assertiveness and sassiness at the end. The ascendance of the New World is complete, with jazz as the vehicle for change.

Krenek played all the notes most threatening and enraging to the Nazis, especially since the opera was the biggest hit in Europe during the late 1920s and early 1930s. *Jonny* was the ultimate nightmare for the Nazis, who as early as 1927 denounced it as "Jewish nigger filth," an obscene catch-all term for jazz, and later declared Krenek a degenerate in the notorious 1938 Entartete Musik exhibition in Düsseldorf, which came a year after the Entartete Kunst exhibit in Munich. That Krenek was not Jewish—indeed, not even "half-Jewish," as the Nazis claimed— was irrelevant. Anyone who championed African-American culture in the homeland was automatically Jewish in sympathy, if not in fact. Even worse, Jonny's affairs with European women made explicit the racial mixing that jazz darkly implied. Indeed, jazz summed up everything abhorrent to national socialism: blacks, Jews, modernism—all manner of impure Americans and Americanisms mingling culturally and carnally to bring down German culture. Because of this single opera, Krenek was forced to emigrate to America in 1938. (Even in New York *Jonny* was considered shocking.)

The odd thing about *Jonny* is that it doesn't sound decadent at all. The jazz-band sequences in scenes 3, 7, and 9 have the a wholesome cheeriness characteristic of the Whiteman Band rather than the dusky sophistication of Milhaud's or Weill's jazz crossovers. Furthermore, jazz is set against numerous other musical styles, dissonant and diatonic, winning the day only at the end. In its actual music, this notorious jazz opera is really not very jazzy. It was the idea of the piece, established in Krenek's brilliantly subversive libretto, that created the sensation. In the waning years of the Weimar Republic, even a little jazz was dangerous.

Brochure cover for the Nazi *Entartete Musik* (Degenerate Music) exhibit. Jazz, Jewishness, and blackness, objects of Nazi hatred, were celebrated by émigré composers. (Weill-Lenya Research Center, Kurt Weill Foundation for Music, New York)

The most threatening jazz polluter of all was Kurt Weill. Krenek is credited with writing the first jazz opera, but he composed no others (sadly, he never regained such sensational notoriety, lapsing, ironically, into the very Germanisms that *Jonny* so nimbly subverts and remaining obscure for the next sixty years). Whereas Krenek was only a theoretical composer of jazz opera, Weill was the real thing. Addicted to sexual and blood-transfusion metaphors, the Nazis reserved some of their most hysterical rhetoric for Weill's jazz operettas. "The most conspicuous aspect of Weill's music is jazz rhythm," railed the *Nationalsozialistische Monatshefte* in 1931; Weill was guilty of perpetrating an insidious "transfusion of negro blood" into the culture of Mozart and Wagner.[34] Beginning with *Royal Palace* and continuing through *Mahagonny, The Threepenny Opera, Happy End, Der Silbersee, Der Zar lässt sich photographieren,* and *The Seven Deadly Sins,* Weill allowed jazz and related forms of American dance music to infect his style in a fundamental way rather than merely in isolated sequences. Even Weill's First Symphony, written under Ferruccio Busoni's tutelage in 1921, has a chorale that forecasts the sinister charm of the "Alabama Song" in *Mahagonny*. In Weill's world, German chorales, sinfonias, marches, and fugues all sound jazzy. The contaminating transfusion was total and sustained.

Weill was happily obsessed with the darker, sexier, more decadent aspects of jazz, whether in the sultry saxophone-percussion continuo of the Weill cabaret jazz band, the slinky seductiveness of numbers like "The Bilbao-Song" and "Surabaya-Johnny" in *Happy End,* or the sexually provocative "commercial love" duet in *Mahagonny*. The cheery bounce of the Whiteman-Krenek model held no more interest for Weill than the designery abstractions of the Stravinsky approach. The initial model seemed to be Hindemith, whose fox-trots and shimmies originally puzzled Weill in his nontonal modernist days. Weill wrote to Hindemith in 1925 that "the way you drew the fox-trot of your Kammermusik No. 1 into the sphere of serious music would be the right thing in this case [that of *The Threepenny Opera*]: refined popular music or a caricature thereof."[35]

Weill's cabaret jazz was on the abyss of caricature, but it was mainly a refined version of the real thing, so much so that it was really a new form. Like Ravel, Weill was perfectly aware that he was reinventing jazz rather than reflecting it. "It is not jazz-music in the American sense," he wrote his publisher, but rather "a quite special, new sound."[36] Weill's vocal numbers slyly cross over from art music to entertainment and back. His cabaret and blues songs are full-blown specimens of their idioms—indeed, some of the sexiest ever written—yet become classical music again the instant the number has ended and the formal expressionist music surrounding it returns. This constant transit between genres gives them a special mobility and tension.

In 1929, Weill shrewdly asserted that a skillful use of the "elements of jazz" would produce "easily graspable melodies that superficially bear a strong resemblance to light music." Weill understood that jazz itself bore this sneaky resemblance to lighter popular music, not just the serious composer's re-creation of it. When jazz is really cooking, it is "not catchy" so much as "rousing" and provocative. The subtle but powerful difference was what Weill played on, making his music profoundly different from the amiable jazz pastiches of the Satie-Auric persuasion. Weill was determined to have it both ways, to reach a large audience while not abandoning "the intellectual bearing of the serious musician." Jazz enabled him to do so. Music needed a new language, both serious and communicative, that would enable musicians to "carry out our intellectual tasks—the tasks of the artist in his time—in a language that is acceptable and understandable to all." Jazz provided that language.[37]

For Weill, the key was irony: "The intellectual bearing of this music is thoroughly bitter, serious, accusing, and in the most pleasant cases, still ironic."[38] Again, Weill is talking not just about his own music but about the elements of jazz upon which it is based. He understood that jazz itself was frequently ironic, even when pleasant. That is part of its unique pleasure: a strange doubleness, or in jazz parlance, coolness. The irony has to do with the disproportion between emotional fervor and a cool exterior, ultimately a protection against vulnerability in a threatening world. Jazz is the most important outgrowth of the mysterious doubling of innocence and sophistication, passion and calculation, which Berlioz observed in Gottschalk, the granddaddy of all jazz musicians. Coolness and toughness set against an almost primitive emotionality: that is what Weill, the ultimate European jazz ironist, is all about in his Berlin cabaret-jazz period.

Weill's new sound had a double edge in another sense, too. Adorno pointed out that the expected anthem and chorale cadences in *The Threepenny Opera* and its progeny are denied and their harmonic embroideries deliberately cheapened in ways that force the listener to confront the brutality of bourgeois capitalism. But the dusky exhilaration and lyricism of these scores also undermine the orthodox Marxism affirmed by Adorno and his colleagues, including Brecht. This deliciously salacious music is too anarchic for any form of political correctness, especially the puritanism and totalitarianism of communism. (The Soviets knew this even if Brecht didn't; Weill remained conspicuously unperformed in the Soviet Union.)

Weill's jazz operettas really are decadent, subversive of all social systems and ideologies. His horrendous vision of the brutality of market capitalism is clear enough: no anticapitalist tract is more devastating than *Mahagonny* or *Threepenny Opera*. But he disdained communism as well, sneering that Brecht composed Karl Marx whereas he composed music. As Charles Rosen pointed out in regard to Mozart, the sensuality of great music subverts all authoritarian systems, and Weill's violent eroticism was no exception. Although he winced at the Nazi campaign of vilification waged against him — the Entartete exhibit called his music "the triumph of the subhuman, of arrogant Jewish impudence" — Weill was heroically deserving of the "Entartete" label. He was the quintessential jazz degenerate.[39]

Entartete eventually became a badge of honor for others as well, most explicitly Bartók, who demanded that the Nazis include him on the list of Düsseldorf degenerates. Although his "decadence" credentials were not as sterling as those of Weill and Krenek, he was a passionate believer in cultural pluralism and an early opponent of fascism. In 1931, he had protested the fascist attack on Toscanini and after 1933 refused to perform in Germany; four years later he disallowed broadcasts of his music in Germany and Italy. Bartók was also a jazz fan, who, like Ravel and Milhaud, was eager to hear the latest bands when he visited New York. Indeed, he was fond of saying that jazz had technical and spiritual parallels to the primitive cross-rhythms of his beloved Eastern European folk music.

Like Weill, Bartók relaxed into a more overt lyricism once he arrived in the New World. His closest approximation to jazz was *Contrasts*, which he began writing in 1938, before he immigrated to America. *Contrasts* demonstrated Bartók's vision of jazz as compatible with European dance music. Written for the King of Swing, Benny Goodman, and premiered by Goodman, Bartók, and Szigeti at Carnegie Hall, it is Bartók's most overt New World gesture, full of bluesy clarinet riffs and dizzying syncopations, especially in the "Sebes" finale. Yet the outer forms and modal harmonies are derived from Eastern European dance music, so that the jazz element, aside from the gesture to Goodman, is mostly limited to the work's extreme rubato and the squealy brightness of the clarinet coloring. *Contrasts* did not come out of nowhere: the two pianos and percussion in Bartók's sonata of that name are treated like a sophisticated jazz ensemble; the heady syncopations, especially in the first movement, are more swingy than a great deal of real jazz.

A number of émigrés experienced a mellowing, a new accessibility, after landing in the New World. Or was it, as Krenek asserted, a new realism acquired through adversity? Beginning with Dvořák, European composers derived not only a sense of adventure and openness from America but also a new commercial opportunity; both aspects have always been part of New World mythology, and both have been fulfilled to an unusual degree in music.

In the last decade of the twentieth century, as movie and New Age music gained ascendancy and accessibility increasingly became a near obsession with even the most serious composers, some began to view this pattern as mirroring the historical movement of concert jazz through the century, as it passed through modernist adolescence before arriving at a calmer maturity. The conductor John Mauceri, a neo-Romantic ideologue, argued the flip side of the pro-Berlin, anti-Broadway view of Weill, dragging Weill's colleagues in for good measure; in the 1920s "Weill belonged to the same wrong-note diatonic school as early Hindemith, Shostakovich, Stravinsky, Schoenberg, Copland, Milhaud and countless others. 'Sour' happy music, with sickly harmonies over a peppy rhythm, became the tired cliché of the 1930s. . . . Once this transitional period (a musical adolescence for Stravinsky, Weill, and others) had been passed through, each found a unique and important adult voice."[40] In the 1990s, history circled back half a century, the rhetoric about sickly music — degenerate, perhaps? — recapitulating the Entartete diatribes of national socialism. Politicized musical camps that create either/or scenarios, rather than celebrate the complexity of art, remained as strong as ever.

But the development of symphonic jazz in Europe has never been linear. The earliest jazz experiments of Ravel, Milhaud, and others were some of the least sour and most soulful, and the use of jazz parody as an artificial jump-start was already on the way out by the 1930s, as pointed out by the British composer Constant Lambert in his remarkable 1934 book *Music Ho!*

The chapters "The Spirit of Jazz" and "Symphonic Jazz" are the most perceptive look at the subject of the period, and one of the most prescient of the century. Picking up where Ravel left off, Lambert prophesied that jazz, real and symphonic, would easily outlast critics who pronounced it a superficial, passing trend. But Lambert went further, asserting that jazz would be the most significant symphonic idiom of the century. Lambert recognized the coming centrality of jazz for highbrow musicians, while unsentimentally diagnosing its problems and predicting their solutions. He was one of the first to recognize that jazz was not only a style and a trend but a sensibility, one that would define the modern period long after the Jazz Age of the 1920s and early 1930s. Popular mythology locates the literary signature of jazz in F. Scott Fitzgerald, but Lambert finds it in an earlier source, the *Waste Land* period of T. S. Eliot. In Lambert's reading, Eliot both reflected and helped create the new funk of the twentieth century. Eliot represents the "same rapprochement between highbrow and lowbrow" that occurs in jazz: in Eliot's early poetry "we find the romantic pessimism of the nineteenth century expressed in the music-hall technique of the twentieth century lyric writer, not ironically but quite genuinely. 'This the way the world ends, this is the way the world ends, this is the way the world ends, not with a bang but a whimper' echoes not only the jingle of the jazz song but its sentiment. Whimpering has become one of the higher pleasures." In this jazz-Eliot fusion, the higher pleasures of whimpering, a new variation on Romanticism, have "suddenly achieved the status of a 'school,' a potent influence that can meet the highbrow composer on his own terms."[41]

To those who might argue that Eliot is far too highbrow an analog to a form so primitive and barbaric (adjectives regularly applied to jazz in the 1920s and 1930s by both champions and detractors), Lambert simply answers that "it is to its sophistication that jazz owes its real force." And it is the African-American heart of jazz that is most sophisticated: "The superiority of American jazz lies in the fact that the negroes there are in touch not so much with specifically barbaric elements as with sophisticated elements. . . . In the best negro jazz bands the irregular cross-accents are given so much more weight than the underlying pulse that the rhythmic arabesques almost completely obscure the metrical framework, and paradoxically enough this 'bar line' music often achieves a rhythmic freedom that recalls the music of Elizabethan times and earlier, where the bar line was a mere technical convenience like a figure or letter in a score." As for the many who consider these syncopations "abnormal or artificial," Lambert, in an extreme version of Stravinsky's view, counters that "it is the lack of rhythmic experiment shown in the nineteenth century that is really abnormal. . . . It is remarkably deficient in purely rhythmic interest."[42]

As for jazz harmony, it too is highly sophisticated, partaking not only of spirituals but of the "harmonic richness" of Debussy, Delius, and other jazz-oriented impressionists. Future generations of musicologists would debate precisely who took what from whom when, but for Lambert the point was that so many divergent elements—the rhythmic "arabesques" of African folk music, the "unctuous melancholy" of nineteenth-century hymns, the dreamlike ambiguities of the "Debussy-Delius school," the "intoxicating low spirits" of the Eliot age—all came together at the same moment of mutual sharing to create the quirky chemistry that is jazz. As an early champion of Delius, who influenced his own work, Lambert cannot resist suggesting the possibility that "Delius, who has been equally subjected to the influence of Anglo-Saxon church music and its negro variant, provides the link" between these diverse traditions.[43] As noted, that influence began in the 1880s and lasted throughout Delius's life. (Percy Grainger told Duke Ellington about the Delius link, turning Ellington, through recordings, into a confirmed Delian.) But Lambert is careful to state that the Delius connection is just a possibility. The exact origins of jazz, dogmatic pronouncements notwithstanding, remain a mystery.

Lambert's advocacy of jazz is full of pungent caveats. One of the first to diagnose Noble Savage clichés in jazz commentary, he excoriates "poor-white negro propagandists whose sentimental effusions must be so embarrassing to the intelligent negro"; just as scathingly, he denounces the antijazz diatribes of "the crusty old colonels, the choleric judges and beer-sodden journalists who imagine they represent the European tradition, murmuring 'swamp stuff,' 'jungle rhythms,' 'negro decadence.' " (The most entertaining beer-sodden journalist who hated jazz, H. L. Mencken, escaped Lambert's wrath.) Lambert deplored the trendy, cool aspects of jazz, which he recognized as a new form of snobbery and pretentiousness; he saw that by the 1930s, jazz tropes had become an empty formula latched onto by chic mediocrities. Similarly, in a startling forecast of jazz and rock used as Muzak, he described the degeneration of jazz into "a sort of aural tickling, a vague soothing of the nerves . . . a drug for the devitalized."[44] (This view of jazz as a drug, similar to Paul Rosenfeld's in America, was an intellectual variation on antijazz preachments of religious fundamentalists, who later used it again to attack rock and roll.)

Despite these vices and difficulties, symphonic jazz, Lambert insisted, was destined to be the wave of the future, following the collapse

of serialism and the "antique-fancying aridity" of neoclassicism. (The
link between jazz and neoclassicism was a dead end as far as he was
concerned.) Jazz was an "internationally comprehensible" language; its
"intoxicating melancholy" captured the spirit of the age, but its potential
for future use was much broader. Its richly divergent sources, emotional
resonance, and rhythmic sophistication provided a "more plastic basis"
for exploration by concert composers than any folk music since the
dances that inspired Bach and Mozart. Indeed, Lambert went so far as
to claim that "the scoring and execution of jazz reach a far higher level
than that of any previous form of dance music." Jazz inverted the traditional relationship between highbrow and lowbrow: "Chabrier's *Fête
Polonaise* has an harmonic and orchestral elaboration far beyond anything imagined by the popular valse writers of his time, but the modern
highbrow composer who writes a fox-trot can hardly hope to go one
better than Duke Ellington, if indeed he can be considered as being in
the same class at all."[45]

Ellington and other black artists were the chief inspirations for
Lambert's music and admiration, not Tin Pan Alley, the Whiteman
Band or, in Lambert's words, the "nauseating blubbering" of Al Jolson:
"Although Tin Pan Alley has become a commercialized Wailing Wall,
the only jazz music of technical importance is that small section of it
that is genuinely negroid. The 'hot' negro records still have a genuine
and not merely galvanic energy, while the blues have a certain austerity
that places them far above the sweet nothings of George Gershwin."[46]
Lambert thus allied himself with the anti-Gershwin crowd in American
intellectual circles, which included jazz enthusiasts like Edmund Wilson and Virgil Thomson, while many Europeans, including such unlikely candidates as Schoenberg, celebrated Gershwin's genius.

The problem with "The Spirit of Jazz" is a repellent streak of anti-
Semitism, the curse of the age, even among ostensible progressives. To
be sure, Lambert recognized the Jewish contribution to jazz, stating that
"the importance of the Jewish element in jazz cannot be too strongly
emphasized" and recognizing the "link between the exiled and persecuted Jews and the exiled and persecuted Negroes." And he delighted
in lampooning the anti-Semitism of others. Even if the Jewish contributions to jazz were "sufficiently recognized, it would hardly abate the
fury of the colonels and the columnists, for from their point of view,
the Jew is just as much an enemy of the British and Holy Roman

Empire as the negro." Still, it is hard to overlook Lambert's attribution of a "masochistic melancholy" in jazz rooted in the "Jewish tempera-ment" and his accusation that the Jews "have stolen the negroes' thun-der" in their expropriation of black music."[47]

Aside from this ugly subtext, Lambert's comments on nationalism and ethnicity are of considerable interest. His point of view is that of a foreigner commenting on the American scene, and not surprisingly, he saw the future of highbrow jazz resting mainly with Europeans, who had the necessary aesthetic distance. "The Americans seem to live too near Tin Pan Alley. . . . They suffer from the immense disadvantage of being on the spot." The Gershwin school consists of "sophisticated trap-pings" rather than lyrical essence; it is "the hybrid child of a hybrid . . . ashamed of its parents and boasting of its French lessons."[48]

Not that Europeans didn't have their own disadvantages: the French tended to be too parodic and "frivolous," the Germans too sol-emn—though there were definite exceptions. Lambert was one of the first to fully comprehend the "grandeur" and "poetic sordidness" of Weill's operettas and to perceive that Weill had been a New World composer long before he set foot in America. He astutely placed Weill in an American literary context: Weill had captured the "dusty pano-rama of American life" and its "drably tragic background" more au-thentically than any American except William Faulkner. In the same class was Milhaud's *La Création du monde*, which Lambert recognized early as a milestone of symphonic jazz, a "brilliant" example of "the compromise possible between popular idiom and sophisticated construc-tion." These works opened "an avenue of progress," extending the "har-monic language" of jazz without losing sight of its spirit. It was this spirit of jazz that was important, and anything that diluted it was a fraud, whether it was the overembroidered "Lisztian" aesthetic of the Gershwin school or, at the other extreme, the "atonal fox-trots" of European mod-ernists, whose mood was "hopelessly at variance" with the idiom.[49]

Many of Lambert's definitions and diagnoses have proved remark-ably durable. A large portion of the musical community—from reac-tionaries like John Philip Mason to modernists like Paul Rosenfeld—denounced the whole idea of symphonic jazz and predicted its quick demise. But as Lambert foresaw, it survived and emerged stronger than ever by the end of the century. Indeed, one might ask, what consistently inspirational aesthetic existed for serious composers at the end of the century besides jazz? Furthermore, its most inventive exponents often continue to be Europeans who compose in a basically tonal style. Lambert's judgment of Ellington as one of the most influential composers of the century has also been upheld: "He has crystallized the popular music of our time and set up a standard by which we may judge not only other jazz composers, but also those highbrow composers, whether American or European, who indulge in what is roughly known as 'symphonic jazz.' "[50]

Lambert provided not only a poetics for the genre but a model. One of the most elegant examples of the aesthetic he advocates is his own *Rio Grande*. Written when Lambert was only twenty-three, for an unusual ensemble of brass, percussion, chorus, and a piano of concerto prominence, it has a genuine blues sensibility and plays with syncopations that suggest both African sources and the Latin American dances that fit its setting (though curiously, Lambert champions only the former). As he later contended in "The Spirit of Jazz" the jazz element is "earnest," not "frivolous." An evocation of the languid "grandeur" of jazz, *The Rio Grande* moves freely from jaunty dance music into dreamy piano cadenzas, distant vocal solos, and delicate percussion riffs that gradually fade into the soft enchantment of Sacheverell Sitwell's imagined Brazilian night. Nothing neoclassical regiments the Lambert-Sitwell magic. Lambert's claim that the spirit of jazz, like early Eliot, is really a new form of Romanticism may seem questionable (more for the latter than the former), but *The Rio Grande*, at least, validates it.

Jazz elements find their way into other Lambert pieces, most notably the solemn Concerto for Piano and Nine Instruments, but nothing else in his output matches the originality and charm of *The Rio Grande*. As with Rachmaninoff's C-minor Prelude and Sibelius's *Finlandia*, Lambert bitterly complained about the public clamoring for *The Rio Grande* at the expense of other works, but one can hardly blame them. Richard Rodney Bennett's judgment that it is one of the most perfect specimens of symphonic jazz is hard to dispute.

Lambert's work as composer and critic illustrates the surprisingly vital and sustained tradition of concert jazz in England. British composers influenced by jazz tend to be relatively un-self-conscious and natural about it, incorporating it with little fuss or fanfare. Cole Porter provides their motto: "Let's do it!" Sometimes no jazz label appears at all. William Walton gave his early *Portsmouth Point Overture* a jazzy swing that shakes it loose from the squareness of Elgarian pomp and circumstance; insistent syncopations also pulse through his riveting First Symphony, giving the sober melodic material a startling eloquence. Walton's earlier, lighter *Façade*—one of the best cabaret comic-jazz pieces because of its genuine humor—reveals Walton's immersion in jazz from the beginning of his career.

The most peculiarly fractured case of jazz in British music is that of Benjamin Britten. In addition to the jazzy numbers in *Paul Bunyan* and *This Way to the Tomb*, Britten wrote vivid blues and cabaret songs ("O Tell Me the Truth about Love," "Night and Day," "Calypso") for the cabaret artist Heidi Anderson, with lyrics by W. H. Auden, Britten's fellow traveler in America. The intensity of Britten's absorption in the New World he inhabited for only a few years is matched only by the total rejection of his American persona after 1945, when he became a proper British composer. As Donald Mitchell pointed out in 1993 (until which time there was a virtual conspiracy of silence about these suppressed songs) "It is the astonishing fidelity of the gestures that leaves one a shade discomposed. Can this really be Britten? . . . Was it that inside the Britten we know so well, there was another Britten who might have (literally) swept the stage with his brilliant entertainments?"[51] Here again is the duality, the New World "second personality" identified by Berlioz in his Gottschalk review a century earlier. For whatever reasons, Britten chose to suppress this childlike persona until the end of his life, when he remounted and revised *Paul Bunyan*.

Malcolm Arnold's use of the idiom has been more consistent and is sometimes startling in its subtlety: the jazz episode in the 1950 Concerto for Piano Duet brings airy repose rather than agitation; like many delicate concert-jazz episodes in twentieth-century music, it performs the function of a scherzo. The most elegant and ambitious of Arnold's jazz-related pieces is the blues he wrote as an elegy for Django Rheinhardt, which became the second movement of his Guitar Concerto. Double basses pluck a hypnotic jazz pattern under sexy slides and bent notes for brass and strings as the soloist spins out a haunting blues tapestry. As with the Concerto for Piano Duet, this brooding slow movement suddenly springs to life as a blues scherzo, demonstrating again how naturally the idiom adapts to and enriches traditional structures. The guitarist Eduardo Fernandez, one of the concerto's most articulate executants, writes: "Instead of drawing from the usual Spanish well (and fishing out the usual trite clichés), Arnold chooses to take jazz as a source (at the very least, an equally valid idiom for the instrument.)"[52] Arnold continued to write for instruments associated with jazz. Composed for Benny Goodman, his 1974 Clarinet Concerto no. 2 concludes with a rowdy movement called "The Pre-Goodman Rag," a testament to Arnold's lifelong admiration for jazz and a tribute to the American dance-band sound. In the first movement, Arnold solves the stubborn problem of what to do with the improvisation element in jazz by instructing the performer to "improvise cadenza, as jazzy and way out as you please," thereby restoring to the cadenza its historical improvisatory function.[53] The cool, sinuous slow movement parallels the blues interlude in the Guitar Concerto.

Like Lambert and Arnold, Michael Tippett regarded jazz as an essential form, maintaining that in the twentieth century jazz and blues serve the same function once met by a Purcellian ground bass and Monteverdian chromaticism. Tippett's insistence on the centrality of jazz is powerfully articulated in the 1970 Symphony no. 3, in which he first attempts to find spiritual succor in the wake of the Holocaust, Vietnam, Hiroshima, and other horrors by invoking the Beethoven Ninth. The attempt fails, with Beethoven's relatively mild dissonance overpowered by the greater discord of contemporary reality: Beethoven and Schiller cannot speak to or dignify the nightmarishness of the twentieth century. But the blues can, as the four extended blues sequences in the finale demonstrate. The flügelhorn solos in the "slow blues" numbers, inspired by Miles Davis and Louis Armstrong, have an eloquence that temporarily soothes the soprano's despairing commentary on humanity's capacity for violence. The blues in the Symphony no. 3 therefore pick up where the spirituals in Tippett's A Child of Our Time left off during the Nazi era. This time, however, Tippett, like Dvořák, created his own African-American music rather than quoting it. For Tippett, spirituals and blues continued to be a profound, if temporary, release, a way of dealing with the darker side of reality summarized by the soprano, who intones a grim shopping list of everything from disease, madness, and carnage to the indifference of God.

Tippett, like so many other European composers, regarded jazz and blues not just as a sound but as a vision. Its many satellites—blues, ragtime, and swing—met the idiosyncratic needs of composers with sharply different sensibilities: Stravinsky found new rhythmic possibilities; Ravel, new modes of fantasy and sensuality; Weill, new layers of irony; Tippett, a new spiritual toughness.

Tippett's getting the blues typifies Old World experiments with jazz forms since the beginning of the century. Weill put it most trenchantly when he said that jazz inspired "easily graspable melodies" that contained within themselves irony as well as pleasantry, poetry as well as bitterness, melodies that combined intellectual substance with emotional punch. Dvořák had said it in the 1880s with his statements on Negro spirituals: for Old World artists, New World music offered universality and simplicity, a seemingly unlimited range of feeling in an instantly graspable form, without loss of sophistication or intellectual challenge.

Tippett had known this for nearly half a century, since his infatuation with Bessie Smith's recording of "St. Louis Blues." Smith was on his mind when he wrote his First Symphony and, forty years later, influenced the Third as well. The libretto of the Third, like that of *A Child of Our Time*, is both awkward and eloquent; it is full of American allusions, some subtle, others explicit: a touch of Eliot ("We fractured men / Surmise a deeper mercy"), a touch of Whitman ("O, I'll go whirling with my armpits / glistening . . ."), an overt reference to Martin Luther King ("I have a dream"). The penultimate stanza is a riff on King's "I Have a Dream" sermon. King's vision of universal human solidarity in the face of evil, juxtaposed with Beethoven's, leads to a final, tender blues solo on the flügelhorn. "What though the dream crack?" asks Tippett at the end. "We shall remake it." More than Tippett's text, the blues have the "huge compassionate power" to point the way.

This is an Old World symphony in the process of becoming New World. An early example of what is glibly called postmodernism, the Tippett Third makes wailing flügelhorn blues compete with everything from Beethoven to strident expressionism. That the blues win hands down, delivering the most beautiful moments in this convoluted, curiously fascinating symphony, demonstrates that in the last third of the twentieth century the Old World still needed the life-giving songfulness of the New. America may have been implicated in Hiroshima, Vietnam, and other brutalities deplored by Tippett, but in music its legacy was life giving.

The ability of jazz idioms to rescue European music from worn-out serial, minimalist, and expressionist formulas continued throughout the century. One of the most powerful examples among nontonal composers was Stefan Wolpe. The quintessential New World musician, Wolpe was an interdisciplinary artist influenced by painters and writers as well as musicians, by popular culture as well as elite. The paintings of Wassily Kandinsky and the sounds of jazz bands, in which Wolpe performed in both Berlin and America, engendered an explosive, mobile aesthetic. Utterly free as well as freewheeling, Wolpe refused to embrace any of the trendy mid-century musical orthodoxies he encountered at Black Mountain College or C. W. Post, where he made his living after a five-year stay in Palestine following his flight from the Nazis in 1933. Instead, he himself was the influence on John Cage, Morton Feldman, Ralph Shapey, the poet Charles Olson, and many others in the arts, including jazzmen such as Eddie Sauter and Dick Cary. (Charlie Parker apparently hoped to study with Wolpe but was never able to.)

Consequently, Wolpe's music is difficult to pin down. It is too fluid to have an easily identifiable signature sound, yet each piece makes a strong impression, creating from its content a new form—the legacy of Kandinsky, according to Wolpe scholars—a philosophy Emerson had advocated much earlier. Wolpe says all he needs to say in a given piece, then moves on to something else. Each work is fiercely independent, with its own world and personality, a manifestation of what Alex Ross, in a provocative article on the Weimar Republic, calls "the Berlin syndrome: every artistic step had to be sold as 'new and improved,' not as the continuation of a process begun in previous works."[54] Like his colleague Kurt Weill, Wolpe was an artist whose commitment to change and freedom, to the endlessly novel, constituted his identity. Not surprisingly, he flourished in the New World, the capital of the New and Improved.

Of Wolpe's jazz-derived pieces, the masterpiece may turn out to be the 1950 Quartet for Trumpet, Tenor Saxophone, Percussion, and Piano. Like Weill, Wolpe integrated American pop and jazz idioms so thoroughly into his style that he created an utterly new sound. Unlike Weill, however, Wolpe moved away from tango and cabaret (characterized by such 1920s works as "Blues and Tango") toward New Orleans polyphony, bebop, and what came to be called Third Stream, the elements of which became a springboard for his kinetic rhythm and counterpoint. The quartet opens with a wild riff for snare drum that sets the piece in motion. From there it rockets out of sight, each polyphonic line independent yet unified by an atmosphere of jazzy exuberance and a jazz-band motif in octaves that keeps returning as a tiny ritornello to bolt this eruption of energy into some semblance of order. The minimal pit-band jazz sounds of tenor sax, trumpet, snares, vibes, and drums convey the essence of polyphonic New Orleans jazz even as they create a new sound. The piece runs only eight minutes yet seems much longer because so much is going on. In the most revolutionary sense, this quartet is the definition of cool.

The vitality of jazz in European music blazed through the century. Some of the most striking experiments came from the avant-garde. In the 1950s Hans Werner Henze, moved by Weill's example, incorporated jazz in the ballets *Labyrinth* and *Maritona* as well as in the multicollage opera *Boulevard Solitude*. Jazz continued to rock the Soviet Union: in 1957–58, Kara Karayev, following the lead of his mentor Shostakovich, wrote a series of Noctures for jazz orchestra and issued a manifesto on the importance of black music similar to Dvořák's; in 1966, Rodion Schedrin, defying the Union of Soviet Composers, created an original amalgam of jazz and serialism in his noisy Piano Concerto no. 2, one of the most gripping jazz fusions of the 1960s. Every conceivable species of jazz-related pop material seemed to be useful, with the most cerebral composers often opting for the most banal subgenres. Although Luciano Berio's Sinfonia, his most celebrated large-scale work, is not a jazz piece per se, the pop vocal style of the Swingle Singers gives it a surreal swing that works hauntingly with Berio's stream-of-consciousness collage. It is largely because of this pop sensibility that the Sinfonia is so much fun compared to numerous dreary mid-century pieces from the European avant-garde. Like Tippett, whose Third Symphony follows the Sinfonia by a year, Berio invokes Martin Luther King, again to bequeath a moment of healing serenity on swirling chaos.

The European avant-garde continues to rely on jazz and its offshoots. Berio's feel for nontraditional jazz finds poetic expression in miniatures such as the 1985 "Luftklavier," with its mysterious ostinato and ecstatic repeated notes. The Finnish composer Veli-Matti Puumala's *Tutta Via* (1992) unveils a mesmerizing jazz pulse that magically organizes the violent, seemingly random noises exploding through the earlier part of the piece. The program notes for the premiere recording describe this ending as a "liberating jazz sequence";[55] the powerful notion of jazz being a liberating force in a stuffy world gets a new spin: as with Tippett and Berio, the liberation is toward greater stability, organization, and coherence. British composer Peter Maxwell Davies, who grew up on 1930s dance music, demonstrated in his 1969 *St. Thomas Wake* that a fox-trot could combine with a seventeenth-century pavane. The idea of jazz as the new Purcellian ground bass continues to flourish and is especially valuable in a postmodern reality where any grounding, any tradition, is comforting. An overt example of a Purcell-jazz fusion is Poul Ruders's 1995 Concerto in Pieces: Purcell Variations for Orchestra, featuring wa-wa brass, shivery bent notes, and a blues solo for alto sax reminiscent of Ravel in its sheer glamour and sexiness.

Jazz continues to liberate more conservative European composers as well. Shortly after the British film composer Stanley Myers completed his swan song, the 1991 Concerto for Soprano Saxophone, he told his son, "Now, perhaps, I can call myself a real composer."[56] A lifelong jazz fan, Myers used it as a way into a new impressionism, exploring delicate, misty sonorities that erupt into a full jazz-band climax only at the exuberant end. Reveling in the sheer joy of music making, this piece demonstrates the rich possibilities of symphonic jazz at the end of the century.

One of the most consistent players on the jazz-classical field is Richard Rodney Bennett, a longtime practitioner of the genre both as composer and as performer. Bennett plays both ends of the jazz-classical circuit. Works such as the 1964 *Jazz Calendar* are straight jazz rather than symphonic hybrids. But the 1990 *Concerto for Stan Getz* is a formal concert piece. Commissioned by its legendary dedicatee, this tense, spiky concerto turned out to be a memorial, aptly signified by the suave blues "Elegy" that constitutes the second movement. This concerto is in the tradition of the Benny Goodman pieces by Bartók and Arnold, a linkage in which celebrated American jazz musicians join forces with European composers whose musical styles they find congenial. Getz chose a relatively nontonal composer who fit his progressive predilections, resulting in a final experiment for Getz and a new one for Bennett. (Lambert underestimated the ability of jazz to blend with atonal harmony; indeed, Berg had used jazz in *Lulu*, to brilliant effect, as would Wolpe, Schedrin, and Berio.) According to the saxophonist John Harle, who premiered the concerto in Getz's sad absence, the concerto is a "celebratory tribute to the possibilities of using jazz harmonies in conjunction with the composer's own freewheeling serial techniques. . . . The language of Concerto for Stan Getz arises out of a true cross-fertilization of ideas."[57]

This cross-fertilization continues. What little resistance remains is a vestige of the snobbery of post-Wagnerian culture. In an earlier time, hybrids and crossovers were commonplace. Mozart and his contemporaries wrote dances, not merely music in the style of popular dances. The New World therefore restored something the Old had lost. Here again is the elegant circularity of the New World Symphony phenomenon, where Europeans use the New World to rediscover something in themselves, something lost in time or atrophied by convention. In this sense, the jazz craze that began in the 1920s was the rejuvenation of a tradition, not just a trend. Had it been the latter, it would have ended long ago.

Lukas Foss once told me that the European love affair with jazz is "absolutely in the tradition of European music to base yourself on folk music. For Bach it was Lutheran hymns, for Beethoven marches, for Schubert the Lied, for Brahms Viennese waltzes. We love to have our roots in folk music because it's like fresh flowers, with a wonderful fragrance and smell. Besides, jazz is terrific. And extremely virtuosic."[58] As such, jazz fit into a tradition of European performance as well as composition, bequeathing a new species of virtuoso, from Benny Goodman to John Harle. The importance of performance in the story of symphonic jazz cannot be underestimated: Ernest Ansermet, who brought the gospel of jazz to Stravinsky in 1918, was in love with the artistry of Sidney Bechet, whose clarinet playing was a continual source of astonishment; as we have seen with Schulhoff, Tippett, Lambert, and other composers, the qualities of a specific performer or band, as much as the music itself, often initiated the jazz obsession. This is one sense in which jazz, as Lambert suggested, may be more versatile than earlier folk musics: it engenders an endlessly renewable, always contemporary star system as well as a source of musical ideas. Like Liszt and Paganini, the new virtuosos are great improvisers who continue to plant new flowers.

Composers and executants of the spirit of jazz therefore reinvented the alliance between peasant and aristocratic culture so familiar to Haydn and Schubert. It is a testament to the power of jazz and its many

Paul Whiteman (center) and members of his band during a tour of Germany, 1926. For many Europeans, the Whiteman Band was synonymous with jazz. (American Jazz Institute, Rutgers University)

spin-offs that it continues to give the culture a unifying energy. After all the isms of the twentieth century—serialism, neoclassicism, primitivism, dadaism, minimalism, postminimalism, neo-Romanticism—it is still standing, still vital, still capable of recharging the batteries of a bland, increasingly corporate culture.

Canonical in the best sense, jazz is indeed the classical music of America, as President Clinton asserted, but it has become the classical music of Europe as well. As predicted by Ravel and Lambert, America's jazz influence on Europe has been consistent and far-reaching. From Kurt Weill to Malcolm Arnold, Europeans have written some of their freshest, most enduring work under the spell of jazz, ragtime, or swing. At the end of the century that marked the beginning of the movement, European concert jazz has become increasingly popular, and forgotten pieces by Shostakovich, Britten, Schulhoff, and other early composers in the idiom have suddenly become hot. Jazz works that seem to have fallen into oblivion—Spike Hughes's *Harlem Symphony*, for example—will surely join the revival.

The influence of jazz on Europeans is one of the most cheering cultural stories in a century of numbing horror. In a mutually enriching dynamic, Europeans hungry for upbeat art in the midst of two world wars brought an outsider's freshness, sharpness, and variety to a form that already used their medium and their instruments. Ravel, Schulhoff, Shostakovich, Bartók, Tcherepnin, and Siegfried Kurtz, among others, took the next step, mingling jazz with European folk dances to create the newest kind of New World Symphony.

As Cornel West points out, jazz is "a major metaphor of American culture," connecting the New World to both Europe and Africa. Jazz is where real integration occurs, mixing races, cultures, and sensibilities in a unified design. There is "no jazz without Africans and no jazz without European instruments." Jazz created a multinational dynamic that moved in many directions at once: to West and other black intellectuals of his persuasion, the fusion of European instruments with African-American content showed that "white civilization is as much part of my heritage as anybody's";[59] for Ravel, Weill, and others, jazz connected European culture in an electric way to the diverse mélange of black, white, Latin American, and Caribbean sensibilities that constitute the New World.

West points out that the same phenomenon jazz initiated has dramatically influenced other popular American forms. Jazz is the "benchmark of American popular culture," and related genres such as rock and rhythm and blues now assume a similar status in Europe. The Beatles, certainly the most powerful transatlantic current in the popular music world, "proudly admit" to being influenced by African-American rock and blues.[60]

For better and worse, rock has taken over the international pop-music scene and has even invaded the work of concert composers such as Steve Martland, whose "Principia" and "Shoulder to Shoulder," with their screaming rock rhetoric, were composed for rock bands and marketed for pop yet whose meticulous syncopation requires classical precision. As with symphonic jazz, older, traditional forms are part of the backdrop: the most extreme case, *Crossing the Border*, uses strict polyphony, including chaconne, as well as baroque ensemble structures and rhythms. In the 1980s and 1990s, Martland's rock-inspired creations helped generate a young, new British audience for classical music. American composers strive to create a similar opportunity, often with gratifying results, at least artistically: Steve Mackey's *Dancetracks* and other pieces for guitars and computers, for example, have a surreal charm; Michael Daugherty's *Motown Metal* combines 1960s rock with a 1990s techno beat to explore a noisy, new urban landscape. If rock and roll seems to lack the complexity and richness to sustain a merger with art music, we should remember that few in the 1950s predicted it would last long in any form.

By the last decade of the twentieth century, the hundred-year-old New World Symphony paradox had reached its apex, as major American composers such as Ellen Zwillich and John Harbison solemnly invoked Handel, Schubert, and Mahler, and as Europeans let their hair down with jazz, rock, rhythm and blues, and even country. The Old World impulse to forge a tradition, even in the New World, has created a New World Symphony continually vital and fresh, a mythology come to life. By 1993, the senior critic for the *New York Times* was able to say that "for all its false starts and compromises, American popular music has touched the world it lives in, confronted it with exuberance and invention. Finger-snapping Europeans still envy the newness of American music and make their own imitations of it. American composers look across to Europe and long for all things old. Nobody wants to be who they are."[61]

Who we are, of course, is highly subjective, especially in art, where identity is a question of choice and imagination. Despite the modern fetish for authenticity, for real spirituals and pure jazz, Dvořák was right: the spirit of the New World, the ideal, is what matters, an American "color" that is often kept alive most brilliantly by Europeans in search of what Julian Barnes called a necessary exotic; they seem to know instinctively that America is an idea, a picture of possibility most poetically invoked through music. In another recent example, the Viennese composer Robert Starer used "the feeling of jazz, never a direct quote," the "unique flavor of the blues," never an actual blues tune, from the beginning of his career: in the 1947 String Quartet no. 1, composed the year before he came to America, and in the charming 1996 piano pieces in *The Contemporary Virtuoso*, in casual minatures such as "Aquamarine" and in stately gestures such as the *Annapolis* Suite. For Starer, as for so many Europeans, jazz provided not just a rhythm and chord structure but a basic mood and sensibility, in his case a melancholy serenity.[62]

In 1929, Kurt Weill, one of the earliest to foresee the advantages of going American, wrote: "Anyone who has worked with a good jazz-band will have been pleasantly surprised by the eagerness, self-abandon, and enthusiasm for work which one seeks in vain in many concert and theatre orchestras."[63] What was true in 1929 continues to be so today: for both players and audience, jazz provides a rare release from the self. The achievement of Weill and his colleagues was to seize upon this mode of liberation and bring it into the stuffy world of concert music. By the end of the century, and as far as anyone could see beyond it, the sublime self-abandon Weill so admired was still igniting the European scene.

A small but telling indication of the shift toward jazz in Europe came halfway through the century, when Poulenc wrote that he was finally curing himself of his "jazz phobia." In a 1951 letter to Milhaud, he confessed that thirty years after the premiere of La Création du monde, he could finally enjoy the piece, even love it: "I used to feel quite estranged because of my phobia about jazz. Now I see in it only very beautiful music."[64]

Notes

Introduction

1. Michael Wood, interviewed by the author, September 10, 1996.
2. Julian Barnes, *Cross Channel* (New York, 1996), 207–08. See also Michael Wood, "Another Country," *New York Times Book Review*, April 21, 1996, 12.
3. Wood, interview.
4. C. Vann Woodward, *The Old World's New World* (New York, 1991), 83.
5. Joanna Bruzdowicz, liner note, Bruzdowicz's *Trio of Two Worlds*, Pavane CD 7355.
6. Ibid.
7. Ralph Waldo Emerson, *Selected Essays*, ed. Larzer Ziff (New York, 1982), 102, 104.
8. Olivier Messiaen, *Music and Color: Conversations with Claude Samuel* (Portland, Ore., 1994), 121.
9. Lukas Foss, interviewed by the author, August 20, 1996.
10. Percy Grainger, *The All-Round Man: Letters of Percy Grainger*, ed. Malcom Gilles (Oxford, 1994), 121.
11. Michael Tippett, *The Twentieth Century Blues* (London, 1991), 248–9.
12. Elizabeth Liddle, interviewed by the author, January 20, 1997.

Chapter 1: The Legacy of the Sorrow Songs

1. Cited in Michael Beckerman, ed., *Dvořák and His World* (Princeton, 1993), 96.
2. Emerson, *Selected Essays*, 102–03.
3. Cited in John C. Tibbetts, *Dvořák in America* (Portland, Ore., 1993), 375.
4. Cited in John C. Tibbetts, "Dvořák in America," *American Record Guide*, September–October 1992, 8.
5. Louis Cheslock, ed., *H. L. Mencken on Music* (New York, 1961), 98.

6. So low is its repute that *The American Flag* was not even raised in performance during the 1993 centennial of Dvořák in America ("Dvořák and the American Connection," Alice Tully Hall, New York City, November 6, 1993).

7. Cited in David Grayson, liner note, Dvořák's Cello Concerto, Sony CD 67173.

8. Cited in Beckerman, *Dvořák*, 140.

9. Ibid., 204–05.

10. Ibid., 96, 138.

11. Ibid., 138.

12. Ibid., 96.

13. Ibid., 172.

14. Cited in Steven Ledbetter, liner note, Dvořák's *New World* Symphony, Telarc CD 80238.

15. Cited in Beckerman, *Dvořák*, 141.

16. Jan Swafford, *The Vintage Guide to Classical Music* (New York, 1992), 109.

17. Cited in Sarah Rothenberg, "Dvořák in America," program note, Lincoln Center *Stagebill*, November 6, 1993, 20B.

18. Cited in Jim Svejda, liner note, Dvořák's *New World* Symphony, Teldec CD 73244.

19. Cited in Knut Frank, liner note, Dvořák's *New World* Symphony, Sony CD 47547.

20. Cited in Tibbetts, *America* (1993), 375.

21. Richard Taruskin, " 'Nationalism': Colonialism in Disguise?" *New York Times*, August 22, 1993.

22. Cited in Tibbetts, *America* (1993), 377.

23. Cited in Beckerman, *Dvořák*, 180.

24. Ibid., 183.

25. Ibid., 180.

26. Adrienne Fried Block, "Dvořák's Long Reach," in Tibbetts, *America* (1993), 158–59.

27. Cited in Tibbetts, *America* (1993), 376.

28. Leon Botstein, remarks made at "Dvořák and the American Connection," Centennial.

29. Cited in Beckerman, *Dvořák*, 183.

30. Ledbetter, CD liner note, 3.

31. Cited in Ledbetter, CD liner note, 5.

32. Cited in Beckerman, *Dvořák*, 138.

33. Ibid., 375.

34. Cited in Rothenberg, 20B.

35. Cited in Beckerman, *Dvořák*, 371.

36. Mencken, *On Music*, 92, 93, 94, 95, 96, 100.

37. Ibid., 93, 94.

38. Michael Beckerman, address delivered at Baruch College, New York City, November 29, 1992.

39. Cited in Rothenberg, 20B.

40. Beckerman, address, Baruch College.

41. Interview with Kurt Masur, Lincoln Center *Stagebill*, March 1991, 22.

42. Zdenek Macal, interviewed by author, August 15, 1993.

43. Cited in Christopher Palmer, *Delius* (London, 1976), 6.

44. Cecil Gray, *Musical Chairs* (London, 1948), 191.

45. All citations from the *Koanga* libretto are from the 1973 reconstruction by Douglas Craig and Andrew Page; rpt. Angel LP liner note (see n. 49, below).

46. Not until the fiction of Anne Rice did modern culture witness anything like this passionate, open embrace of Louisiana black magic by a white artist.
47. Cited in Gloria Jahoda, *The Road to Samarkand* (New York, 1969), 149.
48. George Washington Cable, *The Grandissimes* (New York, 1880), rpt. in Francis E, Kearns, ed., *The Black Experience* (New York, 1970), 207, 199, 217–18.
49. Douglas Craig, Andrew Page, liner note, Delius's *Koanga*, Angel LP 3808.
50. Christopher Palmer, liner note, Delius's *Appalachia*, London CD 425156.
51. Cited in William Tortolano, *Samuel Coleridge-Taylor: Anglo-Black Composer* (Metuchen, N.J., 1977), 75.
52. W. C. Berwick Sayers, *Samuel Coleridge-Taylor, Musician* (London, 1915; rpt., Chicago, 1969), 69, 97.
53. William Dean Howells, "Introduction to 'Lyrics of Lowly Life,'" in *The Complete Poems of Paul Laurence Dunbar* (New York, 1896), ix.
54. Ibid., 90.
55. W. E. B. DuBois, "Of the Sorrow Songs" (1903), rpt. in James Weldon Johnson, ed., *Three Negro Classics* (New York, 1965), 380, 382, 386.
56. Cited in Tortolano, *Coleridge-Taylor*, 148.
57. DuBois, "Sorrow," 378.
58. Cited in Tibbetts, *America* (1993), 376.
59. Cited in Richard Wilson, "Dvořák in America," program note, Lincoln Center *Stagebill*, November 6, 1993, 20L.
60. DuBois, "Sorrow," 382.
61. Cited in Tortolano, *Coleridge-Taylor*, 146.
62. Ibid., 106–07.
63. Paul Gilroy, *The Black Atlantic* (Cambridge, Mass., 1993), 87.
64. Cited in Tortolano, *Coleridge-Taylor*, 73.
65. Ibid., 107.
66. DuBois, "Sorrow," 386.
67. Cited in Tortolano, *Coleridge-Taylor*, 147–48.
68. DuBois, "Sorrow," 382.
69. Cited in Rory Guy, liner note, Sameul Coleridge-Taylor, "Bamboula," Angel LP 38186.
70. Ibid.
71. Cited in Tortolano, *Coleridge-Taylor*, 72.
72. DuBois, "Sorrow," 386.
73. Cited in Claudia Maurer Zenck, liner note, Krenek's *Jonny spielt auf*, London CD 436631. A term used by National Socialists to denounce Krenek's *Jonny spielt auf*, conducted at the 1927–28 premiere by Zemlinsky.
74. Alex Ross, "Influenced by Weimar and Harlem," *New York Times*, June 3, 1996.
75. As part of its Entartete Musik series, London Records has released the Symphonic Songs and numerous other neglected works by Schulhoff, Korngold, Weill, Hindemith, Krenek, and other composers discussed in this book.
76. Cited in Meirion Rowen, ed., *Tippett on Music* (Oxford, 1995), 182–83.

Chapter 2: Hiawatha Fever

1. Berwick Sayers, *Coleridge-Taylor*, 28–29.
2. Paul Lauter, ed., *Heath Anthology of American Literature*, vol. 1 (New York, 1994), 2734.
3. Edward Wagenknecht, *Henry Wadsworth Longfellow* (New York, 1986), 97.
4. Cited in ibid., 22.
5. Ibid., 98.
6. Cited in W. Sloan Kennedy, *Henry Wadsworth Longfellow* (1882; rpt., New York, 1973), 88.
7. Ibid., 89.
8. Thomas Beecham, *Frederick Delius* (New York, 1960), 37.
9. Cited in Tibbetts, *America* (1993), 211.
10. Botstein, remarks at "Dvořák and the American Connection," Centennial.
11. The only recording that delivers the full exhilaration of this music features the orchestra that premiered it, the New York Philharmonic, under Leonard Bernstein.
12. Rothenberg, 20B.
13. Beckerman, *Dvořák*, 217.
14. Stanley Crouch, remarks at "Dvořák and the American Connection," Centennial.
15. Michael Beckerman, remarks at "Dvořák and the American Connection," Centennial.
16. Cited in Kenneth Alwyn, liner note, Samuel Coleridge-Taylor, *Hiawatha*, Argo CD 430356.
17. Berwick Sayers, *Coleridge-Taylor*, 58.
18. Cited in W. A. Chislett, liner note, Samuel Coleridge-Taylor, *Hiawatha*, Angel LP 38186.
19. Cited in Berwick Sayers, *Coleridge-Taylor*, 101.
20. Richard Wilson, program annotation, *Hiawatha*, Lincoln Center *Stagebill*, Alice Tully Hall, November 1993, 20L.
21. Cited in Berwick Sayers, *Coleridge-Taylor*, 57.
22. Cited in Tortolano, *Coleridge-Taylor*, 92.
23. Alwyn, CD liner note.
24. Ibid.
25. Cited in Chislett, LP liner note.

Chapter 3: New Worlds of Terror

1. Cited in Arbie Orenstein, ed., *A Ravel Reader* (New York, 1990), 54.
2. Ned Rorem, "Notes on Ravel" (1975), rpt. in Jack Sullivan, ed., *Words on Music* (Athens, Ohio, 1990), 303.
3. Marcel Dietschy, *A Portrait of Claude Debussy*, 1962, trans. Margaret G. Gobb (Oxford, 1990), 157.
4. Arbie Orenstein, *Ravel: Man and Musician* (New York, 1975), 170.
5. D. H. Lawrence, *Selected Literary Criticism* (1932), ed. Anthony Beal (New York, 1966), 340.
6. Ibid., 346.
7. Cited in Woodward, *The Old World's New World*, 36.

8. François Lesure and Richard Langham Smith, eds., *Debussy on Music*, trans. Richard Langham Smith (New York, 1977), 319.
9. François Lesure and Roger Nichols, eds., *Debussy Letters*, trans. Roger Nichols (Cambridge, Mass., 1987), xv.
10. Ibid., 42.
11. Ibid., 166.
12. From Charles Rosen, *The Classical Style* (1972), rpt. in Sullivan, *Words on Music*, 101.
13. E. T. A. Hoffmann, "Beethoven and the Sublime" (1813), rpt. in Sullivan, *Words on Music*, 118.
14. Edgar Allan Poe, *Selected Poetry and Prose*, ed. David Galloway (New York, 1967), 489, 484.
15. Ibid., 506.
16. Ibid., 491, 446, 491, 484.
17. Marguerite Long, *At the Piano with Ravel* (London, 1973), 99.
18. Cited in Roger Nichols, "Ravel's Lyrical Fantasy," liner note, *L'Enfant et les sortilèges*, Deutsche Grammophon CD 423718.
19. Poe, *Selected Poetry*, 506, 504.
20. Ibid., 499, 500, 446.
21. Cited in Long, *At the Piano*, 71.
22. The speech itself is mysterious. Only the English translation exists: the original script has never been found, suggesting that Ravel made these remarks extemporaneously. For once, this supremely calculating artist may have spoken off the top of his head, revealing how much Poe meant to him and how comfortable he felt discussing at least this aspect of his own art.
23. Lesure and Smith, *Music*, 242.
24. Robert Orledge, *Debussy and the Theater* (Cambridge, Mass., 1982), 104.
25. Lesure and Nichols, *Letters*, 51.
26. Orledge, *Theater*, 103.
27. Lesure and Nichols, *Letters*, 317.
28. Cited in Orledge, *Theater*, 102.
29. Lesure and Smith, *Music*, 100.
30. Cited in Edward Lockspeiser, *Debussy* (1936; rpt., New York, 1962), 115.
31. Orledge, *Theater*, 105, 106.
32. Lesure and Nichols, *Letters*, 235.
33. Ibid., 250.
34. Lesure and Smith, *Music*, 83
35. Lesure and Nichols, *Letters*, 14.
36. Lesure and Smith, *Music*, 81, 21, 262, 278.
37. Lesure and Nichols, *Letters*, 316.
38. Orledge, *Theater*, 110.
39. Lesure and Nichols, *Letters*, 326.
40. Cited in Lockspeiser, *Debussy*, 116
41. Camille Paglia, *Sexual Personae* (1990; rpt., New York, 1991), 572.
42. Cited in Leonard Burkat, liner note, Rachmaninoff's Second Symphony, MCA CD 6272.
43. It is surprising that this case has not been used in psychiatric circles to counteract

the popular notion that psychotherapy tames or compromises creativity. In Rachmaninoff's case it clearly did the opposite.

44. Ewan West, liner note, Rachmaninoff's *The Bells*, EMI CD 63114.
45. Cited in Sergei Bertensson and Jay Leyda, *Sergei Rachmaninoff* (New York, 1956), 184.
46. Cited in Detlef Gojowy, liner note, Rachmaninoff's Piano Concerto No. 2, Sony CD 47183.
47. Edward Said, *Musical Elaborations* (New York, 1991), 99.
48. Karl Aage Rasmussen, "The New Danes," liner note, Ruders's *The Bells*, Bridge CD 9054.
49. Poul Ruders, interviewed by author, November 19, 1996

Chapter 4: New World Songs

1. European Whitmanians were sometimes puzzled by this limitation. Vaughan Williams, for example, was astonished that Whitman "seemed to think that music consisted of nothing but Italian coloratura singers and cornets playing Verdi" (Ralph Vaughan Williams, *The Making of Music* [Ithaca, 1955] 61).
2. Charles Graves, *Hubert Parry: His Life and Works* (London, 1926), vol. 1, 244–45.
3. Vaughan Williams read from Whitman in his eulogy for Parry in 1918.
4. Tippett, *Twentieth Century Blues*, 248.
5. William Stone, interviewed by author, January 12, 1995.
6. Anthony Burgess, "The Answerer," rpt. in Walt Whitman, *Leaves of Grass*, ed. Harold Blodgett, Norton Critical Edition (New York, 1973), 972.
7. D. H. Lawrence, "Whitman," rpt. in Blodgett, *Leaves*, 850.
8. John Updike, *Hugging the Shore* (New York, 1983), 75.
9. Eric Fenby, *Delius as I Knew Him* (1936: rpt., New York, 1981), 194.
10. Ibid., 200. See Joseph Gerard Brennan, "Delius and Whitman," *Whitman Review*, September 1972, 91.
11. Fenby, *Delius*, 35, 36.
12. Cited in Gloria Jahoda, *The Road to Sammarkand* (New York, 1969), 149.
13. In March 1997, an investigative team headed by the violinist and Delius scholar Tasmin Little established through strong circumstantial evidence that Delius's black lover was named Chloe Baker and that she bore a son, Frederick W. Baker, from the affair. According to Little's typically Delian narrative of transience and lost love, Delius returned to Florida in 1897 to find his estranged family, only to discover that Chloe, fearful that he might want to take the child back to England, had vanished.
14. Fenby, *Delius*, 101.
15. Peter Warlock, *Frederick Delius* (Oxford, 1952), 192.
16. Cited in Hugh Ottaway, entry on Ralph Vaughan Williams, *The New Grove Dictionary of Music and Musicians*, ed. Stanley Sadie (New York, 1980), vol. 19, 569.
17. Cited in Arthur Burn, liner note, Vaughan Williams's *Sea* Symphony, EMI CD 2142.
18. Imogen Holst, *The Music of Gustav Holst* and *Holst's Music Reconsidered* (Oxford, 1986), 6.
19. For a thorough explication of the poem, see Monica R. Weiss, " "Translating the

Untranslatable': A Note on 'The Mystic Trumpeter,'" *Walt Whitman Quarterly Review* 1 (March 1984): 27–30.

20. Holst, *Music*, 10–11.
21. Michael Short, *Gustav Holst* (Oxford, 1990), 51.
22. Holst, *Music*, 31.
23. For a rare example of an argument promoting the Broadway Weill over Gershwin, Porter, Rodgers, Kern, and Berlin, see John Simon, "The Threepenny Verdi," *New York Times Book Review*, December 13, 1992, 15.
24. David Neumeyer, *The Music of Paul Hindemith* (New Haven, Conn., 1986), 216.
25. Foss, interview.
26. Interview with Robert Shaw, Manhattan Center, January 12, 1995.
27. Ibid.
28. Ibid.
29. Ibid.
30. Cited in Paul Horsely, program annotation, Hindemith's *Lilacs* Requiem, Philadelphia Orchestra *Stagebill*, Fall 1995, 24C.
31. Cited in Michael Stegemann, " 'Speculating' on Hindemith," liner note, Hindemith's complete Piano Sonatas, Sony CD 52670.
32. Robert Starer, interviewed by the author, August 29, 1997.
33. Ralph Vaughan Williams, *National Music and Other Essays* (Oxford, 1987), 176.
34. Ibid., 39.
35. Baritone Thomas Hampson inaugurated a new kind of Whitman project in 1997 with "To the Soul," a recorded anthology of Whitman settings featuring Hampson as reader, singer, coauthor of the authoritative liner note, and commissioner of one of the settings (EMI 55028).
36. A case in point is John Adams's popular 1987 *The Wound Dresser*, tellingly described in a letter of July 1, 1991, from the publications editor of the Cleveland Orchestra: "As for the piece, everyone seems to like it, but I find it extremely 'safe' and therefore pretty dull."

Chapter 5: Beyond the Frontier

1. Cited in Joseph Kaye, *Victor Herbert* (1931; rpt., Freeport, N.Y., 1970), 214.
2. Cited in Beckerman, *Dvořák*, 179, 177, 163.
3. Cited in Richard Wilson, program note, Coleridge-Taylor's *Hiawatha's Wedding Feast*, Lincoln Center *Stagebill*, November 6, 1993, 201.
4. Michael Beckerman, interviewed by author, November 1, 1992.
5. Cited in Mario Morini, liner note, *The Girl of the Golden West*, Sony CD 47189.
6. W. H. Auden, "Paul Bunyan" (1941), rpt. in liner note, Britten's *Paul Bunyan*, Virgin CD 90710.
7. Speech by Ernest Bloch, recorded on CD of Bloch's *America*, Vanguard 8014.
8. Cited in Beckerman, *Dvořák*, 100.
9. Cited in Philip Haseltine, *Frederick Delius* (London, 1923), 114.
10. Cited in Arthur Cohn, liner note, Varèse's *Amériques*, Vanguard CD 40.
11. Ibid.
12. Cited in Fernand Oullete, *Edgard Varèse* (Paris, 1966; citation from English translation by Derek Cottman, 1968), 113.

13. Ibid., 47.

14. Jacques Barzun, *Critical Questions* (Chicago, 1982), 60–61. Barzun regarded Varèse's achievement as so significant that he included a page on him in materials for the Western civilization curriculum of Columbia College.

15. Jacques Barzun, interviewed by author, September 12, 1995.

16. Oullette, *Varèse*, 57.

17. Louise Varèse, *Varèse: A Looking Glass Diary* (New York, 1972), 102–03.

18. Oullette, *Varèse*, 57.

19. Seymour Solomon, interviewed by author, September 16, 1995.

20. Oullette, *Varèse*, 56.

21. Henry Miller, *The Air Conditioned Nightmare* (New York, 1945), 166, 173, 174.

22. Cited in Sullivan, *Words on Music*, 308–09.

23. Frank Zappa, "Edgard Varèse: Idol of My Youth," *Stereo Review*, June 1971, 62.

24. Cited in Cohn, CD liner note.

25. Cited in Robert Adelson, liner note, *Déserts*, Sony CD 68334.

26. Barzun, interview.

27. Eric Salzman, "Edgard Varèse," *Stereo Review*, June 1971, 57.

28. Cited in Paul Collaer, *Darius Milhaud* (San Francisco, 1988), 63.

29. Ibid.

30. Cited in Edward Downes, liner note, Milhaud's *Les Choéphores*, Columbia LP 6396.

31. Messiaen, *Music and Color*, 162.

32. Ibid., 162, 165, 168.

33. Cited in Jonathan Yardley, review of *Hunting Mister Heartbreak*, by Jonathan Rabin, *Washington Post Book World*, April 28, 1991, 3.

Chapter 6: Broadway, Hollywood, and the Accidental Beauties of Silly Songs

1. Horst Edler and Kim Kowalke, eds., *A Stranger Here Myself* (New York, 1993), 38, 40.

2. Sadie, *The New Grove*, vol. 20, 309.

3. Alex Ross, "A 'Serious' Composer Lives Down Hollywood Fame," *New York Times*, November 26, 1995.

4. Karen J. Greenberg, program note, "The Other Encounter: European Composers in America," American Symphony Orchestra, Carnegie Hall, September 20, 1992.

5. Program note, Korngold's *Adventures of Robin Hood*, Lincoln Center *Stagebill*, Avery Fisher Hall, October 1995.

6. Cited in Tony Thomas, *Film Score* (Burbank, Calif., 1991), 85.

7. Ibid., 84.

8. Ibid.

9. Edward Rothstein, "Film Music Returns to its Roots," *New York Times*, November 19, 1995.

10. Thomas, *Score* 41.

11. Cited in William Darby and Jack Du Bois, *American Film Music* (Jefferson, N.C.), 310–11.

12. Cited in Thomas, *Score*, 43.

13. Otto Friedrich, *City of Nets* (New York, 1986), 34.
14. Ibid., 222.
15. Ibid., 36, 39.
16. Leon Botstein, program note, "Other Encounter," American Symphony Orchestra, Carnegie Hall, September 20, 1992.
17. The pattern could go either way: Dimitri Tiomkin started on Broadway, then, as he put it, "fell under the spell of the motion picture camera" (Thomas, *Score*, 126).
18. Cited in Jürgen Schebera, *Kurt Weill* (New Haven, 1995), 257.
19. Completing the happy outcome of *Lady in the Dark* was the contribution of lyricist Ira Gershwin, who had not worked since the tragic death of his brother, in 1937.
20. Cited in Schebera, *Weill*, 271.
21. Ibid., 312.
22. Ibid.
23. Ibid., 315.
24. Ibid., 313.
25. Ibid., 317.
26. Cited in Donald Mitchell, "Britten's and Auden's 'American' Opera," liner note, Britten's *Paul Bunyan*, Virgin CD 90710.
27. Ibid.
28. Obituary of Benjamin Britten, *New York Times*, December 5, 1976.

Chapter 7: New World Rhythm

1. Carol J. Oja, "Gershwin and American Modernists of the 1920s," *Musical Quarterly* 78, no. 4 (winter 1994): 650. This is an excellent account of the Gershwin phenomenon.
2. Paul West, *My Mother's Music* (New York, 1996), 59, 62.
3. Constant Lambert, *Music Ho!* (London, 1934), 203.
4. Cited in Katherine H. Allen, liner note, *Jonny spielt auf*, Vanguard CD 8048.
5. Cited in Meirion Rowen, *Michael Tippett* (London, 1982), 46.
6. Cited in Schebera, *Kurt Weill*, 46.
7. Paul Rosenfeld, *Musical Impressions* (New York, 1969), 221–22.
8. H. L. Mencken, *Prejudices* (1926), rpt. in Sullivan, *Words on Music*, 359.
9. Gary E. Clark, *Essays on American Music* (Westport, Conn.), 71.
10. Cited in S. Frederick Starr, *Bamboula!* (New York, 1995), 91.
11. Jack Belsom, interviewed by author, March 13, 1995.
12. Barbara Fischer-Williams, "Good Old Giraud," *Opera News*, February 6, 1971, 25.
13. Lesure and Smith, *Music*, 70.
14. Ibid., 278, 275; Lesure and Nichols, *Letters*, 14.
15. Cited in Orenstein, *A Ravel Reader*, 390.
16. Ibid., 390, 46, 458.
17. Ibid., 472.
18. Ibid., 458–59.
19. Cited in Nichols, CD liner note.
20. Cited in Serge Berthier, liner note, "Classics of the Americas," Opus CD 30 9001.
21. Cited in Richard Bernstein, "Jazz's Dark Forces and the Artists Who Love Them," *New York Times*, March 20, 1996.

22. Cited in Orenstein, *A Ravel Reader*, 454.
23. Cited in Keith W. Daniel, *Francis Poulenc* (Ann Arbor, Mich., 1980), 24.
24. Cited in liner note, Milhaud's *Les Choéphores*, Columbia LP 6396.
25. Cited in Herbert Glass, liner note, Milhaud's *La Création du monde*, RCA CD 68181.
26. Darius Milhaud, *Notes without Music* (New York, 1970), 148–49.
27. Ibid., 152–53.
28. Cited in Paul Collaer, *Darius Milhaud* (San Francisco, 1988), 69.
29. Cited in Bruce Adolphe, liner note, "Jazz at Lincoln Center," Alice Tully Hall *Stagebill*, May 7, 1995, 20.
30. Ibid.
31. Cited in Vera Stravinsky and Robert Craft, *Stravinsky in Pictures and Documents* (New York, 1978), 203.
32. Cited in Giselher Schubert, liner note, Hindemith's "Ragtime (Well Tempered)," Wergo CD 60150.
33. Allen, CD liner note.
34. Cited in Schebera, *Weill*, 284.
35. Cited in Stephen Hinton, *The Threepenny Opera* (Cambridge, Eng., 1990), 15.
36. Ibid., 82.
37. Cited in Kim Kowalke, ed., *A New Orpheus* (New Haven, 1986), 73, 331.
38. Ibid., 331.
39. Cited in Schebera, *Weill*, 288.
40. John Mauceri, "Kurt Weill in America," liner note, Weill's *Street Scene*, London CD 433371.
41. Lambert, *Music Ho!* 207.
42. Ibid., 206, 205, 219, 219–20.
43. Ibid., 204.
44. Ibid., 201, 228.
45. Ibid., 222, 207.
46. Ibid., 212.
47. Ibid., 211, 202.
48. Ibid., 222, 223.
49. Ibid., 224–25, 219, 221.
50. Ibid., 215.
51. Donald Mitchell, "Britten's Blues," liner note, Britten's Blues and Cabaret Songs, Unicorn-Kanchana CD 9138.
52. Eduardo Fernandez, liner note, Arnold's Guitar Concerto, London CD 430233.
53. Cited in Piers Burton-Page, liner note, Arnold's Clarinet Concerto, Conifer CD 7560551228.
54. Alex Ross, "The Distant Sound," *New Republic*, January 27, 1997, 35.
55. Juhani Nuorvala, liner note, Puumala's *Tutta Via*, Ondine CD 866.
56. Cited in John Harle, liner note, Myers's Concerto for Soprano Saxophone, London CD 443529.
57. Ibid.
58. Lukas Foss, interviewed by author, August 27, 1996.
59. Cornel West, "Beyond Multiculturalism," address delivered at Rider University, sponsored by American Studies, March 2, 1992; followed by interview with the author.

60. Ibid.
61. Bernard Holland, "If Minerva Could Carry a Tune," *New York Times*, April 11, 1993.
62. Robert Starer, interviewed by author, April 24, 1997.
63. Cited in Hinton, *Opera*, 166.
64. Cited in Sidney Buckland, ed., *Francis Poulenc: Echo and Source* (London, 1991), 189.

Index